Leading Business Change
FOR
DUMMIES®

by Dr. Christina Tangora Schlachter, PhD, and
Terry Hildebrandt, MA, MA, PCC

WILEY

John Wiley & Sons, Inc.

Leading Business Change For Dummies®

Published by
John Wiley & Sons, Inc.
111 River St.
Hoboken, NJ 07030-5774
www.wiley.com

Copyright © 2012 by John Wiley & Sons, Inc., Hoboken, New Jersey

Published by John Wiley & Sons, Inc., Hoboken, New Jersey

Published simultaneously in Canada

For general information on our other products and services, please contact our Customer Care Department within the U.S. at 877-762-2974, outside the U.S. at 317-572-3993, or fax 317-572-4002.

For technical support, please visit www.wiley.com/techsupport.

Wiley publishes in a variety of print and electronic formats and by print-on-demand. Some material included with standard print versions of this book may not be included in e-books or in print-on-demand. If this book refers to media such as a CD or DVD that is not included in the version you purchased, you may download this material at http://booksupport.wiley.com. For more information about Wiley products, visit www.wiley.com.

Library of Congress Control Number: 2012941746

ISBN: 978-1-118-24348-0 (pbk); ISBN 978-1-118-28266-3 (ebk); ISBN 978-1-118-28331-8 (ebk); ISBN 978-1-118-28541-1 (ebk)

Manufactured in the United States of America

10 9 8 7 6 5 4 3 2 1

WILEY

About the Authors

Dr. Christina Schlachter is the creator of *The Leading Change Guide,* a real-world road map for leaders who are tired of too much firefighting and are ready to create meaningful, positive, and lasting change. As CEO and founder of She Leads, Christina's matter-of-fact 12-week transformation process has helped thousands of leaders around the globe reinvent both themselves and their companies. In addition to *Leading Business Change For Dummies,* Christina contributes to numerous business and communication journals and blogs and is a sought-after keynote speaker globally. Christina has been recognized as an American Express Small Business Award winner and is a Lean Six Sigma Master Black Belt.

Christina holds a PhD in human and organizational systems, MAs in education and in organizational studies, and a BBA in international finance and marketing. She is a frequent speaker and lecturer at top-ranked universities, including Stanford, where she received her first master's degree. When not coaching, writing, or speaking with clients about leading change, Christina, also a two-time Ironman triathlete, alternates between swimming, biking, running, and skiing around the mountains of Colorado with her husband, two sons, and their Nova Scotia Duck Tolling Retriever. Christina loves to hear from her readers. She can be found on her bike or in the pool at the crack of dawn, at christinas@sheleadstheway.com, and at www. sheleadstheway.com.

Terry Hildebrandt, MA, **MA**, **PCC,** works with business leaders and their teams to align their organizational culture with new business strategies. Terry is an expert in the principles of evidence-based coaching, contributes to blogs on emotional and social intelligence, and has spoken at business conferences worldwide. Terry holds the Professional Certified Coach (PCC) credential from the International Coach Federation (ICF).

Terry holds a BS in materials science from Rice University and MAs in organizational design and effectiveness and in human development, both from Fielding Graduate University. When not working with his clients, Terry is skiing on the slopes of the Rocky Mountains or traveling with his partner. Terry can be reached at terry@terryhildebrandt.com or www. terryhildebrandt.com.

Dedication

For all the business leaders, managers, and employees who want to create meaningful, positive, and lasting change.

Authors' Acknowledgments

Our sincere thanks and appreciation to everyone who had a part in putting this book together. We are grateful for the wonderful opportunity.

We want to specifically thank the great minds at John Wiley & Sons, Inc., especially the Project Editor, Heike Baird; our Acquisitions Editor, Tracy Boggier; our Technical Editor, Myra Cocca; and our brilliant Copy Editor, Caitlin Copple. To the graphics and layout team at Wiley, you made this book come to life. Thanks to Corbin Collins for stepping in and not missing a step. And a special thanks to Matt Wagner at FreshBooks; without your belief in the project and in us, this book would not have been possible. Also, thanks to Dave Crenshaw for kindly introducing us to Matt Wagner.

To our change management clients who have contributed examples, experiences, and successes, thank you for being such a significant part of the book. Thanks to our executive leaders we coach; your insights and triumphs are a pleasure to share.

Thank you to our great friends and family who stuck by our sides when we were working like crazy to balance writing, family, life, and clients.

And to Christina's husband and brain trust, Michael, thank you for all your ideas, recommendations, and suggestions every step along the way. Your content, commentary, and subject-verb agreement editing make you as much the author of this book as anyone on the cover.

Publisher's Acknowledgments

We're proud of this book; please send us your comments at `http://dummies.custhelp.com`. For other comments, please contact our Customer Care Department within the U.S. at 877-762-2974, outside the U.S. at 317-572-3993, or fax 317-572-4002.

Some of the people who helped bring this book to market include the following:

Acquisitions, Editorial, and Vertical Websites

Project Editors: Heike Baird, Corbin Collins

Acquisitions Editor: Tracy Boggier

Copy Editor: Caitlin Copple

Assistant Editor: David Lutton

Editorial Program Coordinator: Joe Niesen

Technical Editor: Myra Cocca

Senior Editorial Manager: Jennifer Ehrlich

Editorial Manager: Carmen Krikorian

Editorial Assistants: Rachelle S. Amick, Alexa Koschier

Art Coordinator: Alicia B. South

Cover Photos: © iStockphoto.com/SOMATUSCAN

Cartoons: Rich Tennant (`www.the5thwave.com`)

Composition Services

Project Coordinator: Kristie Rees

Layout and Graphics: TImothy C. Detrick

Proofreaders: Jessica Kramer, Lisa Young Stiers

Indexer: Christine Karpeles

Publishing and Editorial for Consumer Dummies

Kathleen Nebenhaus, Vice President and Executive Publisher

Kristin Ferguson-Wagstaffe, Product Development Director

Ensley Eikenburg, Associate Publisher, Travel

Kelly Regan, Editorial Director, Travel

Publishing for Technology Dummies

Andy Cummings, Vice President and Publisher

Composition Services

Debbie Stailey, Director of Composition Services

Contents at a Glance

Table of Contents

Introduction

*W*elcome to *Leading Business Change For Dummies*!

No matter where you look today, change is the one thing that you can count on in business. Social media, new technologies, alliances forming between former competitors, insourcing/outsourcing/right-sourcing, and the growing diversity of global customers are just a few of the external forces in the business news today. Internally, organizations are faced with changes in strategies to meet these demands, diverse expectations from a multigenerational workforce, and significant cost pressures to do more with less.

Basically, you have two choices when it comes to change: Get on board and lead it, or get out of the way and do nothing. When faced with change, some leaders may do nothing except hope the change will go well on its own or just go away, like a nasty little bug. By doing nothing and letting change just look after itself, these leaders may also be stepping aside as competitors rush past them, with customers not far behind. On the other hand, leading change means saying no to the status quo by setting a brilliant vision for the future, communicating the change from the rooftops, and engaging your employees while measuring success every step of the way. Of the two choices, we're pretty sure that getting on board and leading change is the right way to go.

If you've picked up this book, you may be a business leader who needs to launch a change in your company to address one or more of the above internal or external forces. Or perhaps you're a manager who has just been given the task to make a big change happen in your department. Business change can be downright scary, sure, but never fear: You can do lots of things to make your transition smoother, easier, and less stressful. That's why we wrote this book! Whether you are brand new to leading change or are a seasoned change leader, this book can provide you with a road map and the simple yet powerful tools you need to successfully get the job done.

Leading Business Change For Dummies helps leaders become change gurus, ready to take on some of the most difficult changes facing businesses today. We like to think of change as a journey in which you navigate through all the twists and turns to successfully get to your destination. This book is your travel guide, and you can think of us as your concierges.

About This Book

Hundreds of books have been published on managing, leading, and creating change. Some of them focus on step-by-step methodologies, others focus more on how people feel about change, and still others concentrate on the process side of change. We believe that change comes down to doing three things really well:

- Leading with a strong vision of how the change will make the future better
- Ensuring two-way communication
- Engaging employees

Leading Business Change For Dummies focuses on these three aspects of change, giving you a map for leading change from start to finish. We also discuss processes and tools and deliver a boatload of tips to guide you on your change journey. The journey may not always go smoothly, but the tools provided in this book are here to help you avoid the common mistakes and pitfalls that leaders are likely to experience.

Although we're firm believers in the need for senior leaders to take responsibility and set a powerful vision and reason for change in the organization, we also know that leading change is everyone's responsibility, not just the CEO's. *Leading Business Change For Dummies* is a practical book full of tried-and-true, real-world tools and tips that almost anyone in an organization can use. We provide you with an easy-to-apply framework that can immediately benefit your organization, regardless of the size or scope of the change. And because change is a constant, you may find yourself using this book day in and day out to motivate your team, focus on strategic goals, and get results.

This book is for you if

- You're an executive looking at a major shift in your corporate strategy.
- You're a midlevel manager who's been charged to implement a change handed down from the top.
- You're a supervisor or project leader who's just trying to figure out how to make a change work for your team.
- Your organization is facing unprecedented growth that requires doing things differently to meet customer demands — or your industry is shrinking and your organization needs to transform itself to survive.
- Your organization is looking for new ways of working to do more with less while maintaining employee morale.
- You want to make a change or idea happen in your organization and *stick*.

✔ You are an individual contributor or team member who wants to support changes happening in your company.

✔ You want action rather than a methodology with lots of presentations.

✔ You have been doing change management for some time and are looking to learn something new.

Whether you're an executive of a Fortune 500 company who needs to drive a system-wide change, a small-business owner looking to grow the business, or anyone in between, this book can help you make change last.

Conventions Used in This Book

We used the following conventions throughout the book, which you will find in all *For Dummies* books:

✔ All websites addresses and e-mail addresses appear in `monofont`.

✔ When we introduce a new term, we *italicize* it and then provide a definition.

✔ We **bold** keywords and actions in numbered steps.

What You're Not to Read

Although we'd love you to read and enjoy every word we wrote in this book, we know that people in the midst of change tend to be busy. With that in mind, if you're pressed for time you can skip the sidebars, those gray shaded boxes of text. They present interesting side stories or go into more detail on a topic in the text, but you'll still get the important message without them.

Foolish Assumptions

As we wrote this book, we made a few assumptions about you, the reader. Even if only a couple of these descriptions seem to apply to you or your organization, we are confident that this book will support you in whatever change you are leading.

✔ You are a leader in an organization who wants to lead successful change.

✔ Your organization has tried to change, but it hasn't worked very well.

✔ You are looking for a road map, processes, and tools to help you lead the change.

✔ You want strategies that will help you engage employees who will be impacted by the change.

✔ You want to get everyone on the same page about change.

How This Book 1s Organized

Leading Business Change For Dummies is divided into five parts. The first three parts deliver a functional, action-oriented guide for any change effort. The fourth part dives deeper into special circumstances that require unique approaches to leading change. The last part provides a quick summary and reference of key information that every change leader should know. If you would like information on a particular topic, the index at the back of the book is a great reference guide.

Part 1: The Nuts and Bolts: Laying a Foundation for Change

Here's where we lay the foundation. Without it, your house of change will sink into the swamp of failure. Part I is about getting the basics perfectly right so you can avoid common pitfalls in the future. If you have never been through a change or are stepping up and sponsoring change for the first time, Chapter 1 will get you on the right path. We show you how to plan like a pro by developing a plan for change, and you get a glimpse into how important communicating and motivating employees is if you want to make change last. Making sure everyone knows what they are supposed to be doing is so important that we devoted an entire chapter to embracing the change-leader roles. Even if you aren't an official leader of the change, you find some great ideas on how to be a special, not-so-top-secret agent of change.

Part 11: Putting the Plan into Motion

In Part II, we get you started on the road to change. This is where your change leadership toolbox becomes incredibly full. In Chapter 4, we get you moving with ways to create a need for change, build a vision, develop your road map, and engage the rest of the leadership team. With your future looking so bright, next up is setting the goals, roles, and responsibilities to make sure everything you're planning to have happen actually does. Like on any journey, someone is inevitably going to ask, "When are we going to get there?" Well, we have a plan for that too! In Chapter 6, we cover how to keep your eye on progress by measuring the commitment to change and using a change scorecard. Later, we dive into the bread and butter of change: communication. We say quite a bit about communication in this book (okay, that's an understatement), so if communication, or the lack of it, is an issue within your business, this part is crucial.

Part III: Making Change Stick through Thick and Thin

This part provides a wealth of information about what to do when the change is rolling and is powering through to the finish line. If you're following this book's road map, by now you've set a big, crazy, wonderful vision, you're an expert on communicating change, and things are moving. Don't let up on the gas pedal just yet and please don't put this change on cruise control. Maintaining the momentum helps you keep employees engaged and committed throughout the change and makes them believe the change is really happening. Yes, here is where we make sure change is real, not just a lofty goal on a slideshow. Discover how to get over the bumps in the road by helping employees let go of old baggage (travel light!) and by empowering the organization to make decisions and take responsibility for getting over the negative reactions toward change. But change is not all doom and gloom. In Chapter 10, you find ways to celebrate your success and leverage any midcourse corrections to make the change even better than originally planned.

Part IV: Leading Change in Specialized Circumstances

Not all change efforts are created equal. Technology changes involve words like ERP, CRP, and SCM. Mergers and acquisitions may have more rigid communication barriers imposed on the organization. When everything is changing, you can still thrive in chaos with the extra tricks we divulge. In this part we look at six different types of organizational change that require a little extra attention: team and organization change, restructuring change, mergers and acquisitions, technology change, cultural change, and complex change when everything is changing at once.

Part V: The Part of Tens

In a big hurry and need ideas to get started right away? This last part gives you essential principles and creative ideas on leading change along with a final laugh or two. First, we start with ten essential principles of leading successful change that you will want to earmark and come back to again and again. Then, for those employees without the title of change leader, we tell you ten creative ways to lead change when someone else is running the show (things everyone in the organization should be doing when change happens). And when you most need it, we give you a little motivation and energy with ten ways to energize your most valuable players (MVPs).

Icons Used in This Book

Just like signposts along a road, this book uses several icons to point out helpful information that you need for your change journey. Keep an eye out for these symbols throughout the book:

This icon calls your attention to important points that you shouldn't forget. These points are critical for your change effort to succeed.

This symbol provides helpful advice, tips, and words of wisdom that will support your change leadership.

This icon points out potential mistakes and pitfalls that can derail your change effort. Pay special attention to the warning to stay on track.

Where to Go from Here

Where you go from here really depends on where you and your organization are right now. If the company is just beginning to think about change, you may want to start at Chapter 1. However, if you are well on your way and just wanted to pick up some tools, you can start with Chapter 4. If you've already communicated the change and have been working on the change for a while but don't seem to be getting any traction, take a look at Chapter 9, which helps you understand challenges and reactions to change.

This book may be titled *Leading Business Change For Dummies,* but you don't necessarily need a big title to be a leader. If you are part of a change team or just want to support a change happening in your organization, check out Chapters 3 and 19. For tips and ideas on how to deal with specific changes, like restructuring, mergers and acquisitions, or technology change, check out the chapters in Part IV.

No matter what change you are currently faced with in your business, we're confident that you will find in this book strategies, tools, and helpful hints to guide you along the way. Enjoy the journey!

Part I
The Nuts and Bolts: Laying a Foundation for Change

The 5th Wave
By Rich Tennant

"I think Dick Foster should lead the change. He's got the vision, the drive, and let's face it, that big white hat doesn't hurt either."

In this part . . .

The most logical place to start changing is at the beginning. In this part, you get the basics squared away with
the why, what, and who of change, because leading change
is as much about the process of change as the change itself.
In these chapters you find out about the change process and
how to address the need for change. You also take a look at
how you can really lead change rather than simply managing
it. (Here's a hint: through active sponsorship and by leading
by example.)

Chapter 1

Being in Charge of Change

In This Chapter

▶ Comprehending the cycle of change in business

▶ Planning each step of the change process

▶ Communicating and managing change

▶ Working with the people involved in the change

*W*hether your company is changing technology to increase performance, merging with another organization to gain a competitive advantage, or facing strong economic pressures that are forcing things to be different, change is one of the few constants in business. Change can come from all directions and be driven by multiple reasons, but the core building block of successful change always boils down to this:

Successful change means creating a strategy that links the people, the process, and the technology to create a better future state.

And although the motivation or desire for change may come from inside or outside the organization, one element of change is always required: Leaders must inspire and engage employees in change efforts. So even though leaders are in charge of change, they need to involve and motivate the people around them to make the change last in the long term.

In this chapter we introduce the cycle of change and discuss what change leaders like you need to know as you go through the change process. Change is both an art and a science, but a simple formula we outline can determine how successful and sustainable your transformation will be in the long term. We introduce how to create a road map for change and begin to put it in motion. Next, we give you ideas on how to sound the trumpets for change so employees hear the message loud and clear. We then jump right into the people side of change to help you motivate employees and work through possible negative reactions. Finally, we examine how you can make change durable so all your work lasts for many changes to come.

Understanding the Cycle of Change

Businesses can face a variety of changes: Companies merge or acquire other companies, new leadership comes in at the top, new technology is adopted, products and services evolve, and customers grow globally. The list could go on and on. Every change is different, but luckily you can expect and plan for a few commonalities during any organizational transformation. Change can be compared to a journey: You and the organization will be moving from point A to point B. However, unless you have superpowers or are a genie on a 1950s sitcom, you can't just blink your eyes and be transported there instantly. Change takes work, planning, and effort, but in the end the change creates a better future for the organization (if done correctly).

Here are the states you move through during the change process while transforming the organization from A (current state) to B (desired state):

- **Current state:** The status quo, "the way things are done around here"

- **Transition:** The process of how you get to B, including, but not limited to, process, roles, emotions, measures, politics, technology, and so forth

- **Desired state:** Where you want to be

The process of moving through these states is called the *change cycle*. Companies often repeat the change cycle many times in response to competition, changing customer needs, economic conditions, and new technology.

In leading change, consider its two different aspects: the "what" and the "how" of change:

- **What: The content of the change at the desired state.** Identify what's changing in your organization. The change could be a new CEO being hired, a new product being introduced, expanding into global markets, implementing a new product-distribution system, or merging two complementary companies. The *what* of the change is simply the thing, person, or process that will be different.

- **How: The process of the transition phase.** Determine how you will reach the desired state and include the specific steps you will take during the transition phase to successfully lead the change. The process of how change happens is (almost) everything in this book. It involves how you set the vision and purpose of the change, how you communicate the change (and how you deal with resistance when people don't like what they hear!), and how you can include the people who are impacted by the change throughout the process.

How the change is implemented is almost as important as what the change is.

Moving out of the current state: Using SWOT to recognize a need to change

If change isn't easy, why in the world do you want to change in the first place? Pinpointing your need is the perfect way to start the change cycle.

A *SWOT analysis* looks at an organization's *strengths, weaknesses, opportunities,* and *threats.* It's a good tool to help leadership identify what areas need to change in order for the organization to thrive in the future and to help executives begin to frame the need for change. It can also help teams align the vision and goals with the costs and benefits of making the change happen.

Here we take a look at a quick SWOT analysis for a small consulting firm looking to expand its market share.

- ✔ **Strengths:** The company's strengths include knowledge of its offering, strong leadership, and a great product design.

- ✔ **Weaknesses:** The big weakness it needs to overcome is a small customer base and being the "best-kept secret" rather than the best-known firm.

- ✔ **Opportunities:** After considering strengths and weaknesses, leaders recognize a few opportunities: The company could partner with other firms, focus on specific niche marketing, or perhaps work to build its local market.

- ✔ **Threats:** Threats come in the form of large competing firms that may have more recognizable names.

The company now needs to decide what is going to change. In this case, the change involves building the customer base. To convey to employees why things need to change, management should start by explaining that although being the best-kept secret in the industry sounds neat, not being known means not being in business. The company sees the need for change as becoming a recognized name to build a bigger business (more customers) while maintaining its expertise in the field (its strengths).

Building the business case for change is one of the first steps leadership takes when undertaking an organizational change project. For more detail on how to recognize when change is needed and how to spot the indicators for change, see Chapter 2.

Defining the desired state: Deciding where you're headed

After identifying the threats and opportunities, the leaders are faced with a deceptively simple but critical step: identifying what changes they want to make to maximize their opportunities and minimize their threats. Before you can know how to make the change happen, you need to know where to go, and that direction depends on the kind of change you're talking about. Most changes address at least one of the six key change areas:

- Markets and customers
- Products and services
- Technology
- Productivity and business processes
- Reward systems and performance management
- Organizational structures

Although changing any one of these six areas can result in significant change, most likely any change your organization undertakes will not be in isolation. For example, if a company is undergoing a significant technology change, the productivity gains will not fully be realized if processes that manage how work is done don't change as well. The leadership team may decide how to build a larger customer base, but don't neglect thinking about how new products and services may help expand your current customer base.

Checking out the change formula

Wouldn't it be nice if a formula could guarantee successful change? Unfortunately, whenever people are involved, change can be difficult and complicated. But the following formula will get you on the right track to success:

$$\text{Focus} \times \text{Drive} \times \text{Time and Resources} = \text{Change}$$

You have already begun to tackle both focus and drive: *Focus* comes from knowing where you are headed, and *drive* comes from an understanding of why the organization needs to go there rather than continuing to accept the status quo. The last part of the equation is time and resources devoted appropriately, and that factor is where planning comes in — the topic of the next section.

Short change checklist

Are you ready to change? Before moving forward with creating your change plan, use the following two-item change-readiness checklist to make sure you have the right reasons and the right vision for change:

✔ **Do you have a solid focus on the future?** Set a vision of the change. In a few sentences, describe the business case for change and what the organization will look like after the change is successful — and ask others to do the same.

✔ **Does the organization have a strong drive to change?** Know your threats and opportunities. How will the change help you respond to threats and opportunities the organization is facing? List the benefits of the change as well as what the organization may have to give up in order to make the change happen.

For a more detailed organizational change readiness assessment, see Chapter 2.

Planning Like a Pro: A Road Map for Change

Planning helps you continue to build a business case that outlines the expected benefits of changing as well as supports the case for change by aligning time and resources for the duration of the change. The plan also solidifies the leadership structure that will be responsible for organizing and managing all the activities during the change.

Your change road map is your map to the future state. By following the key steps in the process, the organization will be on the right track to successful change.

Step 1: Create the vision and motivation to change

For the change to be successful, it must be embraced throughout the organization. And for it to be embraced throughout the organization, the benefits, consequences, and expected results must be understood by everyone and be seen as a top priority by key stakeholders, the people who have a vested interest in the change. (For more on stakeholders, see Chapter 2.) By setting a vision for change and putting the motivation in motion, your leadership team paints the picture of the future.

The vision for change must be easy to understand and be clearly communicated to employees, because complicated theories and visions detached from the reality employees face day in and day out will get change moving as fast as molasses in January. During this stage, leaders clarify the areas for change based on the strategy, long-term goals, and opportunities for the future. They also identify the benefits of change. Piggyback off discovering the need for change and defining where you are headed, change leaders should answer the question: Why should people in the organization want the change to happen in the first place? The answer will be the source of motivation in the organization.

Here are the characteristics of a good vision of change:

- ✓ **Inspiring:** With the effort that change takes, having a vision that gets people going and energizes the organization is essential to motivating employees. It should excite people and garner support.

- ✓ **Simple:** Come up with a vision that you can explain clearly and concisely in just a few minutes. Make the vision easy for everyone to understand and remember.

- ✓ **Focused on the future:** The vision should focus on the future and create a common purpose everyone can rally behind.

Although we can't tell you one definitive way to create a vision for where the organization is headed, we can clue you in on a few principles that can help you create a clear picture of the future. Chapter 4 contains the details of creating a vision, but to get you started, keep three principles in mind:

- ✓ **Be strategic.** The opportunities to change may be infinite, but the capital, resources, time, and energy are not. Get strategic so you know where to invest. Being strategic means investing in the areas of the business that will diminish the threats and capitalize on the opportunities.

- ✓ **Think multidimensionally.** Change is not a single checkbox — it's a multidimensional endeavor. If the organization realizes that it must perform better to meet future opportunities and threats, everything from work processes, information, and technology tools to decision making and performance management must be accounted for in the change. With the effort it takes to make change happen, just changing one aspect of the organization may not make the desired measurable change happen.

  Likewise, if the organization realizes that the biggest threat comes from not being structured to react quickly to the market, change can't end with restructuring the organizational chart; change should happen by looking at how information flows through systems and technology as well as how performance is measured and rewarded.

✔ **Establish a strong mandate.** As you embark on making change happen, remember that change can be a bumpy road. Establishing a mandate and vision for change will keep your team energized during the more difficult times. Along the same lines, a leader with little strategic vision or authority to make change happen will face an uphill battle. A strong mandate includes having the right leader be responsible for the change and making sure that the plans for dealing with threats and opportunities of the future are realistic and strategic.

Step 2: Set goals using the SMART framework

After focusing the vision, set specific priorities and goals. A goal describes what is happening and when it will happen, and it answers two questions. First, how do you know a change is an improvement? Second, how do you know you achieved your change goal? Goals are effective when stated in the SMART framework: specific, measurable, action oriented and agreed on, realistic, and time bound.

✔ **Specific:** State the goal clearly and briefly in your goal statement.

✔ **Measurable:** Make the goal measurable by basing it on data, timeliness, quality, or customer satisfaction.

✔ **Action oriented and agreed on:** Make the goal focused on doing something different and make sure all the stakeholders are aligned to the goal.

✔ **Realistic:** Although goals should not be easy or just follow the status quo, goals that are too far out there are unbelievable — and probably unachievable. Find the balance between tweaking the system (the status quo with a little change) and being ambitious enough to make people work a little harder and stretch to make the change happen (not impossible).

✔ **Time bound:** Urgency is part of the change equation. Setting time-sensitive goals helps bring a sense of urgency to the change and keeps momentum going.

The goal statement not only helps the team stay focused on what needs to happen but also helps everyone know when the change will be completed.

For more on how to set goals for a change project, see Chapter 4.

Step 3: Begin to raise awareness

As a change leader, you'll be communicating throughout the change, and it will start from day one. Even during these early stages, you need to start communicating and raising awareness of what's happening and why the changes are vital to the organization's success. See the later section "Communicating Progress with the Five Strategic Messages" to get started on your communication plan, and then flip to Chapter 7 to delve into the details of forming a communication plan that keeps people in the loop and maintains enthusiasm at every step of the process.

Step 4: Build the team

Raising awareness of the change is a lot easier when you have a network of support, or a change team, to guide the change from beginning to end and encourage others in the organization to adopt the change as the project progresses. A change team should include the sponsor, project leader, and change agents.

Because the people doing the work that needs to change are often the most knowledgeable about how to transform the work or organization, front-line employees can be tapped as change agents to help support the project and own the outcomes of the project from day one. When putting together your change team, make sure to include some people who do the work that's going to be affected by the change.

Step 5: Develop an action plan

A change-management action plan shows all the planned change activities, project milestones, responsibilities, and expected benefits. One of the best ways to get started in creating a baseline change-management action plan is to conduct a *change-readiness assessment* that maps the as-is and to-be. To create this part of the plan, document and analyze current practices, levels of commitment, and skills and compare them against what will be needed in the future. This change-readiness assessment is often based on the six key change areas discussed in the earlier section "Defining the desired state: Deciding where you're headed." You know you have a good action plan if you can answer these questions:

- ✔ What are the gaps between the current state and future state of the business?

- ✔ What changes need to happen in the six key change areas in order to realize the organizational goals?

For more details on how to create the change-management action plan, see Chapter 5.

Step 6: Measure results

After change starts to happen, the cumulative effect of the changes builds momentum in the organization. Measure progress against the goals and milestones of the project to monitor how things are going, what has been achieved, and what is still left to do. A midpoint evaluation during larger-scale changes (and a similar one at the end of the change) helps teams to recognize successes and lessons learned. Here are a few questions to answer during this phase:

- ✔ Do we need to make any changes to the drive for change, the focus of the change, or the resources and time devoted to the change? (Remember the change formula.)
- ✔ How is the change being adopted throughout the organization?

For more on measuring results and tracking the implementation, see Chapter 6.

Step 7: Sustain the change

Getting from point A to point B takes effort and coordination, and after the change, the organization will want to make sure the change sticks so all that work wasn't for nothing. Leaders in the company should coordinate rewards and performance measures with the new way of doing business as well as make sure the culture of the organization supports the change, even long after the change team has disbanded. Following are the two questions you should answer during this phase of the journey:

- ✔ **If the organization were to do this again, what would we do differently?** These "do differently" items are part of the lessons learned.
- ✔ **How will the change last in the long term?** Organizational capacity means that the competency to make the change last is part of the business, not just part of the change team.

Consider doing a 90-day post-change review to make sure employees and leaders throughout the organization accept their new roles and organizational structure, understand what they can contribute to continue to sustain the change, and undertake any changes necessary to make sustaining the change more acceptable and productive for the life of the change. We outline the steps for leading an after-change review and discuss how to keep the ball rolling in Chapter 11.

Setting it into motion

With the road map to change planned out, you're ready to implement the changes in the action plan and involve the organization through communication and training on what the new organization will become in the future.

Sharing the vision, direction, and action plan with the leaders most impacted by the change makes it possible for these leaders to prepare and equip their employees for their new roles, new departments, new teams, new processes, and new culture. Change leaders can provide tools and coaching that help leaders in their new roles so the local or team leaders can take ownership of the specific changes impacting their people. This spread of information and involvement helps to minimize disruption and maintain productivity, provides opportunities for input into the plan, identifies training requirements that employees may need, and aligns incentives, recognition, and rewards within their departments.

You are probably seeing some themes in the way change happens: Transformational business change starts with a vision and then involves everyone in the organization to help align team and individual practices with the way the organization is headed.

Communicating Progress with the Five Strategic Messages

The purpose of communication during change is to make sure that anyone impacted by the changes is informed, understands, and eventually supports the new organization. This goal may sound simple, but unfortunately organizational leaders are sometimes preoccupied with making sure the internal intranet or marketing materials look perfect rather than ensuring that stakeholders know what is going on with the change. Sending out an e-mail showing how the plan is progressing is easy. It's a little more involved to target communication messages for specific audiences, provide opportunities for feedback, and make sure communication comes from multiple channels that the target audience prefers, but it's worth the trouble.

A communication plan should include information about the target audience, key messages the audience should receive, how the message will be delivered, and who owns the communication.

A structured and consistent communication plan actively engages stakeholders with two-way communication and keeps the change at the top of everyone's agenda. One size does not fit all when it comes to change, so be sure to include local or departmental customs and current communication channels when communicating the progress of the change. As the progress of the change is communicated, be sure to get feedback on how the change is going for the people (including managers) on the front lines of the change.

A communication plan filled with key messages will get the change off on the right start and answer questions as they come up during the project. These five strategic messages go along with the change road map as you communicate the progress of the change:

- ✔ **Clear, compelling vision:** Communicate a clear, compelling vision that answers the following questions. What is the change? How will the change impact the work of the people receiving the message? What will the desired state look like after the change is implemented? See the earlier section "Step 1: Create the vision and motivation to change" for more on vision.

- ✔ **Importance of the change:** Help employees understand why the change is important. Why do they need to change? Why is the change important to these employees? What's in it for them? How will the change improve the organization?

- ✔ **Goals and objectives:** Explain the specific goals and objectives of the change. Are leaders supportive of the change? Are there examples? Why is the change needed now?

- ✔ **What's happening:** Communicate frequent updates about the change. What is happening with the change? What milestones have been accomplished? Is anyone being rewarded and recognized for helping make the change happen?

- ✔ **Results of the change:** Share the results and benefits of the change. What success stories can be told about the change from customer and employee points of view? How have the metrics changed to show the change is working?

Throughout the change, don't forget to provide information on where employees and stakeholders can get more information and what they can do to help the change happen.

For everyone in the organization to see the need for change and make the change happen, the pain associated with not changing (consequences), the satisfaction with change (benefits), and an overall dissatisfaction with the same old, same old (status quo) must be understandable, simple, and communicated thoroughly. Project team leaders should work with managers throughout the organization to leverage existing communication channels to get the message across loudly, clearly, and consistently.

Check out Chapter 7 for how to create a communication plan for your entire project.

Managing the People Factors

When all is said and done, the success of change is based on how committed the people in the organization are to making the change happen and last for years to come. Even if your organization decides to replace its employees with robots, someone still needs to program those robots and control the switches. (Luckily, artificial intelligence genius Raymond Kurzweil predicts robots will not be as smart as humans until at least 2045.)

So for at least the next few decades, it's the people that matter. Throughout your change, leadership and employee involvement are two fundamental ways to help manage the people factors and make sure the change is adopted quickly and is accepted as the new way of doing business.

- **Committing to change:** Senior leaders drive change by creating a vision for the future, setting the organization's course for the future, and making sure accountability is assigned in the organization.

- **Actively engaging employees in the change:** Changes last when they are visible to employees, and the best way to make change visible is to get employees working on it. Employees are more likely to adopt a new way of doing business when they have been part of the problem-solving process. Leaders can encourage communication, but teams working together to develop the future immediately increase collaboration across departments.

Dealing with negative reactions

Although you and the change team may be jumping up and down with joy to see change happen, not everyone will feel the same way. If change is not handled correctly, negative reactions can get out of hand and potentially derail the entire project.

Keep in mind that the cycle of change is not just about how the change will happen and when the changes will be in place. Chapter 9 focuses on working through expected dips in productivity when working with potentially negative reactions to change, but we give you a preview here.

As change is introduced, most individuals have some apprehension about what is ahead of them. Change is by definition *different,* and doing things differently takes effort. Some individuals may be in denial about the need for change or even actively resist the change. Through an active and involving change plan, led by an exceptional change leader, employees begin to explore and eventually adopt the new way of doing business.

As you can probably guess, different employees move through this change cycle at different speeds, and some employees have greater productivity losses than others when working through each of the change stages. Many people have seen early adopters and innovators who change at the speed of light, and many leaders have had to deal with the laggards of change who only move kicking and screaming. Continuing to focus on the need for change and getting there by rewarding the right behaviors will be your golden key to move you and your employees through the cycle of change quickly and productively, so be sure to praise and reward the early adopters rather than punishing people who resist change.

Motivating to move forward

Substantial or transformational change in an organization is more involved than a simple improvement or flipping the switch on to a new technology solution. To go the extra mile, employees have to be motivated.

Motivating employees and the organization to move forward comes down to aligning people, financial resources, and time resources with an inspiring strategy. Many leaders are being asked to do more with less, and change often asks that as well. Align the action plans with sufficient resources to get the job done and make sure the plan is backed by a vision that people can rally behind. Energy, excitement, and motivation come quickly when the right resources, performance measures, and incentives are aligned to strategic change. (Conversely, burnout, false starts, and lack of motivation to change all come from *not* having the right alignment in the organization.)

Making the Change Durable

Choosing and using a consistent road map for change and aligning it with resources helps avoid bumps in the road and increases the likeliness of success in the future. Durable change comes from managing the process of change like a superstar and having the right content of change. The last ingredient to making change durable is building sustainability into it.

If the old way of doing business is still rewarded, the old way of business will quickly find a way back into the organization after the change team has moved on to other projects or promotions. For example, if the change involves improving product quality so that there are no customer complaints, but the only person being rewarded for customer satisfaction is the sales guy who goes out in the middle of the night to service a customer complaint, the change will not last. In this case, employees should be rewarded for improving product quality to prevent service calls in the first place. A good change in rewards structure would be to reward the sales guy for pulling the manufacturing team together to find out what happened and make sure the product is fixed so it never happens again. It is human nature to do what you are rewarded for doing.

Is your change durable? Your durability checklist should include the following actions:

✔ Support employees as they understand how they are personally connected to the change.

✔ Hold leaders responsible and accountable for the ongoing success.

✔ Create the opportunity for everyone to learn, and provide feedback throughout the change, not just when it happens (but that needs to happen too).

✔ Link desired performance to how people, teams, and the organization will be measured.

✔ Keep it easy. If changes are seen as more difficult than the status quo, the status quo will return. Change may take time to adopt, but the new way of doing business must make a positive impact on how work is done if the change is to last.

Chapter 2

You're the Boss: Addressing the Need for Change

. . . .

In This Chapter

▶ Deciding whether your organization is ripe for change

▶ Checking in with the key stakeholders

▶ Considering the content and process of potential change

. . . .

*I*n today's business environment, change is constant. Because change isn't going away anytime soon, forward-thinking leaders should *want* to address the change before they *need* to. Instead of dreading change or hoping it won't ever happen to you (which is highly unlikely), assessing and addressing the need for change prepares you and your organization to remain competitive.

You may have heard every imaginable argument against having to change, from "We're the best" to "We're too big to fail" and everything in between. But having the foresight to change at the right time leads to higher accountability within the organization and to clear expectations about how to address current capabilities and future needs.

In this chapter we start preparing you for almost any change that can come your way. We begin by explaining what change signs you should be looking out for on your road to the future. Then you discover some ways to consider how prepared for change your organization is and who the key folks may be in your change journey. We also discuss how to know which type of change your organization needs. At the end of the chapter, you'll be primed to be the change boss.

Spotting Change Indicators

How do you know if you need to change? Wouldn't it be nice if you had a big alarm that went off to let you know you need to change? Although that may seem like wishful thinking, you probably already have that big alarm button. Unfortunately, it may be lost in a swarm of e-mails, reports, and meetings. To dig out the big alarm button, ask yourself whether your company is going through or has been through any of these big change events:

- ✔ **Are you losing market share? Are profits suffering?** If other companies are taking over your market share by offering a product or service that's more appealing to your best customers, start thinking about changing the way your company differentiates itself in the marketplace and brings value to your customers. If someone else is luring your ideal customers (even if they aren't yours yet), the time is right to start changing.

- ✔ **Are your best employees leaving to work for your competitors?** If competitors have a better work culture or more progressive employment practices (flextime or work-from-home options) or are growing and offer more opportunities for advancement, start thinking about how you can change to attract and keep the best and brightest brains in your company.

- ✔ **Has new technology made your products or services obsolete? Or is your company's image simply outdated?** Things change, and they change fast. A good indicator of the need for change is having products and services that are stuck back in 1999. For example, if you're still trying to sell dial-up Internet service, you could use a change.

Sometimes the outdated feel comes from the culture of the company or a product's marketing, not necessarily from the product. Keep in mind that some of the best products and services haven't changed for years, perhaps even decades. For example, Coca-Cola has been around for decades and will still be here decades from now. The product remains stable and reliable, but the company's image changes with the times. Just because a product is old doesn't make it outdated.

- ✔ **Has the company been sold to another one or merged with another company?** If so, your company may have a perfect opportunity to implement change. When two companies come together as one, you can't just change the logo on the business cards and expect business to continue as usual. If no one steps up to manage the merge, issues will crop up in how people communicate, how teams work together, how performance is evaluated, and in hundreds of other people and process issues.

- ✔ **Is the company expanding — either geographically or into new product and market categories? Has globalization resulted in shifts in**

labor and materials costs? As your company grows, you have to identify what you need to change as well as what you should keep the same. Growth is a great thing in business, but growing without recognizing the need to change how the company operates is about as rational as trying to put a 10,000 pound elephant on a kid's scooter: It's not going to happen, and the scooter will probably be damaged in the attempt.

✔ **Do you have a new CEO or leadership team?** High-level personnel changes merit a change plan because they're bound to cause shifts in organizational direction, business goals, and even how individual and team performance are addressed. The change plan should include a strategy to address concerns and ideas of the employees working for the new leadership team.

✔ **Are you implementing a new technology platform in your company?** New technology is exciting, but with new technology comes new processes for work and new ways employees will do the work — in other words, change. If you just implement a new technology without addressing the people and process side of change, you will most likely end up paying for a wonderful tool that nobody can use or plans on using.

Don't sit back and assess whether you need to change how you do business only once a year. Refer back to your business plan frequently to track growth, market direction, and accountability within the organization.

A big mistake many executives make is changing too often, just because everyone else is changing. When you think about your change, make sure you really need to shake things up for long-term success.

Assessing Your Organizational-Change Readiness

Assessing your organizational-change readiness is simply a way of finding out the substantial common ideas that will either enable or confine the change from happening. We're giving away two $1,000-an-hour consultant-type change secrets right here — stakeholder mapping and stakeholder readiness assessment — so listen up.

Mapping your stakeholders

When you start considering change (or if change suddenly happens — see Chapter 4), your next questions should be "Who is it happening to?" and

"What are they going to think about it?" Answering these questions is where your stakeholder analysis comes into play.

A *stakeholder* is any individual or group who will be affected by the change or can influence the change (yes, that may be a very big list). *Stakeholder mapping* is a three-step technique you can use to categorize the influence that key people, groups of people, or departments have on the success of your change. By anticipating the kind of influence — positive, negative, or indifferent — that these groups have on your initiative, you can leverage their power proactively across the organization. Then, with a keen eye into what people think and feel about the change, you can prepare strategies to enlist the support of the people who can help the change happen and find ways to reduce the obstacles that will surely be put up by the people who don't want it to happen. What you're really getting down to is their attitude about the change.

Following are the three steps of stakeholder mapping:

1. **List all the change stakeholders (either groups of stakeholders, like the accounting department, or individuals, such as the VP of operations) and their roles in the organization on the stakeholder analysis.** See the first two columns in Table 2-1 for examples.

2. **Identify whether each stakeholder's influence on the change is high, medium, or low.** Does a certain stakeholder sign the check to pay for the change? If so, the influence is pretty high. Is a particular person in the department the unspoken leader who basically can make anyone agree to anything just by voicing his or her opinion? Yep, that person is high up there, too. You don't need a fancy title to have a good amount of influence. On the flip side, although the office gossipers may talk a lot about the change and *think* they have influence, their influence over the project may be very low in reality. (This step is represented in the third column in Table 2-1.)

3. **Identify whether their influence within the company is high, medium, or low.** This ranking differs from Step 2 because this time you're looking at how much weight the stakeholder's opinion has from an organizational perspective. Stakeholders' organizational influence has a big influence on making changes stick after they're implemented. (We get much more into stickiness in Chapter 11.) See the fourth column of Table 2-1 for examples of Step 3.

When identifying influence, make sure you differentiate the influence on the change and the influence in the company. These rankings can often be related to one another, but they're not always the same.

Your stakeholder mapping will look something like Table 2-1 when it's complete.

Table 2-1	Sample Stakeholder Mapping for New Finance System		
Stakeholder	*Role in Organization*	*Influence on Change Project*	*Influence within the Company*
Annie Brown	CEO	Medium	High
Raajeev Smith	Finance department head	High	High
Stan Black	HR manager	Medium	Medium
Joe Bing	Team leader	High	Low
Finance Reporting Group	Finance	Medium	Low

Assessing stakeholder readiness

Now that you have identified the key players and assessed their importance, you can find out who is going to help you and who is going to try their best to stop anything from changing. The readiness assessment is all about evaluation.

Don't overcomplicate the matter when it comes to change readiness. Using individual or group interviews, sit down with the stakeholders with high influence over the project and ask these power questions to help identify what you need to do to lead change in your organization:

✔ **What has been done to date to build commitment around the change?** Even in the beginning of the change, change leaders can start building commitment to the vision for the change or even the need to change.

✔ **What do you think or know about the forthcoming benefits of this change?** As the change gets moving into full gear, change leaders can start talking about the good things that will come from the change. Will jobs be easier to do when the change happens? Will there be more advancement opportunities in the new company? For more on how to involve employees in the change through two-way communication, check out Chapter 7 on communication and Chapters 8 and 9 on great ideas on how to motivate employees during the change.

✔ **What will you have to give up as a result of the change? What do you think other people will have to give up?** Although most of the change will be for the better, people may be sad about losing some things, like no longer working side by side with colleagues they have been working with for years or having to take the time to learn a new system or process while continuing to do their job.

✔ **What skills and resources do you believe are necessary? Do you have the right number of people and the correct skill sets on your team?** No one likes to admit that his team may need to upgrade its skills, but a change is a perfect opportunity to teach employees new technologies and processes. Understanding what additional skills may be needed to complete the change early on in the change cycle is always helpful.

✔ **Are you excited about the change?** The answer to this question speaks a thousand words. If the answer is "Uh, sure," then change leaders know they have some work to do on creating an inspiring vision. If the answer is "YES! We need this change," you know the change is off to a good start.

✔ **What specific employee issues may affect the success of the implementation in the organization? What other obstacles and barriers may impact the success of the project?**

✔ **Do you believe this implementation will disrupt business? What will the disruptions be? How can we minimize their impact on the business?**

After you have a wealth of knowledge about how your stakeholders feel about the change, you can make an assessment of how ready they are to embark on change. Some of your stakeholders will be excellent change adopters, others will be good change adopters, and, yes, some will be failing a little in the change department.

Are some of your stakeholders doing an excellent job at change and ready to quickly adopt the proposed change within their group or department? You can use these powerhouses of change to push this next change through. Your job will be to help partner these stakeholders with people in your organization who, shall we say, are not as "change ready." You can also use these change rock stars to help you communicate messages about the change and be your eyes, ears, and feet when it comes to making change happen.

Most likely, many of your stakeholders will be feeling neutral or somewhat supportive about the change. Your next step is to keep in touch with these stakeholders on a weekly basis. You want to make sure these stakeholders have every opportunity to ask questions and be heard as well as get any support they need to help make lasting change in their part of the organization. Maybe their group is great at communication but needs help with planning. Plan on leveraging their strengths and beefing up on their weaknesses, and you'll be well on your way to change success.

The best way to beef up weaknesses is to find individuals who can teach and mentor whose strengths complement the weaknesses. For example, if someone is great at strategy but not great at marketing your ideas, you can partner her with someone who is great at the communication and marketing side. Change leaders may find employees in other parts of the company or bring in a consultant to help coach employees on change skills. To make sure weaknesses do not hold you back, find a way to teach employees how to improve in the long run. When it comes to strengthening your weaknesses, live by the saying: *Give a man a fish, he eats for a day. Teach a man to fish, he eats for a lifetime.* Look for ways to teach and mentor weaknesses during change.

And, yes, you will have some skeptics (in the change world, we often call them *laggards*) who need a big push when it comes to change. If people who have a large amount of influence on the change are also laggards, remember that change takes time. If it was easy, well, you wouldn't need a book on it. Categorize what the laggards' biggest barriers are to supporting the change and start brainstorming how to address those issues. Most of the time, simply listening and responding to concerns of those stakeholders who are doubters will move them from pessimists to supporters of the change. We delve into an in-depth discussion on how to overcome resistance in Chapter 9, so flip there for more.

Laggards can become an energy drain. Don't invest too much time with these stakeholders if nothing is happening. If you do, you may end up spending 80 percent of your time on them with very slow or little return, versus 80 percent on those who can champion or help lead the change.

Identify the people who will have the most influence on whether the change will happen and how well it'll happen in the future. Keep these people within arm's reach. They say to keep your friends close and your enemies closer; in this case you want to keep everyone close and your high-influencers (both positive and negative) closer.

Deciding What Change You Need

Deciding what kind of change you need is the pre-work to change in many aspects, because change leaders in the organization need to decide what they are doing before doing it. We explore creating a vision of the change in Chapter 4, but in this section we discuss some ways to determine what change road you want to embark on before you and your organization get moving.

Determining the type of change

When you're making important judgment calls on exactly what kinds of changes your organization needs, you want to consider two things: the content of the change and the process of the change. If you go with the right type of change, employees will respond more positively, processes will function more smoothly, and your life will be light years easier.

To determine the change you want to undertake, first find out if the change is needed in the first place. Assess and prioritize possible changes against other changes in these areas:

- ✓ **Goals and results:** If no actions are taken, will the goals or results of the organization be compromised? If so, change in this area is a high priority.

- ✓ **Mission and vision:** Does the proposed change support the mission and vision of the organization? If the change is aligned with the bigger picture of where your organization wants to go, the change will have a higher chance of success. Otherwise, although the change may be nice to do, perhaps it isn't a great use of limited resources right now.

Prioritizing possible changes allows you to evaluate each change against one another and choose the most important ones to dedicate resources.

When you know that the organization needs to change, you can move on to determining the content and process of the change.

- ✓ **Content:** Are you dealing with transactional change or transformative change? *Transactional change* is primarily task-focused. These changes usually focus on strategic realignment of structures, processes, and systems. Implementing a new customer service program or reorganizing departments are often transactional changes. *Transformational or transformative change* is inspirational change that occurs through radical strategic repositioning and leadership changes, or through turnarounds that enable organizational survival or skyrocket growth. New CEOs and boards of directors being appointed, culture changes, and many mergers and acquisitions are transformational.

- ✓ **Process:** Which parts of the change will be happening in smaller steps (incremental change), and which will occur rapidly and only for a short period of time (immediate). Have you ever felt (or heard) that everything is constantly changing? That's true when it comes to incremental change, like slowly evolving a product line but still supporting earlier products for customers. On the other hand, some changes happen immediately, like switching from an old technology to a new one overnight, sometimes referred to as *flipping the switch*.

After leadership determines the content and process of the change, it is time to pull together the team, create measurements for success, and get moving (we start covering these in the following chapter).

Implementing a tried-and-true change model

The model you use to implement change has a big effect on what kind of change you get. And there are probably as many change models in existence as there are changes, but at its core, all change follows a simple process. The hard part is applying the process to your change and applying it consistently.

We assert that you don't need to recreate the wheel of change. These four steps will get you where you need to be. The wheel that works, no matter what you call it, rolls like this:

1. **Create a vision for change.** Leaders identify the change that is needed and create a picture of what the future will look like after the change happens.

2. **Plan the change.** Planning the change includes creating a team that will make the change happen, developing measurable goals, and identifying ways to include employees.

3. **Communicate the change.** Communication is a big part of change, but not just the communication that comes from the top of the organization. Change lasts when employees are empowered to make changes and their feedback is used throughout the change.

4. **Implement and revisit the change.** After you implement the change, everyone may be tempted to go back to what they were doing beforehand, but change needs constant attention. After the change happens, remember to check back in with employees to see how the change is working and find out if any modifications are needed to make it last.

Here's the change model you want to avoid. Stay far away from the method we like to call *Announce, consult, surface, and move on.* It goes like this: An executive announces a great idea he read about in his favorite business magazine or overheard on the golf course, he hires a bunch of consultants to recommend options for implementing the change, the organization begins to discover the real issue for change (which isn't half as exciting), and the executive moves on to the next big thing. This "announce and go do it now" model almost always ends up as a big old binder and fancy presentations that gather dust on the shelf — not exactly the result you're hoping for with your change.

Even though every effective change uses a similar process, it can be extraordinarily difficult for some companies to do it alone, without a business partner guiding them. Going it alone may cost a company more money than if they had sought guidance in the first place.

A change-theory history lesson

If some nosy person in your organization asks, "Well, what change method are you following?" just let him know that your ideas were inspired by two of the greats in change history: Dr. John Kotter and Kurt Lewin.

Back around the turn of the 19th century, organizational-change pioneer Kurt Lewin described organizational change in three basic steps: Unfreeze the old to become motivated to change, change what needs to change, and then refreeze the new to make it stick. Similar to our real-world model, we recommend making sure change sticks by revising measurements and changing structures to make change last long after the change team is done with the work.

Taking a chip off the old block from Lewin, in the 1990s Dr. John Kotter came up with an eight-step methodology that focuses on getting leaders to address change by creating a powerful vision and sense of urgency to change, forming a powerful team to guide the change, following an action-based plan, and making sure the change is embedded as the way to do business. Both Kotter and Lewin have a strong emphasis on leadership-driven change that motivates employees with an urgent need to change.

These two grandfathers of change are the basis for our real-world model: create a vision of the future, make a plan, communicate like crazy, and revisit the change to make sure it is working. And remember, whether you're setting the vision, planning, communicating, or making the change last, remember to engage employees every step of the way.

Chapter 3

Embracing Change-Leader Roles

*R*esilient leadership is pivotal in the change process. Whether you're in a formal leadership position or an informal leadership role, as a change leader, you will help set the plan for change, gain commitment for the change, communicate the change, and demonstrate ownership of the change. You may also find yourself preparing the organization for the change, selecting the right people to work on the change effort, and ensuring an effective process of change. So when we say you need to embrace the role of a change leader, we really mean *embrace* it, because that responsibility is here to stay, and you can't delegate it down to other members of the organization. Someone else can write up a project plan or an e-mail, but sponsoring success is going to have to come from you.

Of course, you may still need or want help. Leadership during change is rarely a one-man or one-woman show. You can manage some obstacles and barriers you'll face during the change yourself, but other issues require the influence of other leaders to shepherd the project to success.

In this chapter we look specifically at the roles and responsibilities of leaders during change, examining what each role should focus on throughout the change process. We also highlight one of the most critical aspects of leadership during change: leading by example. Because no change is exactly like any other and the change process isn't just a matter of flipping a switch, you find out when you need to push a little more, when you need to engage others to help you, and when you need to step back and let change just happen.

Recognizing the Call for Leadership

When your business is changing, you can respond in one of three ways:

- ✔ Do nothing and let it look after itself.

- ✔ Manage it by sending out e-mails, creating a project plan, and having lots of meetings and a great internal website about the project.

- ✔ Lead the change by creating a vision, communicating change with passion, and inspiring employees by empowering them to make the change happen.

Did you guess that the last option is the best approach? Brilliant!

In this section, we cover how leadership differs from management and how to lead by example.

You can think of change like going on a trip. Your current state is where you are today and your desired state is where you want to go. Unless you have the power to blink your eyes and get you there, you have to do a few things first: find a place to stay, pack your suitcase, decide who is coming with you, get delayed in airport security, and so on. All these details are the transition. Your business change is no different. You want to get to your future, but you have to do some things to get there. And here's the big kicker for leading change: Your goal is to lead the change so the road from here to there is as smooth as possible!

Understanding the difference between managing and leading

How often have you committed to something 100 percent just because you read an e-mail or went to a meeting? Probably not often — or ever. People don't change because they are told to; otherwise, everyone would eat perfectly because the doctor said to and children would always listen politely and use proper manners.

Writing e-mails, making a beautiful project website and project plan, and having lots of meetings will only get you so far during a business change. These activities are simply the management of change.

Managing change is defined by making sure that steps are checked off. *Leading change* is making sure the change is giving employees the tools and information they need to make the change happen (and last). Communicating change is critical, but communication while leading change focuses on interactive dialogue, not just messages.

Sometimes simply managing a change works just fine. For example, if you're just planning to change the mailroom hours at your company, go ahead and communicate the message (see Chapter 7) and then switch over to those new times. But if the strategy of the business is changing, if the change impacts people (jobs, pay, roles, management structure), or if the change will alter the way you do business, leading change will make you and your change a success.

Business change involves working with human behavior. To generate lasting results, you need to align people around a common goal that everyone has committed to. And you need to strive for efficiency while achieving that goal. If you embark on business change by leading it, your change will result in an organization-wide commitment to making change happen that can be seen, heard, and felt by the business.

What does it take to lead change?

- ✔ **Set an example for others to follow.** Commitment is not just about saying the right thing; it's about doing it. We discuss leading by example in detail in the next section.

- ✔ **Involve employees and get buy-in.** Nothing gets people invested like the leader asking for their opinion and then listening to it. Good change leaders know that listening to employees' ideas and engaging them in business decisions is one of the main ingredients to developing a motivated and innovative workforce.

  Employees need to be engaged in the process so they gain ownership of the change and want to make the change last.

- ✔ **Make procedural and structural changes, but don't stop there — make things look different.** If you desire a culture that rewards results, make sure people see results on the walls, in meeting rooms, and when they walk into the office in the morning. If you want people to focus on team behavior, tear down the large walls that separate teams (literally!). A small change like rearranging workspaces to help tear down the walls of "silo" departments can do a tremendous amount to boost conversations and interaction.

Don't get too caught up in physical changes and neglect real procedural change. Creating more open work environments with colorful and modern chairs is great, but if you still need to get 26 approvals on 14 different forms to buy a pencil, change will just be on the surface.

As a change leader, you can take the first steps by personally making the change happen in your own team or department. Take the first step by walking the talk and making things look different by asking employees what the change means to them and then acting on it.

Leading by example

When a leader leads by example, maintains interest, and holds the pedal to the metal to keep intensity and commitment at their highest levels, the rest of the organization usually picks up on it, and people increase their own belief in the change. Regardless of your role, you have a great opportunity to make change happen by simply making the change happen with your own leadership style first. Whether you have a team of 100 employees or just manage your own work, think about what you can personally change to be more aligned with the vision of the future for the organization.

The best leaders make change an organizational value by expressing, modeling, and reinforcing the principles in day-to-day operations. Have you ever had a manager who wouldn't walk the talk and who gave only face time to important issues rather than really working on them? We bet it was a pretty miserable experience. While implementing change, leaders must demonstrate integrity and act consistently with what they're asking of the organization's members. Following are the four key actions that a leader should take to effectively lead by example:

- ✔ Express the desired behavior.
- ✔ Model the desired behavior through decision making and day-to-day activities.
- ✔ Reinforce the desired behavior through forms of recognition and rewards.
- ✔ Endure to the end.

Suppose that during a large technology change at your company, a new reporting system is implemented, but most of your team still is using spreadsheets to do work. Leading by example means you toss those formulas and worksheets and embrace and use the new tool. If you are asking someone else to do something, make sure you are willing to do it and are doing it, too.

Here's another example. Many companies are trying to change to better support a culture of work-life balance, but if you're replying to e-mails at midnight, your own balance is pretty out of whack. You can say to employees, "Take time for yourself," but if you're not doing it, your employees will have a hard time doing it.

Leading by example is not always as black and white as those examples, but it's the foundation for respect from others in your organization. If you want people to show up to meetings but you're frequently leaving the room to answer phone calls, your employees and peers will think you're insincere. If you want to implement a new performance-measurement system that rewards results but you constantly reschedule performance-discussion meetings with your employees, the change will be seen as superficial.

When leaders' actions are inconsistent with their words, they can destroy the trust needed for an organization to effectively implement change. Even the most intricate and well-orchestrated plans will fall on deaf ears when the trust and credibility of the change leader is lost.

Doing a changing-by-example audit

Leading by example seems easy enough at first, but in reality it takes practice. Because leading by example is so far-reaching, we recommend you take a personal audit of the example you want to set for the change. The two areas you want to address in your personal "changing by example" audit are what you physically and mentally give attention to and what new skills you're mastering in the new environment.

  ✔ **Attention:** Where do you spend your time and energy? Are these items aligned with the goals of change? If not, what needs to change to make sure your calendar reflects the new way you want others to work?

  ✔ **Capabilities:** Have you taken the time to learn the skills you need as a change sponsor, change agent, or change advocate (see the later section "Role Playing: Assuming Different Roles during Change" for details)? If you take the time to learn how to become a better change expert, everyone around you will follow your example. Do the same for the new capabilities you'll need in order to operate in your new business environment.

What you do and how you do it is equally important when it comes to mastering the change process and the new way of doing business.

Sneaking in examples

When it comes to changing by example, the rubber really hits the road when new skills are ready to be put in action. Until things are really done differently, you can say one thing but do something else. When the time for action comes, everyone can see who isn't walking the talk.

Do any of these situations sound like your organization?

  ✔ Skills and knowledge are assumed, not taught or developed. People learn on the job or through water-cooler conversations.

  ✔ Quality issues are dealt with after the fact, rather than eliminated earlier in the product development process. Employees may be rewarded for being the hero and saving the day for a customer when a product breaks rather than employees being rewarded for stopping the problem before it happens.

  ✔ Individuals complain about not having information, clearly defined roles, or straightforward responsibilities, but they then run as fast as they can (the other way) when asked to adhere to new standards.

If you're nodding your head, we have great news for you: All of these situations can easily be turned into opportunities to lead by example. If skills and knowledge are assumed in your organization, have other employees (often your change agents and advocates) step up and teach classes. If you praise teams who get up at midnight to go fix something, start turning your attention to the teams that actually got to sleep through the night because they did things right the first time. If individuals complain about not having clarity, allow them to create the clarity for the new change.

Leading by example doesn't have to be a huge shift in the way things are done — small changes can add up to a big change in total.

Role Playing: Assuming Different Roles during Change

For each change leader, the authority and responsibility to remove barriers and provide adequate resources must be within reach. But the change leader must also have the softer skills necessary to get everyone on board with the change. Regardless of the leadership badge you may wear during change, these softer skills are common and essential for all roles. Beyond anything else, change leaders are individuals who

- Influence people
- Facilitate and drive discussions for answers
- Make decisions

Multiple levels of leadership commitment, resource support, and hands-on involvement are critical for successful change. Because each leader within your organization has different formal leadership capabilities (spans of control and authority) as well as informal competencies (political influence, leadership style), they take on distinct leadership roles during the change.

The three main roles to be be filled by you and other leaders within your organization are change sponsors, change agents, and change advocates. Each role is pivotal to the success of the project in its own special way. In this section, we make sure you're comfortable with the tasks associated with each role. Table 3-1 shows you a quick overview of what each change role is responsible for during sequential stages of the change. The following sections explain each role in more detail.

TIP

All leaders involved in the change process must share the same view of the change and what it's intended to accomplish; we dive into how to come up with shared vision and measures in Chapter 4.

Table 3-1	Responsibilities of Change Leaders		
Change-Cycle Step	*Role of Change Sponsor*	*Role of Change Agent*	*Role of Change Advocate*
Seeing a need for change	Encouraging organization to take risks and change direction	Taking the risk to make change happen; owning the change	Challenging the status quo; encouraging peers to do the same
Deciding where you're headed	Building change into the organizational strategy	Making sure the real change is part of the organization strategy	Making the strategy work
Developing the road map for change	Involving others to build the plan for how change will happen	Accepting and owning the road map; making the road map happen	Voicing concerns with the plan; recommending ideas
Setting it into motion	Providing resources to support the change	Aligning the resources to make change happen	Enacting the plan
Communicating the progress	Sharing ownership of communication plan; acting as a spokesperson for change	Relating communication to employees' day-to-day work	Informing peers of the change
Dealing with negative reactions	Working with senior leaders to resolve conflicts	Networking within their area to resolve conflicts	Raising issues with the change
Motivating to move forward	Giving recognition for the change; monitoring results	Getting recognition for the change; measuring results	Getting recognition from peers and leaders for making change happen
Making the change durable	Working with team to design the new structure to support lasting change	Making the new structure real	Operating in the new way of doing business

Sponsoring success

Many of the change activities we explore in this book come under the banner of sponsoring change. *Sponsoring* a change means that you have the responsibility for the processes that are being affected by the change and the formal authority to make the change happen. Needless to say, sponsoring success is a pretty big deal.

Sponsors usually come in two varieties:

✔ **Initiating sponsor:** Typically a high-level executive who has both the vision and authority to launch the change effort

✔ **Sustaining sponsor:** Picks up the responsibility for his or her part of the organization

That being said, you may very well be or work with someone who is the perfect blend of both these roles. During most large changes, only one or two people are the official sponsors of change.

If you are sponsoring a change, what exactly have you signed up to do? We're so glad you asked. Following is a rundown of what you'll be doing as you sponsor successful change:

✔ Describing the compelling need for the change and communicating its benefits to others within your organization

✔ Providing resources such as people, money, space, and tools for the change to happen

✔ Making time available in the organization to allow the change to move forward

✔ Being available to the other change leaders, project leaders, and change-team members to resolve issues and set direction

✔ Personally demonstrating the desired behaviors wanted from the change

✔ Communicating to your organization the key messages and ideas in the communication plan

Did you fall over in your chair? Are you running the other way? Although this list may seem like a lot of things to take care of, remember you aren't going to do it alone. Not only do you have this trusty book at your side, but you also have a team of leaders within your organization to help you. This is where the change agents and change advocates come into play, so don't sweat it, and keep reading the next two sections.

The need for change is often seen first by people who aren't in a position of authority or power. Therefore, engaging employees in the change through two-way communication and cross-functional teams is very important. Change happens when leaders can bridge strategy and vision to real problems and opportunities in the organization.

The change sponsor's primary roles are to validate that the change is happening through the dedication of resources and to provide a compelling reason for change to happen.

Being a change agent

Sponsors are the ones building the plan and providing resources; *change agents* are the ones who get the plan off the ground. Change agents are embedded within the organization at the department or regional level, so they're always within arm's reach of the people doing the work that is changing. Think of change agents as field agents who find out what's really being said about the change, help to correct any discrepancies in the change, and make sure everything runs like clockwork throughout the change plan.

Change agents fill both a formal and informal leadership role during business transformations. Change agents possess a broad understanding of the business, especially in their functional area. Because of their close communication with the project team, they're one of the best sources of information for what's happening on the project.

So what exactly does a change agent do? You get a good overview of what change agents do in each stage of change in Table 3-1, but the following list addresses change agents' overall responsibilities and roles:

- ✔ Being the single contact source for specific change in their areas
- ✔ Ensuring that whatever changes happen meet the needs of people doing the work
- ✔ Actively working to demonstrate the desired behaviors
- ✔ Assisting in the training assessment process
- ✔ Helping with the transfer of knowledge for new roles and processes
- ✔ Gaining knowledge of the new change before it happens
- ✔ Assisting in the identification of area-specific communication needs
- ✔ Communicating key messages and ideas in the communication plan

When identifying a change agent for a project, ask yourself two questions. Is this person fully committed and passionate about the future of the company and making the future real? Is this person genuinely in a position, either formally or informally, to influence others, or would the role be better filled by someone with more credibility or authority?

Serving as an advocate

Change agents and change sponsors are formal positions within change projects, but one informal role, the change advocate, is what makes change happen successfully and efficiently. Change advocates can either be self-elected or be a standing, cross-functional team of front-line resources in non-supervisor and non-management positions. Either way, they're responsible for providing guidance and feedback to the change agents, change sponsor, and project team on critical decisions and approaches during and after the life of the program.

Change advocates understand the business needs and are passionate about facilitating positive change. With this in mind, following are the four most important qualities change advocates possess:

- Living in the future, but understanding the past and present of the company
- Being fueled by passion, and inspiring passion in others
- Possessing a strong ability to self-motivate
- Understanding the people and processes around them (how things really work)

The fact is, anyone can be a change advocate as long as he or she is willing and able to facilitate change and be personally accountable for making change happen in an area of work.

Change advocates fill informal roles within change projects, but that doesn't mean they are an optional part of the process. Some of the most compelling changes happen when change advocates simply live and breathe the change and share this experience for change with others. Nothing supports change more than telling a story of how the change is helping you to do more or create better results. We talk more about creating a vision for the future in Chapter 4, but you don't always need to speak of some grand vision of the future to inspire people to do things differently. Sometimes the best change is driven by peers advocating the new way of doing things.

Change advocates can make a world of difference by being wonderful storytellers. Change advocates, because of their hands-on, non-management role, can put the problem and solution in black and white, in a less threatening manner than more-formal or senior roles can often do.

For an example, start by taking a look at how a particular change is communicated by a change sponsor:

> **Change sponsor:** *Over the past five years, we have faced some of the toughest economic challenges in our history. But we have fought for survival and made personal sacrifices, and we are leaner, stronger, and faster than ever before. The future is bright, and, with the significant changes we are making in our products, we will be the number one company in our market in the next two years.*

This message is to the point and maybe even a little inspiring. But look how different the story is when a change advocate talks about the exact same change:

> **Change advocate:** *Five years ago, half my department was laid off after the markets tumbled. As I looked at my friends packing up their desks for the last time, not really sure how they would tell their families they no longer had a job, I made a vow to myself that this would not happen again. I know personally how hard it has been to let go of products and processes we have been building for over 20 years. But because of these changes we're making, yesterday we hired back some of those same people who lost their jobs five years ago, and let me tell you, it is good to be back together again. Change is tough, and change is making a difference, and it is a difference I want. Will you join me?*

You can see how each role you can play during change is critical for success. Whereas change sponsors bring the resources (money) and the vision for the future and change agents are the eyes, ears, legs, lungs, and arms of the change, the change advocates are the ones who often make the heart of change beat.

We recommend creating a front-line council to make sure the views of employees throughout the organization are heard. A *front-line council* is a formal group of change advocates who get the inside scoop on information and actively campaign for the change.

Working with Your Change-Leadership Style

The world is filled with all types of people, so you shouldn't be surprised to find out that leaders come in all types, too. All leaders will be able to possess all these skills to an extent, but everyone has their preferred style. The key to being able to drive results is knowing your leadership style and then being able to use it to its fullest when leading change. The icing on the cake is being able to adapt your leadership style to fit the needs of the organization.

This book looks at a number of aspects of change and how organizations can successfully navigate through change. Maximizing your own change-leadership style focuses more on your own capabilities and style and how those fit in to the overall organizational strategy.

Great change leaders know their style, apply it appropriately, and adapt it as necessary. Maximizing your leadership style is about knowing your work style, knowing how you interact with peers, leaders, and your team, and understanding how you can adapt your style to be effective in the change environment.

That being said, to make organizational change happen, you may have to do a little work on how you work with others. Sorry, no getting around that, but we promise to make it as painless as possible.

Plan to use both modes of change leadership. Although a shared style of leadership is often the best way to make change last, some days you may have to make a decision to get the ball moving again when little or no time is available for debate.

Knowing your leadership style

As a leader, you're challenged to align the needs of different individuals and teams with the strategy and changes happening in your organization to drive results. Understanding your own leadership style and how to apply and adapt it during change goes a long way to helping make change seem like a nice walk in the park (well, maybe not that easy, but you get the point).

Although every organization is unique, two basic leadership approaches drive decisions and results in most organizations (and at times can limit any results from happening). In this section we take a peek at the main ways things get done in organizations.

Hierarchical leadership

In hierarchical organizations, the flow of information is like a pyramid. It has a clear order and defined levels of leadership, and who has authority is obvious. This increased administration often delays the change, but the roles and responsibilities are crystal clear.

Hierarchical organization sometimes gets a bad reputation for not being free flowing with information and for taking too much time to have ideas for change move up the chain of command, but in reality these organizations have a sense of stability and focus on completing the task at hand. Change doesn't happen quickly in hierarchical organizations, but when the boss says change is going to happen, it often does, because he begins the process and the organization is set up to make processes work. During the storm of change, the stability of how information flows down the pyramid in the organization provides a sense of calm. As long as the change follows the same process and procedure, change can happen, even if it moves at a snail's pace at times. Organizations and leaders who thrive in hierarchical environments pay close attention to procedures and standards and value clearly defined performance expectations.

Are you in a hierarchical organization? The benefit of this organizational structure is consistency. The downside is, well, consistency. Although a change may happen like clockwork after it's put in motion, the initial impetus for change tends to get caught up in paperwork.

If you find yourself working with a hierarchical boss, use the structure to your advantage to create change. Ask your boss to push the idea up the chain of command and focus changes on how they will improve the processes and procedures within the organization. You also want to get a strong group of change agents who can translate the decision to real action on the front lines.

Are you a hierarchical leader yourself? If you like structure and think dotted lines are for kids coloring books, not organizational charts, you may need to take your resistance to new ideas and opportunities down a notch, especially if you resist ideas because "that's not the way things have always been done in the past." Ask change agents and change advocates in the organization for their ideas on how to solve problems. You may even enlist a peer to give you an alternative point of view — preferably one that's not just from the top looking down.

Although some two-way discussion takes place between the big boss and the second-biggest boss in hierarchical organization, people sitting on the bottom of the pyramid may feel they are often the recipients or targets of change, with little back-and-forth discussion happening at their level because the decision and discussions already took place. Hierarchical organizations can consider implementing skip-level talks (talks that have employees speak directly to a leader a few levels up the chain) to get involved in the change earlier in the process.

Some hierarchical leaders are also *top-imposing leaders,* who tend to have the hardest time implementing lasting, meaningful change because they decide what's going to happen and then hand it over to employees to make it work. In a hierarchical environment, the change flows in something of a step-ladder fashion, but top-imposing leaders look more like an ivory tower in the sky with peasants down below. If you work with this type of leader, don't despair. With the right coaching, top-imposing leaders can reduce the emphasis on controlling people and conditions by listening more to employee ideas and being more accepting of those suggestions. Coach these leaders to recruit change agents and advocates to tell it like it is, and then make sure they don't throw them out on the street when they tell the truth. Show these leaders that by listening with patience they may just find answers to the problems the organization is facing right on the other side of their desk.

Top-driven leadership can dictate the vision but then rely on employees to make their own decisions about how to make the vision come alive. This system creates a greater sense of shared ownership from the bottom up.

Shared leadership

Collective organizational styles and change leaders who focus on doing things together tend to see change happen the quickest and with the most acceptance. Although the change sponsor is still in charge of the change, sponsors work closely with change agents and the recipients of change to make sure the *right* change is put in place, even if it doesn't come from the top. In this type of environment, the emphasis is more on involvement in the decision-making process rather than who is making the decision. It sounds like a pie-in-the-sky ideal change environment, and, frankly, it can be.

Keep in mind the downside to these shared organizational change structures during change: Without a specific boss to call the shots, your organization may experience confusion and even power struggles between leaders to show who's in charge. But when managed well, a shared ownership change style possesses a speed of communication and adaptability that other groups envy, in which employees are encouraged to make changes that are right for the organization.

Are you in a shared organization? Lucky you. You probably have been told you have a voice in change, and you actually do. If find yourself in this type of a structure and love change, stand up and let your ideas be heard — and then get ready to get to work, because you may find yourself being responsible for making those great ideas happen.

Are you a "let's do it together" leader? The one downside of having a change-adaptable shared style is making sure that crystal-clear accountability is assigned for what happens next. Even though the responsibility can be shared, decisions still need to be made. Make sure you and your change agents and the recipients of the change know how and when a tough decision may have to be made for the benefit of the team.

Adapting your change-leadership style for optimal success

The real key isn't what type of change leader you are; it's how you use your style to deliver results. There's no absolutely right way to get change to happen and stick. No single mode of communication or leadership suits every person's needs. Being able to adapt leadership styles is what sets change leaders apart from those only capable of managing change.

However, change, innovation, and ownership come when people are involved in the process, not just told what to do. If a command-and-control style of leadership works for your organization, that's perfectly fine, but change is about challenging the status quo. The more that change agents, change sponsors, and change advocates can have equal but different voices during the change process, the more likely change will stick long into the future.

If a sudden crisis situation hits an organization, leaders may need to make decisions that are not shared or inclusive. If this happens, stepping up the communication and being open about why a decision was made by a select few rather than a larger population is the best alternative. And don't forget, even though a change decision may have been made quickly, all the work to make the change last still needs to happen, which is where you can include multiple opinions and ideas from employees.

Most organizations use multiple types of leadership styles. Your company may have a very clear pecking order, but within your department or peers, responsibility and ideas may be shared equally.

The way to maximize results through your change-leadership style is to think of change in two related and intertwined, yet distinct, work streams:

- ✔ Make the project a success.
- ✔ Make the company sustainable with a shared purpose in the long term.

Any leadership style can make a project a success. Even the most top-isolated, clueless-about-reality leader can get from point A to point B on a project plan. But you probably want a little more out of change than just saying, *woohoo, we changed,* and then letting things go back to how things were done before.

You can hire any consulting company to come in and create a change plan, write up communication materials, and provide training on the new way of doing business, but you can't hire consultants to maximize results in the long term. That change has to come from you and your leadership team.

We're not going to tell you to go and change everything about you (see, we promised this wasn't a self-help book), but adapting your leadership style to maximize results looks something like this:

- ✔ Stepping out of your comfort zone when your leadership style or structure doesn't get the intended results
- ✔ Realizing when you need to step out of your comfort zone before the results don't turn out the way you want them to

So when do you use different styles to make things happen? We don't have a crystal ball or psychic capabilities, but we can tell you that the following adaptability options will get you tuned into your own supernatural leadership powers:

✔ **Blend communications from the top bosses with those of advocates on the field to beef up your communication and make it a conversation.** Ongoing change needs robust, dialogue-based communication. The trickle-down method of communication rarely works at the speed change needs, so balance a shared-ownership change style with clear messages from the top. Target at least 50 percent of communications to be dialogue based, not top-down presentations. (For more on communication, head over to Chapter 7.)

✔ **Create a clear line of sight to strategic initiatives for all employees.** *Line of sight* means all employees know how their actions impact the bigger picture. Although shared leadership styles are great for ownership, they sometimes fall short in listing out how what one person does impacts another aspect of the business downstream. (Hierarchical organizations and leaders tend to excel at providing line of sight.)

✔ **Prominently reward new behaviors and accomplishments.** Regardless of style, by acknowledging people and teams that change, you can help propel others to make changes. People do what they are rewarded for, so look for the new behaviors and let people know you appreciate the change. For more on rewards and motivation, check out Chapter 8.

When you start adapting your style, you will start to hear different comments in your organization as well. First, the murmurs may sound like, "Maybe this is different." Then they'll move to, "This *is* different." By the end of the process, people who may have been critical at first may be transformed into change advocates, saying, "What can I do to make it happen?"

Part II
Putting the Plan into Motion

"Okay, who wants to kick off a discussion about the importance of change?"

In this part . . .

Great change starts with a vision and need for change and ends with a perfectly executed plan. The heart of change work comes down to these elements: leadership with a strong vision of how the change will make the future better, two-way communication, and engaged employees. In this part you roll up your sleeves and get to work on all these areas.

Whether your organizational change flew in overnight or came after years of strategic planning, this part gives you the tools to make the change happen. You build your toolbox for change with a solid change road map and find out who the best candidates are for the change team. You review the fine art of project planning and find ways to integrate the people side of change with the process of change. We also take a peek at change scorecards to help you measure success. Finally, you bring everyone into the loop by developing a communication plan that will deliver on the communication trifecta: getting the right information out to the right people at the right time.

Chapter 4

Assembling Your Change Toolkit

In This Chapter
▶ Creating a vision everyone can support
▶ Assembling the change dream team
▶ Keeping the change process ethical

*Y*ou're ready to get moving. In Part I, you discover how to begin brainstorming and managing the organizational change process within your organization. And starting right here and now, you need to start filling your change toolbox. With what, you ask? With the right mechanisms for aligning your strategy, values, goals, and processes from top to bottom throughout the change project. You also need to assemble your core team who will help you cross the finish line. This task isn't easy, and you may feel somewhat overwhelmed. But we're here to help.

In this chapter, you come to an understanding of the steps you take to guide the process of change, and you find out how to use these steps to bring about the desired results. We also help you make sure you're addressing change from an ethical point of view. With all the new tools you receive in this chapter, you'll be able to get your change team up to speed quickly and get that change rolling.

Looking to the Future State: Steps to Get There

As you fill your change toolbox, focusing on three core steps helps you move your organization from the current state (today) to the future state (where you want to be):

1. Building an inspiring vision

2. Creating a change road map

3. Factoring in what's helping or hindering change

Think of these steps as your hammer, glue, and saw. With them in place, you can do just about anything. Check out the how-to info on each step in this section.

Building an inspiring vision

Whoa, Nelly! Before you can get too far in leading change, you have to first define your vision of the future. What will the future look like when the change has happened? This vision so important because it keeps you moving forward and gets you through the transitional bumps in the road. It's a clear, compelling statement that gives everyone a picture of where you're headed. A vision usually considers the elements of products, services, customers, relationships, employees, technology, and culture and has supporting details that describe how the vision will be achieved. And you better make sure that the vision is inspiring, too. We also talk about how to create a vision that makes people want to get involved in this section.

There is no time like the present to create a clear vision. Right after you decide what kind of change is needed and necessary, start crafting a vision that will inspire others to make the change happen.

Voicing your vision

Your vision should set expectations and help you continue moving toward the end goal even if obstacles are in your way. Having that clear vision of the future state of the organization is a powerful tool in creating stability when chaos is all around you, and it will help you create an accurate image in people's minds of what they can and can't expect.

To emphasize the importance of the vision, imagine an Olympic hurdler during his race to the finish line. If the racer begins to stutter-step every time he gets to a hurdle, he loses time and momentum (not to mention he may not make it over the hurdle directly in front of him). But if the racer maintains momentum with the end goal in mind, he looks as if he is gliding over the hurdles on his way to the finish line. A vision helps the organization focus on the end goal — not just the hurdles everyone must overcome to get there.

What makes a good vision? For one thing, it is driven by senior leadership but created by many people at different levels and supported by the change leaders in the organization. We know many great changes have come from grassroots efforts, but the vision of large-scale, lasting change must be defined by someone who can control and inspire the change. A leader shouldn't lock himself in a plush executive office, type up a fancy vision on cardstock paper, and then tape it up around the office for all employees to see (yes, we know leaders who have done this, and we don't recommended it!). The best visions are created when senior leaders sit down and listen to opinions and ideas, explore the marketplace for opportunities, and integrate these ideas into a clear picture of what's possible. The vision is a statement of the organization you want to be, and therefore it must speak to everyone in your organization — not just those up in the corporate office.

Great visions are also specific and clear. Don't spend time creating a vision of the future that's as clear as mud. A vision must address what the future looks like, when it will happen, and how people can get involved. The vision must state the capabilities the organization will have in the future.

A really successful vision is also highly inspiring. We've devoted a whole section to that aspect; keep reading to find out how to motivate everyone with the vision and win their full support.

Inspiring a shared need

As a change leader, you will work relentlessly to generate understanding and consensus around your vision. How will you answer your local staff when they ask why they should invest in the change? What is it going to do for them? Why should they give this project their attention?

You inspire people by communicating a reason for why people need to get out of their comfort zone and do something different. People need to be convinced that the status quo must change. This issue is the *WIIFM*, or *what's in it for me?* Chapter 7 walks you through the process of creating good WIIFM answers for your employees.

Change needs a catalyst. Look for the *change driver* — the business need for the change. The change driver is either a problem that people need to address or an opportunity that will further the strategic value of the organization. The change driver (or drivers) must offer a reason to change that is more compelling than people's natural attachment to the status quo or comfort zone.

Although your change may seem like a no-brainer in your mind and perhaps in the minds of other change leaders in the organization, that feeling may not be felt throughout the organization. A shared need is the fuel that gets the change fire going.

When you've pinpointed the change driver, make sure you don't muddy it up in your communications about the vision. Think about how different these two visions are:

- ✔ We will stop having issues with quality next year.
- ✔ Working together, we will improve the quality of our products next year so that all our customers are delighted with their experience.

Making a personal connection to change

We love this story about an energy company's vision for the future: A CEO at the energy company decided it was time to change the company's entire technology infrastructure to help it better monitor equipment, break down the silos created by antiquated systems, and improve its ability to proactively respond to environmental concerns. The CEO and his senior leadership team started off by stating that the vision of the future was to improve productivity in the plants and be more environmentally friendly. You can imagine that very few people outside of corporate headquarters were chomping at the bit to undergo this massive change with such a mundane vision. But then the CEO got smart: He went out to the plants and asked the people who do the work what would inspire them to change the way they do business. A senior foreman told this story:

"Five years ago there was explosion at the plant that threatened to pollute our community. This threat could've been avoided if we'd had the right data. It endangered the lakes our children swim in and the skies we watch at night. For ten days, everyone came together to stop that from happening. We weren't worried about overtime, and we didn't care who caused the disaster. We wanted to make sure our community was clean and safe. If the systems you want to put in can stop that from happening again, you bet we will join in."

As you probably can imagine, the CEO and his change team reformed the vision of the change project that evening: *The new system within the company will give us the information we need to deliver energy products and keep our communities we operate in safe and clean.* Now that statement sounds a little more inspiring, don't you think?

You may have meant the same thing in both statements, but only the second one will impress employees with an inspiring shared need.

We aren't saying you need to be a cheerleader and spell out V-I-C-T-O-R-Y every five minutes, but you can't be a downer. No one is going to jump and rally around a depressing vision, so channel your inner cheerleader and ask people to do something great. Great visions bring emotional response, either through the story of why the change is taking place or through vibrant language and images.

Keep your vision genuine. If a vision is just so out of the touch with where the organization is today, employees may find it unbelievable and not act on it.

Inspiring a sense of urgency

After you inspire people to change, you need to inspire them to want to change *now*. A sense of urgency may be incredibly obvious if your organization is faced with economic or market-driven challenges, but it's not always that clear cut. The easiest way to create a sense of urgency is to describe how a behavior is causing an undesirable consequence.

You may be able to identify some change-driving consequences through your answers to the following questions:

- ✔ What is the competition doing? Is it taking away customers?

- ✔ What do our customers want? Have their needs changed over the years?

- ✔ How will our company stay in business in the long term? What changes need to happen to make sure people's jobs are secure?

- ✔ Does the change impact the communities in which our employees live? (Maybe increasing revenue is important for the CEO, but you need to tie that need back to how that increased revenue will make a difference for the front-line employees.)

- ✔ How is the future different from what happens now?

- ✔ What market opportunities have opened up recently?

- ✔ What current problems are we experiencing?

One word that tends to be forgotten when creating shared urgency is the word *shared.* The executives may feel a sense of urgency to change established systems in order to create bigger profits for the company, but that's hardly a rally cry for change because it will make the processes of a system work better. But if executives can convince workers that changing the system will help make sure their community (and workplace) safer, they just may get people up and moving. The shared need has to come from the heart, even if it is driven by numbers on a balance sheet.

The shared need must show that doing what you have been doing isn't an option anymore. Keep in mind that the behavior you're trying to encourage or discourage with the sense of urgency can't have a "because we're telling you to do it" feel. Surprise, surprise — people don't want to be told what to do; they want to experience something and decide by themselves to act on it. Here are some great examples of urgent and shared needs for change:

- ✔ After the BP oil spill in the Gulf of Mexico in 2010, many energy companies decided they needed to look at their own safety procedures to make sure they didn't have a similar fate.

- ✔ Many organizations used the collapsing financial markets as a reason to look at their strategy and decide how they would come out of the recession successfully.

- ✔ After the September 11 World Trade Center attacks, Cantor Fitzgerald lost approximately two-thirds of its employees. The company used the crisis to look at how it did business and reinvented itself as a stronger, more profitable company.

Even if you don't have as urgent of a need as an energy company after the oil spill or national tragedy, you can still inspire your employees to do what's best for the company and what is best for their personal job satisfaction, and making it personal can make a big difference. (Flip to Chapter 7 to find out more about telling employees what's in it for them.) Organizational change will make the company better, but linking the organizational change to the personal change and benefit of employees creates urgency. If you are having trouble creating urgency, ask your fellow change leaders these questions to get an idea of why the change needs to happen. Does the current state put people or measurements at risk? Are regulatory bodies requiring this change? Is changing the current state critical to the future operation of the company? If no actions are taken, will financial, customer, or employee targets be compromised?

When you change, you are either addressing a problem people need to fix or an opportunity that will further the strategic value of the organization. You do not (or at least should not) change for the fun of it. If you find it hard to create shared urgency, go back and look at why you are changing in the first place.

Above all, be authentic in your vision. We discuss the importance of doing the right thing later in this chapter (see the section "Keeping Everything Ethical"), but telling the truth about the future develops a sense of respect and trust throughout the organization. To get your change project done, a vision must be real — not just smoke and mirrors.

An inspiring vision and shared sense of urgency don't mean you need to sugarcoat the outcomes of the project, just balance them. If the major end goal is to reduce expenses or reduce headcount, say so, but also discuss the importance of the other elements of change.

Here's a bonus: After you've crafted the perfect vision that inspires and is appropriately urgent, that means you've also generated some key messages that you can use in your communication strategy. Head to Chapter 7 for more on communicating your change.

Creating a change road map

Your inspiring vision gets people moving, and the change road map tells them how to get where they need to go. Too often, desperately needed changes fall short of their desired results because change leaders don't really understand how to lead change or have a clear map of how to get there.

Your change road map has two parts:

✔ The strategic part maps out where you are and where you want to go, laying the groundwork.

✔ A 30-60-90-day road map defines what you will do to reach the strategy over the next 30, 60, and 90 days. This part gets the wheels moving.

Making a strategic road map

Your strategic road map, indicating where you're beginning and where you want to end up, should cover the following areas:

✔ **Why do we need to change?** In order to answer this question, you need to know what's happening now. Figure out where you're starting from so that you can define what changes are needed to get to the future. (We help you find that starting point a bit later in this section.)

✔ **What are the two or three key changes that are taking place?** Change is often like an onion; you have to keep peeling back information and ideas to get to the core of the change. When you keep uncovering new information or new changes that are needed, even the best-scoped project can start becoming a little bit out of hand. So identify when and how the changes will be assessed and prioritized. Some changes may be strategic; others may be driven by economic concerns. The important piece is knowing how the organization will prioritize changes. Not all processes and changes are created equal, and the road map helps decipher which changes are absolutely critical and which ones will support those critical changes.

✔ **Where do you want to go?** Visions are needed to inspire change, but goals and measurements will eventually show that the change did what it set out to do. Measuring success in the road map addresses how benefits will be measured and tracked. These measurements will include how the company is doing from a financial, customer, process, and employee perspective, as well as key milestones that will happen during the change. (We devote Chapter 6 to measuring change.)

✔ **How will the change last?** Even if the change you're undertaking is not focused on changing the culture, the change road map should specify how ready the organization is for change and how the change will last. Actions may include creating a powerful, two-way communication strategy or changing reward systems to make sure individuals and teams are rewarded for doing what the change wants to accomplish.

To really define the starting point, change teams usually conduct a current-state analysis to understand the current capability of processes, organization structure, data, and technology. This examination isn't meant to place blame, because many problems can be systematic; it's just to understand what's really going on. So often, people in organizations are not all on the same page because they have been operating in the current state for so long and can't provide an objective view of what's really going on. Conducting a comprehensive assessment of the current state and using that information to make decisions leads to an effective change plan.

A comprehensive current-state assessment combines measurements of how key functions and processes are performing, with honest, objective answers from leaders on their *perspective* of how things are working. This assessment can help identify, prioritize, and evaluate change recommendations as well as provide valuable suggestions to help solidify the vision and urgency of the change. A fact-based assessment should be based on the results of your SWOT analysis (Chapter 1) and balanced-measures scorecard (check out Chapter 6 on how to create one), complemented by objective recommendations from change leaders on how the current state is operating. Consider asking change leaders the following questions to identify the effort that moving from the current state to the future state will take.

✔ **What is happening today that is driving the need for change?** The answer to this question gives you good insight into the barriers and opportunities the change may face.

✔ **What do you have to do to make sure the change happens?** You want leaders to feel responsible for the change by communicating the vision, offering resources to help, and removing barriers that could stop the change.

✔ **Do we have the time, people, and financial resources to make the change happen?** Remember, change can't happen without resources.

Creating a 30-60-90-day road map

Different changes take different lengths of time to happen, but after you map out the change plan (in the preceding section), you're ready to take planning to the next level and commit to when you're going to get things done. At this point in the change cycle, you won't have the full project plan developed, but putting together a plan for what will happen by 30 days, 60 days, and 90 days (and so on) will keep your team on track with the short-term goals. Check out Table 4-1 as an example. (Use the 30-60-90 day outlook as a guideline and build out the schedule further when these initial milestones are met.)

Table 4-1	30-60-90-Day Road Map Example		
Aspect	*30 Days*	*60 Days*	*90 Days*
Why do we need to change?	Conduct a current state assessment. Integrate current state assessment into vision and reason for the change	Share results of current state with leadership team. Share vision, actions, and goals with employees.	Create a front-line council to help communicate the need for change to employees.
What are the 2–3 key changes that are taking place?	Meet with leaders and employees in the organization to decide what types of changes are needed.	Decide on 2–3 critical initiatives for the change based on current state assessment; develop teams to create the tactical plans for those initiatives.	Communicate to employees what changes are happening and when.
Where do you want to go?	Define goals for the change.	Create a scorecard with metrics and goals for the change; edit based on the current-state assessment.	Communicate how teams will be measured against the change goals and metrics.
How will the change last?	Review current performance targets; conduct SWOT analysis. Create two-way communication forums to help support change in the long run.	Identify what organizational culture norms, behaviors, and individual skills may need to change to make the change last. Create a plan to make the changes to skills, norms, and behavior happen.	Share plan and new rewards structure with the company.

The purpose of your 30-60-90-day road map is to guide your next steps as you keep moving towards the future vision. It provides an accurate view of what needs to change in order to reach your goals.

Making a list of what's helping or hurting change

You probably already can tell that a bunch of things impact change beyond just processes and measurements. When you're building your change tool-box, to make sure change sticks, you will want to look at the entire picture of your organization to see what's helping and hindering change. Some people may call this step *looking at the system;* other people talk about the *holistic approach to change.* Call it what you want, the important part is that you consider all the elements that are going to make sure your change happens, lasts, and delivers what you want it to.

Here's an overview of the areas your list should address as you explore what's going to push you forward and what may have the potential to hold you back:

- **Business process:** The business process covers what work is performed; how information, products, and services flow throughout the organization; what rules, policies, and procedures are in place; and the physical environment. Business processes that may be hurting the change could be a lack of information sharing between teams or leaders, causing undesirable results. For example, we often see organizations excited about entering new product or service markets, but then they move so fast with the process they forget to build quality and internal communications into the process. This can cause new products to enter the market that may not meet customer expectations; other times services change without a consistent process to communicate all the changes internally, causing confusion between departments.

  After business process, technology is one of the easiest things to blame when change stalls or fails. If a company is running an antiquated system, changing business processes can be problematic. Check out Chapter 15 for ideas on how to make technology work for your change, not against it.

- **Corporate culture:** Culture is hard to pin down, but it can hurt or help a company trying to change. A culture that rewards performance and accepts new ideas from anywhere in the organization can be a great help in making change happen fast. On the other hand, when a culture only undertakes change when a senior-level person comes up with the idea (rather than letting the ideas come from anywhere), the culture could hurt any change efforts. Chapter 16 goes into detail on how to successfully move culture in the direction of positive change.

- ✔ **Organization structure, job roles, and skill sets:** A workforce that gets continuous training and has opportunities to take ownership can be a great help in making change happen. On the flipside, if people don't have the skill to do a job or are not encouraged to update their skills, no matter how wonderfully you lay out the change plan, the change can't happen (in other words, it will hurt the change efforts). Be sure to encourage employees to keep their skills fresh and reward the employees who do so — these employees will be big advocates for change.

- ✔ **Management and measurement systems:** This one area can single-handedly impact how long the change will last. If personnel (compensation and incentives) and organization (process measurement and policies) are not addressed, things will quickly go back to the way they were before the change. If you want the new behavior to stick, you have to change the way the behavior is measured. Without an incentive to change, the change will be slow at best.

Another important area to look at when deciding what's helping or hurting change is the external stakeholders who impact how you do business. These stakeholders may be customers, suppliers, or even competitors.

Putting Together Your Change Team

You have heard it before, but getting the right people on the team is absolutely critical to your project's success. If you have the right team, you will gain buy-in to the project more efficiently, communicate the project's vision and goals more clearly, help institutionalize the change, and of course, get the change done.

In this section, we help you assemble your change dream team from the people at your organization. The people who do the work on a day-to-day basis must be behind the change. Outside experts (consultants, coaches, business gurus, psychics) telling front-line staff what to do will not have lasting impact.

Gathering the right folks

A perfect change team is an asset to your change toolbox for two reasons:

- ✔ These people, with their pool of process knowledge, are the think tank for the project.

- ✔ The team is there to help you. We know you may want to do it yourself, but remember: You're an advisor and leader, not the only doer!

So what makes the perfect team? Consider these personnel aspects when picking your team:

- ✔ **Who:** When creating your team, make sure front-line staff and supervisors are involved. Change teams need to look and feel like the population you're changing, so they should include workers affected by the change as well as committed leaders. Involve people who can be advocates for issues that may be impacted by the project.

- ✔ **How many:** The ideal team size for large change projects is a core team of 8 to 12 people. If you're undergoing a major change that impacts multiple parts of the business, you will need this number of people to help represent the various functions and ideas within the business. Any number more than 12 gets a bit chaotic; any fewer than 6 fails to represent everyone affected. Your job is to find the happy medium.

- ✔ **Skills needed:** Although you may really like someone and want her on your team, make sure the team has the right mix of skills to get the job done. The right mix of skills blends leadership skills that encourage open communication and idea sharing, strong technical skills applicable for the position, and strong talents in facilitation, conflict resolution, and team building. Yes, skills can be taught, but if they aren't taught quickly, anxiety will start to fester and people will wonder if the change can really be implemented.

Teams work best when they have clear sponsorship or authority from executive leaders, consist of front-line staff who are passionate and educated about the change, and are led by a change leader who facilitates change based on knowledge and skill.

Committing leadership

As a change leader, you know your main goal is to sponsor the future state with bells and whistles. But encouraging and guiding the change is not only up to you. Committing executive leadership (and then the leaders underneath them and on the front lines) to change will sustain the momentum of the project. Leaders who are passionate about the change will serve as helpful hammers and nails in your toolbox.

You probably have spoken with some leaders in your company, and many of them are likely on board with the changes. These people are your change agents and change sponsors (refer back to Chapter 3 for more on change-leader roles). But don't relax yet; you need to make sure the actions of these leaders are in line with their verbal commitments. While getting your ducks in a row, ask yourself the following questions:

✔ **Are the leaders communicating the vision and goals of the project?** Committed leaders don't just send out an e-mail; they hold meetings, participate in change-team events, and provide resources for the change when asked.

✔ **Are the leaders recognizing that employees have a voice in the change, and are they helping employees reflect on what needs to happen?** If leaders are holding one-on-one meetings and team discussions about the change, you know they're on board with the future vision.

✔ **Are the leaders responding to the needs of their employees?** The icing on the cake is when leaders ask for feedback from employees, reflect on it, and then respond openly to any concerns or ideas raised by their group.

If you cannot answer "yes" to all these questions, take a step back and assess whether or not the change will last in the long term. Some leaders may need a coach or training on what's required to lead change. Try to work with these leaders to understand why they are not raising their hands and cheering. If coaching and training do not work, it may be time to recruit new leaders who are more fully on board with the change.

Creating the change-team charter

After your change team is in place, make sure all members know what they need to do next. This step is where the change-team charter helps. The *change-team charter* is a document that defines the goal of the change, who will be working on the change, and the big milestones for the change. Chapter 5 covers the importance of planning out the team charter utilizing the GPRI (goals, process, roles, interaction) model. Just as planning the change leads to a more probable outcome of success, planning out the team's purpose and way of working increases the probability of a successful change.

In addition to listing out the goals of the project and team, the processes for how the team will operate, the roles of team members, and how the interpersonal communication will work on the team, a charter should also include a list of what resources will be available to the team. You can assemble the best team in the world, but without any means of getting the work done, a team can get exasperated. In addition to listing the financial resources (which are important), make sure your team charter also addresses how team members will secure additional human resources, management resources, and physical resources as well.

Aligning the team with a SMART common goal

As you create your team, you will begin aligning that team to the common goal of the project. This process begins on day one, so make sure the goal is well defined.

The common goal for the team is often the goal of the project, but just as you spend time developing and communicating the vision and shared urgency of the project, make sure you spend time ensuring everyone in the change team has the same picture of the common goal in mind. The goal of the project and the vision for change are related but not the same thing. The vision sets the inspiring picture of the future, but the common goal simply describes what progress and events will happen when.

After the goals for the project are developed, put them in the 30-60-90 day strategic plan to help the team frequently review the progress the team is making.

When working up your goal for the project, be sure you're developing a SMART goal. A *SMART* goal is specific, measurable, action oriented and agreed on, realistic, and time bound. Here are the questions that should be considered:

- ✔ **Specific accomplishments:** What specifically does the team intend to accomplish? Don't just write down the vision. Be very specific about what you will (and will not) do.

- ✔ **Measurements:** What are the specific numerical goals to measure the results? Using data and measures to track change (even if it seems more subjective at first) helps make sure your change continues to stay on track.

✔ **Action oriented and agreed on:** Will the goal actually help you do something different? And are most stakeholders in agreement that the goal is important? You can bring the stragglers into the fold with the tips in Chapter 8, but make sure you have support from the core people.

✔ **Realistic:** Is the goal actually achievable? Keeping momentum and enthusiasm going is difficult if people know the goal isn't very realistic.

✔ **Time bound:** How long will the goal and change take? Strive to designate a time frame for this change to take place.

Here is a great example of a SMART goal a team can support:

> *With changes to our technology systems, we will achieve a 90 percent improvement in wait time between patient arrival and seeing a physician in urgent care department in the next six months.*

When you have a goal on paper, the change team sponsor or leader should take the time to ask the team these questions to make sure your team is aligned with the common goal:

✔ **Is the team leader willing and able to do the job?** Be honest. You have put a lot of time and energy into just getting ready for change, and sometimes that can be overwhelming. Make sure you and your team are in it for the long haul. If the leader is daunted by the work that will be necessary, scale back or slow down with the change rather than rush ahead and let it fizzle out midway.

✔ **Does the team understand and agree with the reason for the team, the resources, and the time frame?** Change leaders and teams can (rightfully so) get caught up in the excitement of change and assume everyone is on the same page. Take time to review and check in with individuals to make sure everyone is on board before the change ship starts to sail.

If the team members can't describe the goal in one or two crisp sentences, they may be unclear about their task. Teams who lose focus of the goal will have trouble seeing the change through to the end.

Supporting cross-functional teamwork

One of the best things about having a diverse change team that supports cross-functional work is that the team will help drive buy-in throughout the organization because the team members come from various stakeholder groups and have credibility with their "home" team. *Cross-functional teams* include individuals from the different areas that will be impacted by the change.

Cross-functional teams were the hot thing back in the 1990s when people started bragging about how they were so matrixed and dotted-lined into someone else. Today's cross-functional teams dealing with change need to up the ante a bit. Here's how you can support cross-functional teamwork during change:

- ✓ **Encourage self-direction.** Organizational charts are great, but if you pick the right people and have a well-thought-out plan and a clear vision, the team can start deciding what to do to reach its goals. Your role as a change leader should focus on where the team needs to go; let the team decide how to get there.

- ✓ **Recruit leaders who facilitate discussion, ideas, and options.** Cross-functional teams that quickly fizzle out are led by imposing leaders who micromanage every line on their fancy Gantt chart.

- ✓ **Allow cross-functional teams to be diverse.** Novice change leaders tend to pick people just like them to work on the team. Don't make this mistake. It takes all types of people to make change happen, so select people to work on your team who have skills you may not have. Balance out strong data- and project-management employees with individuals who connect well with people and emotions.

- ✓ **Know that the team members weren't born yesterday.** You picked these team members because of their track record, so let their past experiences shine. Give team members enough opportunity to share their past experiences and incorporate these personal lessons learned into the project and communication plan.

Keeping Everything Ethical

We often use the terms *ethics, morals,* and *values* interchangeably, because they all tie back to doing the right thing. When you lead change, you have significant influence over the behavior of others, the policies the company follows, and the values and principles demonstrated throughout the organization. No matter what change road maps and change teams you have in your toolbox, don't forget to bring along your ethics. To make sure you're leading the right change (that is, the ethical one) even when you're faced with tough decisions, follow these guiding principles of ethical leadership:

- ✔ Focus on organizational success, not personal agendas.

- ✔ Create mechanisms for employees to disagree and the opportunity to discuss these disagreements without consequences.

- ✔ Make tough calls while taking into account the values, feelings, and emotions of others.

Whether you're leading a technical transformation or merging companies, your best approach to leading change is constant, clear, honest, and relentless. Regardless of all the benefits of the proposed change, clarity and honesty are going to be what make people want to join you in leading change — and, just as importantly, make them trust that you're taking them in the right direction.

Chapter 5

The Fine Art of Planning for Change (Or Dealing with the Unplanned Kind)

Does this scenario sound familiar? You're working on a change initiative, it kicked off perfectly, employees are doing their jobs exactly as expected, and energy for the project is focused and moving. And then all of a sudden (or so it seems), the project begins to slow down. People move on to other jobs, perhaps even to other companies. Another project comes up or a barrier is put in the way, and your project that was once on the path to success is stalled like a rusted-out car. What happened?

If your organization is like most, change initiatives progress quickly until they become 90 percent complete, regardless of their impact, scope, or purpose, and then remain at or around 90 percent complete forever. Very few major change projects are implemented perfectly on time, under budget, and with the exact same staff that started the project in the first place. Why, you ask? It's because 90 percent of projects are stalled by external pitfalls that block the way and because the projects aren't following a comprehensive plan. Examples of external pitfalls include a competitor releasing a new product, a global recession that changes demand for your products, or new technology changing the way you go about running your business. Internal pitfalls can include lack of involvement of key staff, poorly defined action steps, or insufficient communication, to name a few.

To help your change project beat these odds, you need a comprehensive project plan in place. A good plan helps you maneuver past internal and external pitfalls that otherwise could block the way to the success of the project, its processes, and your organization as a whole.

This chapter provides tools you will use in project planning as you lead change (and just about any other project you need to get done, too). Here, you discover the ins and out of creating a winning project plan and using the GRPI model (goals, roles, process, and interpersonal relationships) to quickly inform people of how the change initiative is being run. We also equip you with ways to focus on the vital areas of the project, avoid scope creep, and understand how to identify what's absolutely critical to fully accomplish the change goals. Then we walk you through how to tie all these plans together as you develop a project charter to guide you and your organization through anything that comes your way during the change. Finally, we help you plan when you're facing unexpected change.

This chapter covers the basics of project planning for change, but if you need more in-depth discussion on project planning, you can get on the right track by picking up a copy of *Strategic Planning Kit For Dummies,* by Erica Olsen, or *Project Management For Dummies,* by Stanley E. Portny (both published by Wiley).

Creating a Winning Project Plan: What's Going to Happen

Although your overall goal is to lead lasting change in your organization (see Chapter 4 for details), your *project plan* is a short-term design to help create change. Think of the project plan as a blueprint for building a house, only the house is the change you're trying to achieve. You need the blueprint to make sure the house gets built, but the end goal is not a marvelous blueprint, it is the extraordinary house. That being said, without a blueprint for change, you will have a vision for the future of your organization with no clear idea of how you're going to build this great future. A winning project plan specifies *how* you're going to get to your desired future state.

Project planning is part science and part art. Established tools and frameworks provide a method for delivering results. Following step-by-step instructions to map out the time, budget, and resources you'll need is often the easier side of project planning. The art side of project planning, the part you have to feel out as you go, is sometimes more difficult, especially when it comes to working with the emotional reactions of the people involved in and impacted by the change. We encourage you to start thinking of project planning not just as a piece of paper but as a mindset of how you do business. It is a disciplined approach to leading change and perhaps even managing the chaos during the transition period. Both of these elements should be in place as you create your project plan.

Checking your readiness to launch

Most project-management methods have common fundamental areas: scoping, planning, managing, and closing. Before you can begin writing a project plan, you need to spend some time thinking about these areas of the project. If you can answer the following eight readiness questions, you're well on your way to creating a winning project plan:

✔ **Scope**

- What are we trying to do?

✔ **Planning**

- When will we start?

- Who will do the work and make decisions?

- How long will the project take?

- How much will the project cost?

✔ **Managing**

- What work needs to get done?

- How will we make sure the work gets done?

✔ **Closing**

- How will we know we have been successful?

If you were able to answer all eight questions with no trouble or hesitation, you can jump ahead to creating your project charter and moving ahead with your change plan (we discuss the charter later in "Using project charters to stay on track"). If you feel that your answers may need a little more oomph (technical term) or substance, don't worry. You are in the same place as 99 percent of other change leaders when they begin embarking on change. Now is the time to move straight into project planning basics to get your project moving. The tools in this chapter help you get to the point of being ready to launch your change.

Planning to succeed

How are you going to do all this planning? Well, the first answer is that you won't do it alone. You shouldn't be expected to know everything about the project, and that's why your fellow change leaders, change agents, and project team are there to support you. In Chapter 4 we focus on getting your team, vision, and shared needs aligned and ready to roll; now you can use that marvelous team to make sure the plan is realistic, actionable, and measureable.

Even if people are ready to get changing now, you still have time for planning — if you make time for it. If you don't do it, you most likely will be playing catch up later. So wouldn't you rather plan to succeed instead of pulling a few all-nighters dealing with risks you should have known about and tried to mitigate before they happened?

Doing the following things will make your life easier during the planning phase:

- ✔ **Identify the types of project management in your organization that you have used in the past:** Don't start from scratch if you don't have to. You may be surprised to find that your organization has a project-planning method or template you may be able to modify to meet the needs of your change.

- ✔ **Piggy-back onto existing project management tools:** Some organizations already have program offices in place or perhaps even project managers. If your organization has this resource, use it! If not, the Association of Project Management and the Project Management Institute have wonderful resources available on their websites for new and experienced project managers. You may want to consider joining these organizations to access a wealth of tools and information.

Project management is about creating an environment conducive to getting critical goals accomplished during your change plan.

Looking at the elements of a project plan

If you have been on a project before (and who hasn't?), you may think that putting together a project plan is basically creating a project schedule or Gantt chart. Although having a project schedule is absolutely critical, the schedule is just one piece of the project-planning puzzle. This section covers the elements of a project plan to get you on the right path to successful change.

Focus on making the project plan comprehensive but easy to read. We recommend writing a one-page project plan for executives to review and a longer version for the change team to utilize.

Writing a project problem statement

The problem statement is a one- or two-sentence description of the symptoms arising from the problem to be addressed. It often parallels a business case for change quite closely, but the problem statement is more specific and focused than the business case. For example, *"Turnover in our research department has increased from last year's level for three quarters in a row, reducing our knowledge base and limiting new product development."* A problem statement then focuses on a key element of that larger issue: *"Experienced engineers have left the company three times as often as last year, contributing to a significant reduction in new product introduction."* Problem statements usually answer these questions:

- ✔ What's wrong?
- ✔ Where is the problem appearing?
- ✔ When did the problem happen (time frame)?
- ✔ How big is the problem?
- ✔ What's the impact of the problem on the business?

Defining the goal of the project

Making a great project plan is a waste of time if you aren't certain of where you want to go. Defining your destination, the goal of the project, should be pretty easy because all you have to do is state what you expect to get out of the project. If this step sounds familiar, it's because it ties straight back to the vision of the change, discussed in Chapter 4.

Be specific about what the project is aiming to accomplish and make sure to define measurements around how you'll know the goal has been met. To help you come up with the goal of the project, refer back to your vision from Chapter 4 and refine it by asking yourself these questions:

- ✔ **What are you trying to get done? What do you want to happen? What end result(s) do you expect to achieve from this project?** These answers are the team's change objective, and it often starts with an action verb like *improve, control,* or *increase.*

- ✔ **How will you know that any changes have resulted in improvements?** Use SMART factors later to describe your results. To make sure you have SMART goals, make sure the goal is *specific, measurable, action oriented and agreed on, realistic,* and *time bound* (see the nearby sidebar for more info).

- ✔ **Who are you trying to reach?** List audiences in priority order to make sure you're focusing your goal in the right direction. You may want to refer to the stakeholder mapping section in Chapter 7 if you need more help determining who your audience should be for the change project.

Getting SMART

After you have set the vision for your change, you're ready to get SMART — that is, to set a goal that's specific, measurable, agreed on and action oriented, realistic, and time bound.

SMART goal planning has a number of variations, but the bottom line is to make goals that are easy to understand and clear for everyone working on the project. When you start your change project, take a minute to consider how SMART your goals are:

✔ **Specific:** Are goals well defined and clear to anyone who may read them?

✔ **Measurable:** Will you know when your goal is achieved?

✔ **Action oriented and agreed on:** This A gets double duty. Make sure the goal focuses on doing something different and that all stakeholders are aligned to this goal. You may still have some stragglers who don't yet agree (see Chapter 8 for working through resistance), but the goal should have the support of multiple people in the organization.

✔ **Realistic:** Although an inspiring vision is needed for change, goals have to keep at least one foot on the ground. Make sure goals can be completed with the given resources, knowledge, and time. Make goals and vision genuine so employees have a reason to believe the change will actually happen.

✔ **Time bound:** When will the goal be accomplished? Have a clear deadline to make sure actions don't loose focus during the change.

Here are examples of a SMART and not-so-smart goal:

✔ **Not-so-smart goal:** Our company will change to exceed customer expectations around quality.

✔ **SMART goal:** Our company, with the support of senior management, will implement (action oriented and agreed on) a quality program to improve first-time quality to 99 percent (specific and measurable) by June 2013 (time bound). (As long as the company is willing to devote resources, this goal is realistic too.)

We'll illustrate creating a goal statement with an example. Say your change project's problem statement is focused on how customer information isn't available to everyone in the organization. Your project goal is to have the entire sales team, customer-service team, and marketing team (measurable and specific) using a new customer-relationship software to cross-sell to and support your customers (action oriented) by the end of the year (time bound). This goal seems realistic because it is related to the various team's job descriptions, so it's fully SMART. It also addresses what you're trying to get done and who you're trying to reach, so it's an excellent goal.

Many organizations have lots of numbers floating around, and drowning in a sea of them is easy to do. Revisit the project goal and problem statement regularly to keep in mind what the team is trying to accomplish.

Setting quality standards

When it comes to getting a project done, the two ends of the quality spectrum are using the quick-and-dirty method (which often lacks quality) and following previously established standards. Here is where doing a little research on best practices in your industry can really help, so that you can set goals that are competitive. Of course, not every project needs to pass the white glove test, but as a change leader you need to define what standards of quality are required. Will a review council be established to look at the milestones, or will a quality audit make sure deliverables for your change are acceptable?

The important thing is not necessarily which standard you pick but how well you communicate that quality standard to the rest of the organization. All the key players need to clearly understand what is required and how success will be measured each step of the way.

Allocating financial, human, and physical resources

Nothing gets done without resources. Whether these resources are financial, physical, or human, identifying the necessary resources up front (or lack of them) alleviates a tremendous amount of pain in the future. If you need a project manager, identify the person to fill that role. If you need financial resources to make a technology change, let senior leaders know how much money you need and how you came up with that number. (If you're facing resistance with gaining resources for the project, you may want to take a glance at Chapter 9 on managing resistance.)

Outlining governance structure

You may have the best plan in place and have all the project resources you could possibly desire, but you still need to know who's running the show. The governance structure puts down on paper who is making each decision.

By identifying resources, you determine who will do the work, whereas the governance structure shows who oversees the project and makes key decisions on what will get done in what time frame with what level of investment. Please refer to the "Roles and responsibilities" section later in the chapter for more about these assignments.

Noting critical milestones

Critical milestones, also referred to as *critical-path items,* is just a fancy term for things must happen before going any farther. We discuss these action items in the later section "Identifying critical successes and critical paths."

Identifying dependencies and risks

Risk management is one of the most bypassed areas of project planning for large changes. Who wants to stand up and talk about the risks of the project not being an overwhelming success when you're just starting? That's like telling a bride on her wedding day that her marriage has a 50 percent chance of failing — not a really pleasant conversation.

Change teams also sometimes avoid talking about the project's *dependencies,* the factors they're counting on in order for the project to succeed. For example, a team may require the support of the IT department to make necessary changes to information systems in order to track the progress of the change. This need may require the IT manager to shift priorities and workloads to accommodate this request. We discuss dependencies along with risk because they're simply risks that you want to have happen.

But dependencies and risks don't need to be intimidating, because every large change (and small change) holds potential risks and dependencies that can cause problems or delays. Your goal is to highlight them so they can be avoided or reduced through advance planning (sounds much better than failure, right?).

Risks and dependencies usually fall into a range of categories: people, knowledge, funding, materials, equipment, data quality, and market/customer/external concerns. When you identify risks and dependencies, you should ask yourself the following questions:

- ✔ **What risks and dependencies do we know of?**

- ✔ **What is their potential level of impact on the project timeline and cost?**

- ✔ **How likely is each risk to cause problems? How likely are we to have something we depend on not happen?** *Very likely, somewhat,* and *not at all* are just fine as categories. You don't need to put too fine a point on this.

Identify ways of reducing the risks or their impact if they do happen. Create a plan for if the risks happen or if the dependencies fail to happen. We go into more detail on assessing and managing risk in Chapter 6.

Scheduling

The most important reason to have a project schedule is to give you and your change team a way of monitoring tasks. Now is the time to list out all those critical milestones (or critical-path items; see "Identifying critical successes and critical paths") and list what specific tasks are needed to complete each big step. Your spreadsheet or project-management software should be able to provide a template to create a robust project schedule.

Because a project schedule is a critical path in project planning (you can't go forward without one!), we take a quick look here at what makes a good schedule (hint: it's not a wonderful software package with pretty charts). A great project schedule identifies the major tasks or deliverables that need to be completed and then groups subtasks together according to how you can make these major tasks happen. The tasks should always imply action. For example, if your major task in the project plan of getting to work in the morning is making coffee, your subtasks may be: grind the beans, fill the water in the coffee maker, push the *On* button, warm the milk, pour the coffee, and stir in the sugar. Your subtask may instead be getting in the car and getting your local barista to make your cup of joe, but that's where the art of project planning comes into play. There are many possible ways to make a great cup of coffee. The subtasks nail down the specific approach you plan to use in your project.

Many, many tools are available to create project schedules, from the simplest plans created in Microsoft Excel and Numbers to more advanced Gantt charting and Project Tools. DotProject (`www.dotproject.net`) is an open-source project-management tool.

We have known some fairly highly paid consultants to spend weeks, if not months, glued in front of their computers, ignoring family, friends, and clients to make the perfect schedule. But making a perfect schedule is impossible — you can't plan the next two years with certainty. You're much better off creating functional pieces of deliverables or critical things you must do, planning out the overall timeline of the project, and then working through the project schedule in portions. We aren't saying you should be vague or careless; rather, be realistic. Things will happen that will cause dates and tasks to change. Trust us and tear yourself away from that computer screen. Your family and friends will thank us.

The GRPI Model: Getting a Grip on How Change Will Happen

The GRPI model for project and team management is one of the most user-friendly, can-be-done-anywhere models out there. The GRPI model is simply a way of organizing your team around the project plan in a way that makes sense. *GRPI* stands for

- ✔ **Goals:** Clearly define the team's mission and establish objectives that conform to the SMART approach (that is, goals that are specific, measurable, action oriented and agreed on, realistic, and time bound).

✔ **Roles and responsibilities:** Clearly define each team member's function and the interrelationships between individual and team roles, objectives, and processes.

✔ **Processes and actions:** Identify and define processes inherent in and essential to the project's success (such as problem solving, decision making, and so on).

✔ **Interpersonal relationships:** Ensure open communication between team members, encourage creative and diverse contributions from all members, and discourage "groupthink" (quickly coming to consensus without critical reflection).

By enhancing your project plan with the GRPI model, you get a one-two punch for project success: a solid plan to make sure everyone knows what is going to happen (the project plan) and a structure of how it will happen (the GRPI model). Additionally, using the straightforward GRPI acronym is something most people in organizations can relate to, remember, and grasp with little or no project-management or team training. Use the GRPI acronym as your checklist to make sure you have everything accounted for in your project.

We recommend creating both a project plan and a GRPI model for your change project. Although most elements of a project plan fit perfectly into the GRPI model, the project plan gives you a very detailed listing of what's going to happen when, and the GRPI model details how it is going to happen.

You may feel like you're reiterating what you already completed, but each part of your change plan serves a different purpose. The vision is used to communicate and motivate others, the project plan describes in detail what you're accomplishing, and the GRPI checklist makes sure your change team knows how to get the project done.

Goals

The first part of your project plan covers the goals of the project and the problem statement. Make sure to include the vision of the project (from Chapter 4), the goals and deliverables of the project (from your project plan), and the scope of the project (which we cover in "Staying Focused on What Matters Most" later in this chapter).

Roles and responsibilities

The *R* in GRPI stands for roles and responsibilities. This information pulls heavily from the governance structure part of your project plan. A RACI chart is a simple yet effective tool for assessing roles and responsibilities, ensuring the right people are involved (that is, that you have the right management or governance structure). *RACI* is an acronym for

✔ **Responsible:** Who is responsible? List the individual or individuals (limit this role to one or two people) in charge of getting the job done.

✔ **Accountable:** To whom is the responsible person accountable? Make note of the individual or individuals (again, limit this role to one or two people) who have ultimate decision-making and approval authority. It is typically the owner of the budget or resources.

✔ **Consulted:** Who do the responsible and accountable parties need to get input from? The consulted group is the individuals or teams who should provide input into a decision or action before it occurs.

✔ **Informed:** Who needs to know about the change/project? This group is the individuals or teams who must be informed that a decision or action has taken place. Be sure to include people who will be most impacted by the change.

Your overall change project will have one big RACI chart as part of the governance structure, but a great next step is to put the RACI model into your project plan as well. After you have completed your RACI chart at the project-schedule level, take a step back and get some perspective on it. Watch out for the following red flags:

✔ **Does one person have lots of responsibilities?** You will want to make sure this individual can stay on top of so much.

✔ **Are too many people accountable?** If too many people are accountable for one activity, it most likely means you don't have the right person making the final decision. Having too many people accountable for an outcome can muddy the water of who really will make your project the one that gets completed.

Processes and actions

The processes-and-actions section of the GRPI model focuses more on how the work will get done rather than on what is getting done, which you covered in your project schedule (see the earlier section "Scheduling" for details). In this section of your GRPI model, cover four big "hows" of how to get the plan done:

✔ **Decision making:** How will decision making take place? Will decision making be in the hands of the project owner (the accountable person), or will the team make decisions and then propose the final solution to the boss? Stating these rules upfront saves time at the end of the project by making sure decisions don't need to be revisited.

✔ **Problem solving:** You may also want to discuss how you will work through problem solving. Will problem solving be done individually or as a team? Neither method is better than the other, but you can see how conflict will quickly arise if one person expects to handle all the problem solving on her own and the rest of the team thinks group discussions are needed for anything that happens.

✔ **Conflicting opinions:** What will you do in the face of conflicting opinions? Conflict happens on teams. Entire books are written on conflict management (we have a chapter on it; see Chapter 9). But like all planning that goes into making change happen, laying out the groundwork to make sure people know how to escalate conflicting opinions will put the team in control of resolving tough situations.

✔ **Communication:** How will the change team stay connected through communication? You probably know that communication is one of the most, if not *the* most, important aspects of making the change happen and getting the change team to work together. If you are working on a large project, you want to make sure that a number of change agents, change advocates, and executives are involved in the project details, so use this area to map how the change team will communicate with one another. At this point you want to focus on communication processes within the change team itself. We go into greater detail on how to communicate to the broader organization and how to develop your communication plan in Chapter 7.

You may be thinking that so many of these processes just evolve as a team works together, and yes, they do tend to create lives of their own. However, when a change team comes together, you don't necessarily have months (and you definitely don't have years) to work these things out. So discuss them upfront in one of your first change-agent or change-team meetings and then revisit them often, because just like a project plan and project schedule, things evolve over time.

Interpersonal relationships

The interpersonal-relationships part of the GRPI model can best be described as how the team is going to work together to get the project plan done. This part of the plan focuses on the team that's driving the change, and you will want to include how your change agents, change sponsors, and change advocates will work with one another and what is acceptable and expected behavior on the team. (For details on the roles of change leaders, see Chapter 3.)

Think of this section as setting down the ground rules for how the project will get done. You may consider addressing some of these key interpersonal areas:

- Are openness and outspokenness valued and rewarded on the team, or should differences be handled in a less direct manner?

- What level of flexibility does the team have in working with one another? Can team members revisit ideas already decided on?

- How will the team value emotions and feelings about what is happening versus rewarding data and facts?

The answers to the above questions are influenced by the overall culture of your organization. Culture dictates the formal and informal ways that things get done in your organization. We go into organizational culture in more detail in Chapter 16. Your change team can create its own subculture, but we recommend you define this in the context of what is happening in the larger organization. For example, is openness between management and employees encouraged and rewarded in your company? What is the level of trust between different levels of management? How is conflict typically addressed?

The interpersonal part of the GRPI model is the ground rules and operating agreements for the team. Although this aspect may seem like fluff to some people, sharing expectations and guidelines builds relationships and fosters productive behaviors on any change team.

 Team-building activities are often seen as an added expense that virtual and global teams don't have the opportunity to participate in. This view could not be further from the truth. When teams are operating in different time zones, it is essential that the change sponsor get the team together (even if it is a virtual meeting) to come to agreement on how the team will operate. We also highly recommend the use of telepresence technology for global teams to "see" each other as often as possible.

Staying Focused on What Matters Most

Organizations, no matter how productive, can only focus on so many things at once. Furthermore, too many simultaneous changes are impossible to track and manage. When you have too many changes happening at once, the problem is usually that the change isn't aligned with the strategic plan and goals of the organization.

The solution is to make sure you're focusing your project plan on what matters most. You can do so by identifying the specific actions you need to take and focusing the change team on actions they need to accomplish.

Identifying critical successes and critical paths

Your goal as a change leader is to help the organization set milestones that help keep the change moving forward. Although not all these milestones (or mini-goals) guarantee success, they certainly are strong indicators of whether or not you will have your vision for the change become a reality.

The easiest way to define markers of success is to think of your change like American football (sorry to all you non–sports fans; just bear with us a for a moment). The team's goal is to keep getting first downs (or moving the ball forward at least 10 yards) until it moves the ball into the end zone and gets a touchdown. Apply this game play to your change project: Your goal as a change leader is to identify what the first downs are for your project and work toward them; in other words, note the meaningful points along the way that show you're making progress and then help your team get there. For example, if you're changing an organizational structure, markers for success may be creating the new organizational chart, communicating what's happening to employees, identifying who will be taking the different roles in the future, and sharing the vision of the new organization with employees.

Now here is where it gets tricky: Some changes are hard to measure when they're in progress. For example, if you're trying to change the culture, how do you measure whether the organization is more open to different ways of doing things? We mention earlier in the book that change in business is both an art and a science, so here is where you may need to brush up on your artistic skills. If you are trying to make the company more innovative, your end measure may be the company's ability to introduce ten new products successfully each year. But that number is an end goal, so you want a marker to indicate whether or not you are on track to getting those new products out the door each year. You could measure each product getting out the door as a marker of success, or you can create a success marker like these: Do teams meet weekly to try new ideas? Do managers allow time for brainstorming creative ways of doing things as part of their monthly meetings? Have you provided training and coaching on ways to be more innovative?

Critical-path items are milestones that are forks in the road — you can't just keep moving forward without making a decision. They impact downstream milestones and the overall timeline of project. If you miss a critical path, the entire project will most likely be delayed (or you'll have to dash around to make up ground).

Two aspects of critical paths you may want to consider are

- ✔ Assigning a resource to them
- ✔ Identifying what depends on them in case they don't happen according to plan

You don't have to think of the worst possible thing that could happen, but be realistic about the potential for the project to be delayed or not adopted fully if critical milestones are not met. You may highlight critical milestones in your project plan with big letters in your Gantt chart, but this is a great place to get visual. For information on how to build a Gantt chart, see *Project Management For Dummies,* by Stanley E. Portny (Wiley).

Stripping out the work that doesn't add value

If you or your team start feeling overwhelmed by action items, you may be focusing on parts of the project plan that have little or no impact on the final goal. To overcome this barrier, have your team list how their part of the project plan fits into these three categories:

- ✔ **Strategic:** These tasks may involve keeping the organization focused on the vision of the future state or continually aligning the change strategy with market forecasts and challenges.

- ✔ **Day-to-day operations:** These actions usually are tasks on your project plan, and if they're not done they'll lead to missing one of your critical-path milestones.

- ✔ **Firefighting/nonvalue:** This no-value-added work drains your energy and time. It's most likely work that should have been done correctly the first time but wasn't.

Now look at how these three categories balance out. If you're not focusing on what matters most, you're probably spending quite a bit of time in the firefighting/nonvalue category and not enough time in the operations and strategic roles. There's no magic number or formula, but a general rule is that no one on your change team should spend more than 10 percent of their time on no-value-added work.

Look at the list of nonvalue tasks and try to identify trends and similarities. Then work with your change team to stop them from happening. For example, if you're spending hours creating presentations and then editing them, you may want to bring on a presentation expert. If you seem to be spending all your time on performance issues for the team, it may be time to reset expectations. If something is pulling you and your team away from focusing on what matters most, stop and change it; otherwise you'll keep doing the same thing, over, and over, and over again.

Avoiding scope creep

Scope creep is a very real concern for even the best change projects and the most robust change plans. You know scope creep when you see it: A project's goal is meant to solve one problem, and then another problem arises and seems to work its way into the original project, and then another problem comes up and is added to what the original project was meant to solve as well.

The projects that get done successfully are meaningful (tied to the change vision and the desired future state) and focused (solving one or two problems, not the entire organization's problems that have been around for years).

How do you limit the project scope effectively and make sure you avoid scope creep?

- ✔ **Be clear on where the project stops and starts.** This step gets back to the project goal. If the goal is SMART, you'll have a much easier time acknowledging when additional work isn't part of the change.

- ✔ **Communicate what is inside of the project scope and what is outside of the project scope.** This advice may seem obvious, but many people assume your change project is going to solve everything in the entire world — and why wouldn't it, with such a great vision of the future? Do not overpromise what the change will do. Be open about what it will and will not do.

    For example, you may have a change that focuses on altering the culture of a company from a traditional bureaucracy to an open, flat organization. You can change management structure, you can change the office layouts, and you may even change how people are rewarded, but you may not be able to take on changing all the information systems that tend to slow down decision making. Anything with that large of a scope may need to fall into the next big change project your organization tackles.

Using project charters to stay on track

After all this work, you're almost ready to get moving. At this point, many good project managers wrap it up and get moving with their project plan and GRPI model. But one final tool helps you pull everything together to keep the project on track. A *project charter* is a one-page document that is usually available for anyone in the organization to review. Each part of the charter covers pieces of the project plan and GRPI model. For a visual of the project charter, see Figure 5-1.

What makes a charter different than a project plan? You can't have a project charter without a clear project plan. Although the project plan has enough detail to get and keep you on the right path, the charter is a high-level plan that the change sponsor has signed. Some teams use the terms *charter* and *project plan* interchangeably, and that's just fine if it works for your team.

Whatever you call the document, make sure the document has one essential characteristic: *it should be evergreen.* By that, we mean that the charter should be reviewed and updated as needed every 60 to 90 days. The best way to keep your project on track and make sure you continue to focus on what matters most (and don't miss any of your key milestone dates) is to keep that charter in front of you and review it with your change agents and change sponsor on a regular basis.

The project plan, the team GRPI model, and the project charter all have similar but distinct duties. Your project plan is the detailed listing of everything that needs to get done for the change to happen, your GRPI model describes how the team plans to work together to get the change done, and your project charter is a one-page document that clearly ties all this information together and gets physical approval of the project through the change sponsor's signature or sign-off.

Change Project Charter		
Name of Project:	Project Statement:	
	Project Goals:	
Change Project Manager:	Change Sponsor:	
Resources		
Estimated Budget:	Estimated Target Completion Date:	
Resources Required: (Input in RACI information)		
Processes		
Critical Milestones:		

Milestone	Date	Responsibility

Project Communication:	
Quality Standards:	
Assumptions, Constraints, Risks:	
Charter Approval:	Project Launch Date:

Figure 5-1:
A project charter is a living document that summarizes the project plan.

Leading Unexpected Change

Even though you may have done your best to identify possible risks to your project, you may still be surprised by things that you would never have been able to predict. Being surprised by winning the lottery is one thing, but no one likes surprises in business. When you wake up one morning and your business is turned upside down (or at least shaken up), *stressed* doesn't even begin to describe how you'll feel. Unexpected change isn't something to be disregarded and brushed under the carpet. When change is knocking at your door and you weren't expecting it, you need to immediately strategize thoroughly on what to do next.

Planning your response to out-of-the-blue changes

A number of challenges happen when you don't have time to plan for change. The biggest of them is trying to plan and change direction when you're also trying to keep the business running. This challenge is real but not insurmountable.

Don't start changing everything at once in response to the change. You need to plan first and *then* act. Although you may feel pressure to move forward as quickly as possible, planning what to do next can be the difference between strategic steps and chaos. Just doing a bunch of things with no plan in place will most likely get you into a worse place than you are by doing nothing.

In this section, we cover areas that need to be part of your action plan to address unexpected change.

Clarify goals and objectives

If an organization faces unforeseen change, one of the first areas you want to address is clarifying the goals and objectives of the company and revisiting roles and specific performance standards. If a big external or internal change happens, you want to be crystal clear on what the business will continue to deliver and who is going to deliver it.

Decide how to shift resources

Lack of resources or changing resources is the outcome of many sudden changes. A fall in market demand, an increase in competition, or instability in the market after disasters all have a significant effect on businesses. When sudden change happens, identify how money, time, technology, and people will be allocated to address the change while the business continues running.

Increase communication

If communication is important during a planned change (and it is!), you can only imagine how critical communication is when the change is abrupt. Although communicating bad news to employees may be uncomfortable, communicating as much as you can immediately after the change fosters a responsive atmosphere, with employees willing and able to adjust to change. Address the change and what you plan to do (even if you're still figuring it out) internally with employees and management, and if appropriate for the type of change and challenge you face, communicate externally with your suppliers and customers.

Show strong leadership

Visible leadership is essential when reacting to change. Leaders can provide clear direction and positive motivation to help employees remain optimistic about the future. During times of unanticipated change, people crave the security that confident, straightforward leaders provide.

Involving key stakeholders and employees to gain support

The best way to get a leg up on a sudden change is to start moving. As you work through unexpected change, you need to get your stakeholders together, and you need to get them together fast. Write up an action plan, be realistic in what can and cannot be done in the short-term and long-term, and engage your stakeholders to help you quickly gain support for the plan.

Having clear and visible senior-management support for the action plan is the first way you can calm the rocky waters left by sudden change. Quickly pull together a map of your stakeholders showing their roles, interests, and authority, and assess who can influence the company to move in the right direction. Ask key stakeholders for their input and support as you conquer sudden change. Bringing these individuals together to discuss common issues helps them to develop a shared understanding of what's happening in the business concerning business continuity, strategic direction, performance, communication, and change management.

If you're trying to get your feet under you again, you'll have little time or need for an organizational-readiness assessment. Ready or not, change is here! However, the stakeholders can help create and prioritize recommendations that are a match for the organization.

Your employees are also an important resource during times of unexpected change. After updating employees on the situation, engage *key employees* — the ones who can influence other employees and support you by developing actions to address the change — by pulling them into the conversation. Unexpected changes in a business can worry employees, so it's more important than ever to keep everyone in the loop of what the leadership is planning on doing to address change. Although getting key employees involved may just seem like one more thing to do, it gives you extra eyes, ears, and legs to overcome sudden change.

The success of the change and future business performance directly relate to how much information can be shared and planned immediately after the change hits. Answering why the change happened without any notice will also help lower the chance of future surprises creeping up on you again.

Chapter 6

Get Real: Staying Realistic about Where You're Headed

In This Chapter

▶ Figuring out the risks and doing something about them

▶ Setting key benchmarks to gauge progress

▶ Marking milestones along the path

▶ Measuring the change progress

*A*fter the vision and shared need are set for your change project, you want to make sure you're moving in the right direction while also staying realistic about where you're headed. Measurements, benchmarks, and a scorecard can keep you on track and provide you with tools that help raise early warning signs when you may be veering off course.

Measuring change isn't easy, but change that's left unmeasured gets you nowhere. Consider the measurement of change and the tracking of change to be like the gauges on your car's dashboard. Although the change may be running just fine, without indicators to tell you how much fuel you have left in the tank, how many miles you have traveled, and where the GPS says you should turn next, eventually you'll end up in the middle of nowhere, unsure of which direction to go and with your resources depleted.

In this chapter we start you off by showing you how to keep track of what risks you need to be aware of during the change and how and when to mitigate their impacts. You find out what, when, and why to benchmark other processes and measures to keep your goals realistic, and you also discover what to track in order to keep your eye on the progress of the change. You'll then be able to develop relevant milestones for your project and measure the commitment to change from your change team and leaders. Finally, you see how to pull it all together with a balanced view of your desired change results.

Assessing and Managing Risk

Change risk is any possible event that can negatively affect the success of the project. Yes, the list of change risks can be long, but your job involves much more than simply thinking about risks or listing them out. You also have to assess the risks, decide whether you're willing to take them, and then manage the risks to the success of change the best you can. As you identify the risks that may obstruct your change, you first review the existing risks and then plan how to respond to them. We tell you how to do that in this section.

Knowing your risks

What risks are out there? You may be in control of risks such as maintaining production levels, training, and aligning human resources to the project, but you may not be in control of some other risks (ones that are customer or market driven). You don't have to be concerned about where the risks come from — the important part of this phase is knowing they're there.

To identify risks, you and your change team can hold brainstorming meetings or do an assessment to identify risks, you can ask experts on the subject what their opinion is regarding the risks (with data to back it up), or you may look at the past history of when something stopped a change before.

Looking at what makes a project likely to succeed

The ways in which organizations combine the following four factors often mark the difference between projects that are very likely to succeed and those that are most likely to fail:

✔ Duration

✔ Team cohesiveness and leadership

✔ Receptiveness to change

✔ Amount of work required

For example, a short project led by a skilled and cohesive team with leadership support, which is implemented in a department that's receptive to the change and requires little additional effort, is bound to succeed. At the other extreme, a long, drawn-out project that's executed by a disjointed team, lacks leadership support, targets a function that dislikes the change, and requires a lot of extra work will fail. Although identifying change programs at either end of the spectrum is easy, most initiatives occupy the middle ground, where the likelihood of success or failure is more difficult to assess.

If you're still having trouble identifying risks or if you're not sure whether you have a complete list, here are the "usual suspects" of risks to your change plan:

- **Financial risks:** Financial risks with your change may include business or service interruption due to the change, or loss of customers if change is not properly executed.

- **Technical risks:** Technical risks can range from not having the right platform to support a large system change to losing data if information systems are replaced.

- **Legal risks:** Legal risks are the factors that could break the law if not handled correctly. These risks range from not having sufficient controls in place to catch insider trading when implementing a new financial-reporting system to not doing due diligence on financial reports during a merger and acquisition. By risking legal requirements, the result may be damaged reputation, loss of customers, or even imprisonment.

- **Safety risks:** Safety risks are the factors that could cause harm to employees, the environment, or customers.

- **Human-resources risks:** Resignations, employees asked to take on additional work, unavailable skills, ineffective training, absenteeism, and poor quality/execution are just some of the many risks that come from the human element in change.

- **Public-relations risks:** Public relations deals with risks to the reputation of your company and your brand. This area includes how the change is perceived in the court of public opinion and the press.

How big? How likely? Analyzing your risks' probability and consequences

After you have your list of risks, you need to analyze those risks. Ask your change team how big and how likely each risk is. Most organizations assign numbers to the size and probability of risk to make the equation more meaningful and action oriented, with higher numbers representing larger or likelier risks. Here are ways to quantify the probability and consequences:

- **How big is the consequence of the risk?** To decide whether the risk is big or small, discuss what the outcome will be if the risk becomes a reality. If the risk could shut down your business, it should be considered of high consequence. On the other hand, if it could delay the project a few weeks or add a moderate amount of additional work for the change team, it may be considered as having a low impact on the overall change strategy. Also think about how much the risk will cost if it happens.

Your change team can decide on a measurement system to rank consequences, but it should reflect the following values for risk:

> **1: Small:** No impact to strategy; impact to smaller teams
>
> **3: Medium:** Impact to timeline or budget; impact to larger teams impacted by the change
>
> **9: Large:** The organization will be impacted; impact to strategy of the change or company

Consequences may include anything from the project not moving at the desired pace to significant financial loss.

✔ **How likely is the risk?** Probability of risk is inherently hard to pin down, just like pinning down which slot machine to use in Las Vegas is hard. Probability can be estimated with a few factors, including history (has this risk occurred in the past?), knowledge (do experts think this risk is likely?), and environment (has the risk happened to your competitors?). You can rank probability in a number of ways, but we recommend the following simple categorizations:

> **9: Almost certain/quite likely**
>
> **3: Likely/good chance**
>
> **1: Possible but unlikely**

These two areas, probability and consequence, combine to give you a simple equation for the amount of risk:

> The probability of an event × the consequences of the event = the amount of risk you have for derailing the change!

Using the exponential rankings of 1 (small), 3 (medium), and 9 (large), you can clearly see which areas are the most important ones to address in your risk plan. The more likely an event is to happen and the greater the consequence, the more attention you should pay to it.

Working with your change team, first identify the risks associated with the project (which you do in the earlier section "Knowing your risks"). Then assess their potential impact and place them on the risk-impact matrix. The risk-impact matrix helps you classify which risks you need to do something about and which risks may not be worth your time and effort to mitigate.

Here's how to handle your priorities:

✔ **A priorities: High probability, high consequence:** Your priority should be on A risks, or the ones with a high likelihood of happening and a high consequence if they do happen. Identify ways to lessen the consequence or probability, and make doing so a high priority.

✔ **B1 priorities: Low probability, high consequence:** These events shouldn't happen, but if they do, the end result could be significant. Identify ways to lessen the consequence or probability.

✔ **B2 priorities: High probability, low consequence:** These events are quite likely to happen, but the change only faces minimal risk from the events. Keep an eye on B2 priorities but hold off on any specific mitigation action for the moment.

✔ **C priorities: Low probability, low consequence:** These risks aren't show-stoppers. Carry on with the change plan, revisiting these risks at key milestones. Your C priorities should be noted and then reviewed as needed (unless you can find an extra hour and have unlimited resources to address everything).

Limiting your risks

After you've defined your risks, the next step is deciding how to respond to them. In general, you can do three things with your risks:

✔ **Risk avoidance:** Take steps to avoid them or significantly lower the probability of them happening. This process means building a change plan that eliminates the causes of the risks. For example, if knowledge on how to do things differently is an issue, then offer training and mentoring to bridge the skill gap.

✔ **Risk mitigation:** Some risks cannot be avoided, so in mitigation, you take steps to lessen the impact/consequence if the risks do occur. Risk mitigation is kind of like buying insurance for the change: You acknowledge that it could happen, but you want to lessen the blow to your change if it does. This step is where contingency plans frequently come into play. Contingency plans may be financial, task-focused, or management/people-focused.

Often, losing key human resources is a concern (a risk) during a change project. If your risk is losing top management or key employees, then make sure you have a plan in place to backfill that talent. (You may also want to try to avoid the risk by making sure you're ready to respond to the WIIFM question — what's in it for me? — from these folks; see Chapter 7 for details.)

✔ **Risk acceptance:** Accept that the risk may happen and proceed as planned. This response is what you will probably do with your C-priority risks. You acknowledge they may happen and are willing to work with the consequences if they do. When you accept risks, you may be willing to work them into the project plan and then get on with the change.

Keeping an eye out: Control and documentation

To close out your risk assessment, make sure you keep an eye on what's happening with the risks you're currently managing and with the risks that aren't an A priority at the moment. The best way to do this is to

- ✔ **Record information:** Keep track of your risk assessment. In other words, write down the results of your assessment and any important details. You also want to write down any actions you're taking on your A priorities (and B priorities if the team decides to work on them).

- ✔ **Track and review:** Throughout the change, refer back to the risks on a periodic basis and during any critical milestone reviews (we discuss milestones later in "Establishing Milestones"). Risks change just like projects change, so you want to make sure your risk assessment is a living, breathing document. Keep it evergreen!

- ✔ **Monitor:** Monitoring is a way of creating early-warning indicators that enable you to activate your contingency plan — or, in the case that you don't have a contingency plan, to create your plan. Having a monitoring system in place lets you know when things are off track. When creating indicators, think about information that is easy to obtain that will provide you with insight that a risk is about to occur.

Developing Benchmarks

After you have your risks under control (or are working toward that), you can start focusing on realistic targets of your change with practical benchmarks to help guide the course of change. *Benchmarking* is the process of defining standards of performance by comparing yourself with others.

In many change processes, when the time comes to set targets for where you want to go and how you will measure progress, you may have difficultly knowing what's good enough for the change. This uncertainty is where benchmarking can come in handy. The goal of benchmarking is to help you set a realistic measurement of success for your change project based on well-grounded ways of doing business and lessons learned from similar teams. Feedback from customers and employees (as well as information from competitors, peers, or other departments) helps you see how your change is performing in comparison to other change projects. When it comes to moving toward the shared vision of the future, knowing who else is moving and how they're doing it helps catapult your change while maintaining a realistic eye on what's possible.

Knowing what "better" looks like

In order for change leaders to have benchmarks for assessing the change progress, you need to start with a clear assessment of how you're doing. Many leaders make the mistake of seeing a great idea out there and then directing a project team to implement it without having a clue about how the company is performing today. After you know where you stand, you can start looking at best practices that others are using.

Best practices are methods, processes, tools, or any number of things that are considered industry standards of excellence. By understanding best practices, your change team can compare your company's practices to what other leaders are doing. You may find that you are behind the learning curve in some areas and perhaps even leading on other areas. Knowing where you stand in terms of best practices is a critical step in setting change goals.

Best (or better) practices can be found many places, both internally and externally. Experts are great at generating ideas (this may be the place you spend your consulting dollars — a much bigger payback than getting a consultant to write up a project plan!). You may also do a good amount of legwork to gather research. Get as much data as you can but also as much as you need. Surveys, observations, self-reports, examinations of official or public documents, and subsets of any of these sources can give you a good idea of what's out there.

Best practices are great, but don't get paralyzed by all that research and data. You should be able to understand what "better" looks like, but don't write a book report on it, because your "better" and someone else's "better" are almost always different. Get the data on how well you're doing, discuss it, and then move on.

The Internet is great for research (stating the obvious, we know). But the Internet isn't always reliable (even more shocking, we know). If you do your research for best practices online, make sure you back up your findings with solid proof. Industry conferences and peer-reviewed journals are reliable sources. Benchmarks are meant to be realistic measures to guide your future change goals, and therefore they should be based on factual information.

Creating practical benchmarks for change

Benchmarking is a great idea, but few organizations know how to do it well. Why? When you're working in subjective areas like change, what's best isn't always clear. Even if you're measuring objective data, benchmarks don't always paint a clear picture of what's happening to the entire organization — just one part of the organization.

When creating benchmarks, you're not trying to define all the benchmarks that could determine success, just a few important ones. But articulating and gaining agreement on the vital few metrics can be your most challenging task in the integration process.

When you're creating change benchmarks, keep these questions in mind:

- **What are the three things that you absolutely want to do better after the change is done?** These goals should be the focus of your benchmarking plans.

- **What part of the process will the change impact?** Benchmarks often look at the end result. When developing your benchmarks, you should look at the inputs, not just the outputs of the process. Processes define how you will create the end result by defining the required inputs and the specific steps to create the outputs. In benchmarking, the "how" is equally if not more important than the "what".

Establishing Milestones

Change projects sometimes seem like they can last forever and ever, so establishing big and small milestones to track progress is critical. The word *milestone* originated from the stones that were set up next to roads to indicate to travelers the distance in miles to a particular destination, and in your case milestones are events or actions that mark progress in your change project. You use them to communicate when your project has reached certain stages and to indicate what is coming up next.

Looking at bigger milestones

Bigger milestones are, of course, more important and more visible, but luckily they're often easier to set and should be aligned to the steps of implementing change we discuss in Chapter 1 and throughout the book. Here are five big milestones that mark the end of these key implementation steps:

- **Build a vision and shared need:** As soon as the vision for the change is set and is beginning to be communicated to the larger audience, you can measure and evaluate whether you're on the right track early in the project. Setting and communicating the vision is the first big milestone.

- **Create the change road map and plan the change:** Although a project plan doesn't make the change happen, the change plan is one of the first tangible outputs of the change, and getting it done right should be recognized as a major milestone.

- ✔ **Committing leadership:** Leadership is often a subjective area that people find hard to measure. We discuss how to measure the leaders' commitment to change in the next section, but after your sponsor, change agents, and change team are aligned, you will have surpassed a big milestone worthy of celebration.

- ✔ **Implementing the change:** Throughout the implementation, you will want to communicate and measure larger milestones such as your critical-path events (see Chapter 5).

- ✔ **Finalizing the change and recognizing results:** This milestone is the no-brainer. After the change happens, you will surely want to celebrate, recognize, and learn from everything that happened during the change. This milestone marks the conclusion of the project.

Setting small milestones

Small milestones do two things: They help generate momentum with small successes along the way to the bigger goal, and they help you gauge how the change is moving. Creating milestones to identify early wins is one way of building momentum. Just like the bigger project goal, smaller milestones must be clear, tangible, and directly tied to the project (don't forget to communicate them — but you'll know all about that after Chapter 7). Small milestones may be getting the change team trained, finalizing the vision, completing benchmarking of better ways of doing things, and establishing communication channels for the change.

Small milestones should be linked to the implementation of the change, too; a rule of thumb is to have a small milestone every two to three weeks during the project. People will become overwhelmed if you tell them weekly or daily how wonderful the change is, and any length of time more than a month between measuring progress and small wins will make people think the change has vanished.

Keeping an Eye on Progress

You probably know by now how important it is to measure by fact, not feeling. So how do you know a change is an improvement? You measure it. The best way to keep an eye on progress is to keep an eye on your data. In this section, we describe how to create simple measures that will help you to track and evaluate your implementation, measure the leaders' commitment to change, and measure the effectiveness of the change on your business results.

When setting up change measures, find out where you are before the change so you can later prove that the benefits of the project have been delivered.

Using simple measurements

Often, organizations get bogged down in measuring everything perfectly and delay making a change until they've collected enough data. But measurement should speed change up, not slow it down. The key is to not track things just because they can be tracked; keep your measurements aligned to the strategy and goals of the change. Your measurements should be relevant to strategy, reflect the outcome you want to achieve, and be based on data that's reasonably easy to gather.

Your first priority for measurement is called your *key performance indicators* and should be linked to the strategy and vision of the change, the processes that are going to change, the impact to the people, and any legal or compliance issues that must be tracked during the change (which is often a key factor in mergers and acquisitions; see Chapter 14).

To keep an eye on progress, just make sure you cover two main parts of data:

- ✔ **Measures to evaluate implementation, or whether the change was executed as planned:** These measurements may be tracking of project plans, critical milestones, and budgets. This type of measure is often objective: Did it happen or not? Did we meet our target dates? Did we meet the budget targets for the change project?

- ✔ **Measures to gauge effectiveness of the change or how well the change accomplished the future-state goal:** These measures should be linked to benchmarks you identified for your change and to goals for the change. Although some of these measures may be objective (are management structures flatter rather than hierarchical?), other parts of the effectiveness assessment may be more subjective (does the organization operate with fewer boundaries, and has teamwork improved across functions and departments?).

You want change to be large and engaging, but you want the measurement of your change's success to be as simple as possible. Note that *easy* and *simple* are not the same thing — doing a little extra legwork to keep your measures simple can give your change team confidence when they're asked to review the measurements frequently. For example, a simple measure could be the results of a few questions on an engagement survey asking employees to rate their perception of the change on employee satisfaction on a scale of one to ten. This measure is simple, but the information isn't easy to gather.

Here is a great example of how to keep an eye on implementation of the change and effectiveness of the change: The goal of your change is to enrich employees' skills and capabilities at the company, and the change strategy chosen is to provide more training and professional development to everyone in the organization. The change team may assess implementation by counting the number of courses now offered within the company or how many professional-development plans have been reviewed by management.

The team can review the effectiveness by talking directly to employees and managers about how their skill sets have increased or how employees are applying learning to their jobs.

Measuring and tracking implementation

The first type of measures are designed to track and evaluate the implementation of your change to ensure your plans stay on time, on budget, and at the right level of quality. You essentially measure whether or not you are doing what you said you would do. You need to answer the following three primary questions:

✓ **Are we on time?** Your project timeline dictates the time frame for your key milestones, discussed earlier in this chapter. You need to track, on an ongoing basis, whether your project is meeting the deadlines set out in your plan.

✓ **What is our quality level?** Each milestone should have key quality levels defined. Sometimes these levels are called *completion criteria,* which specify deliverables along with the level of quality required for the milestone to be deemed complete. For example, one milestone might be "Employees trained on the new process." The training quality measure may include a certification test. The completion criteria could include 100 percent of employees completing the training with a certification test score of 90 percent or better.

✓ **Are we on budget?** Most change efforts have at least some budget allocated to them. Tracking and reporting your expenses is usually an important part of measuring implementation success, unless of course your organization has money to burn.

Many change leaders report on the progress of implementation on a periodic basis to the team and sponsoring executives. The timing of reporting is dependent on the overall time frame of your change initiative. Really short projects may need daily reporting, whereas longer projects may only need weekly or even monthly progress reports. The timing and frequency of progress reporting needs to be negotiated by the team with the change sponsors.

Measuring the leaders' commitment to change

In creating a vision and measures for the project, so far in this chapter we have described the outcome of this change. But in order to ensure that the change happens, you need the appropriate people to be accountable for the outcomes.

What specific outcomes are these leaders being held accountable for? Leaders must unmistakably demonstrate their commitment and support the future state and the changes that will come with it.

The best way to drive accountability is to give leaders ownership of both the implementation and the effectiveness of big and small milestones. Your change team can measure the buy-in and commitment to change through a process of interviews, focus groups, and just plain old observation. This in-depth review helps you learn the unique perspectives of each stakeholder group.

If you want more-concrete measures of leadership dedication to the change, consider these elements of commitment:

- ✔ **Is the leader available and visible?** Committed leaders attend meetings and open their doors to people if they have differing opinions or questions.

- ✔ **Is the leader timely?** Missing deadlines and forgetting to identify the success of small milestones are fairly clear indicators that commitment must be reexamined.

Implementing change and delivering the benefits of the future state requires input and assistance from many people. Promoting shared understanding and ownership of the change helps you more easily achieve your measures of success. The sooner the buy-in occurs, the shorter the time spent by people resisting or merely complying.

Implementing change is not a spectator sport; shared accountability is born from shared participation. Even when the change seems slow moving at best, involving the owners of the future state and the teams they lead helps them be (and feel) part of the solution.

Making the grade: The change scorecard

Change projects exist to provide some improvement in the organization, including performance, profitability, skill sets, or process and product innovation. In order to judge where your project is successful and where you have shortened the gap between the current state and the desired state, you need to take measurements. And people more clearly understand the goals of a project if the measures of success are clearly communicated. In the absence of known measures, people will create their own, especially if employees have made assumptions about job-role changes.

The change scorecard is about measuring the effectiveness of the change effort, as opposed to tracking and evaluating the implementation. It reveals how your change initiative has impacted your organization and its performance. It contains a set of measures from four perspectives, specific targets for each measure, and the actual results achieved. You should create your scorecard early in the planning process, shortly after the visioning and benchmarking process is complete.

Setting up balanced measures

Balance measures, originally developed by Kaplan and Norton, are a popular and influential business tool that looks at your progress from four perspectives: people/learning and growth, business process, customers, and financial. These four perspectives create a balanced view of effectiveness by taking into consideration the interests of multiple stakeholders, including shareowners, customers, the company, and employees. Each of the perspectives have underlying strategies that can be measured as part of the effectiveness of the change.

Here is a description of each perspective, its strategic question, and what types of measures are included:

- ✔ **People/learning and growth:** How can you develop your people and their capabilities? You likely need to include people development and learning to achieve your project vision. Measures may include number of training opportunities, employee satisfaction ratings, employee retention rates, and new-employee recruitment success measures such as percent of critical job openings filled.

- ✔ **Business process:** What must your organization change and excel at to meet customer needs? You may be able to track the speed and quality of business processes or how efficiently new products and services can come to market after the change has happened. Key measures may include cycle time, inventory levels, time-to-market, rework rates, deflect rates, or regulatory costs.

- ✔ **Customers:** How will customers value your product and services after the change? The measures may include client satisfaction, customer loyalty, or quality.

- ✔ **Financial:** How will the change project help the company succeed financially? Perhaps your project can be to reduce operating costs or grow revenue. Key measures could include profit, revenue, operating costs, and stock price.

Although not every change involves every perspective, take the time to consider each perspective to consider its possible contribution and relevance. For example, almost all changes involve employee learning and growth at some level.

Each measure should include the following information:

✔ The specific indicators and their target criteria, so you know whether you have achieved the desired results or not

✔ The methods you use to gather and report the results, including data sources and calculation methods

✔ The specific actual results, so you know you have met the criteria and are making progress in the change initiative

Seeing how your scores compare

After creating your change scorecard, go back and review it against the vision of the change project. Ask your team the following questions:

✔ **Do the measures match?** If not, where are they different and where can you align them to the strategy of the change?

✔ **How achievable are they?** Make sure your measures meet the SMART criteria we outline in Chapter 4: The goals should be specific, measure-able, action oriented and agreed on, realistic, and time bound. Ensuring that your goals and their measures are SMART improves their likelihood of being achievable.

Forecasting the cost of organizational change

Ask most change professionals to give a cost for organizational change, and they most likely will say something about the benefits — higher chance of meeting the change or team objectives, mitigating risks, or higher proficiency of a skill. These payoffs are all well and good, but they are not costs; they are expected benefits and for the most part are hard to quantify unless they don't happen. It may be easy to say that not changing a company's culture could cost millions of dollars, but unless the company goes belly up because the culture did not change, the number is quite subjective.

So how do you quantify the cost of change, whether it is for a change project or a change team? Here are a couple of hard costs that should be accounted for:

✔ **The project team:** If team players are pulled out of their day-to-day jobs, it's a clear cost of change. Smaller changes may just need a leader to work with a group that's already capable of change; but with larger changes or when change has great resistance, the cost of human resources dedicated to make the change happen should be accounted for in the cost of organizational change.

✔ **Tools, methods, and training:** You're close to being an expert on change by now, but the rest of the organization isn't there yet. Change not only takes the time of people leading the change but also requires the cost of training, tools, and methods of getting people up to speed on how to make change happen.

Chapter 7

Getting the Message Out: Communicating the Change

*Y*ou have probably heard the saying, "Less is more." But when you're talking about communicating during change in a business, that saying couldn't be further from the truth! Throw "less" out the window and adopt your new mantra: More communication is more.

When people start feeling the stress associated with major change, they develop an almost insatiable hunger for information. You will hear these questions: What is happening? When is it happening? Why is it happening? Is it happening to me? If you leave a gap in answering these questions, the gap is inevitably filled with rumor, and the rumor mill is the nemesis of change. On the other hand, successfully communicated changes result in project-management utopia: shorter timelines, widespread ownership in the new environment, lower costs due to speed of the change and/or increased efficiencies, and an organization ready to take on future changes.

In this chapter we take you through the process of communicating changes step by step. First we reveal the three big questions you'll encounter as soon as the change starts and help you develop good answers. We then address what you need to do differently when communicating about change, how to create a communication plan that delivers powerful messages, how to address generational and organizational differences in your messaging, and how to build trust as you communicate. By the end of the chapter, you'll feel so confident with your new knowledge and skills that you may find yourself trumpeting the message far and wide. At the very least, you'll have a well-thought-through communication strategy and plan ready to be implemented.

Answering the Three Big Change Questions

As soon as your employees hear that change is coming, you can bet that three major questions will surface even before you have a chance to develop your full-fledged communication plan (see the section "Bringing It All Together: The Communication Plan" for more on how to do that). Early in the change process, people will want and need to know the answers to these three *big* change questions:

1. **Where are we headed, and why?**

2. **WIIFM — what's in it for me?**

3. **How are we going to get there?**

Having well-thought-out answers to these questions sets up the change for success, starting day one. Change succeeds when a powerful case for the change is communicated relentlessly to generate understanding and consensus for that change. By planning for these questions in advance, you can present a case that's strong enough to win over your employees and keep them on your side.

Question 1: Where are we headed, and why?

The first question most often asked when a large change is about to happen is "Where are we headed?" This question is quickly followed by, "Why are we going there?" A powerful vision that rallies people and generates enthusiasm for a brighter future is the best way to address this duo. Although that idea may sound lofty, without a passionately communicated vision, nothing will happen. Imagine if civil-rights activist Dr. Martin Luther King Jr. got up to speak in 1963 and, instead of giving his moving "I Have a Dream" speech, stood up there and said, "Hey, yeah, I think we should probably do something." Not the same effect, right?

When you are starting to craft the answer to the question of where you're heading, think of change like a vacation. Just like your vacation, you need to first find out where you are going before you can do anything else, otherwise you may be packing a ski jacket for a trip to the Caribbean. If you don't decide where you're going, you will probably go nowhere and very few people will want to come along just for the ride.

Let's say, for example, that Top-Notch Typewriting Company, a manual typewriter manufacturer, is making a big change. The company's leaders have finally realized that the marketplace for manual typewriters has dwindled to three or four people, so they're moving to producing the next generation of touch-screen writing tablets. This change will impact the entire company.

Top-Notch's employees are wondering: Where are we headed? If Top-Notch's leaders are smart, they'll give an answer that hits the following points:

- ✓ Top-Notch Typewriting is reinventing its products, service, and culture to provide state-of-the-art writing products to writers across the globe — products customers want and need!

- ✓ Top-Notch Typewriting Company has been focused on supporting those three or four people still using a manual typewriter, and now it's going to provide a product people everywhere want to buy and use.

- ✓ Because Top-Notch Typewriting Company is going to be shutting down 100-year-old manufacturing lines and replacing them with the latest technology, employees will be learning an entirely new skill set and will get the best training and tools in the world to create and support the new services and culture of the organization.

- ✓ Top-Notch Typewriting Company has been a traditional and bureaucratic organization for many years, and now it's going to be innovative, exciting, and on the cutting edge of technology.

Now that's change the company can rally behind! The answer is specific and addresses key information: products (new writing tablets), customers (lots more!), employees (new skills), and culture (state of the art!). If you want to get your message out right, creating a vision of what's changing is one of your first tools to help everyone understand where the change is headed.

Question 2: WIIFM, or what's in it for me?

When you think you have a good vision, put yourself in the shoes of the people going through the change and answer the questions they may have when you begin to communicate the vision. What is this change going to do for us? Why should I give this project my attention when I have 100 other things competing for my time?

People tend to get comfortable in the current state and, after they hear that change is coming, they want to know how this change is going to affect them personally. It makes sense; work is where they spend much of their time, where they make their money, and where they have developed important professional and personal relationships. You, as the leader, must answer the big WIIFM question (What's in it for me?) in a way that resonates with them and encourages them to jump on board.

When a change happens, the vision is often tied to growing business, becoming more profitable, and having teams be more productive. Although these messages are critical and are perhaps the main reason for change, they don't always resonate with the people doing the work. Change projects succeed or fail when employees know and support how they're going to affect them. So if you want people to jump on board, you need to let them know how their lives and jobs will be better in the new environment.

WIIFM drives home how the change affects someone personally. Your answer lets employees know what they need to do when the change is happening and after it happens. And when your answer is a good one, it will get people out from behind their desks and saying, "I am ready to change!"

To give employees the best WIIFM answer possible and start using this critical change tool, follow these four steps:

1. **Explain:** Explain WIIFM to the employees involved in change, letting everyone understand what you're asking them and why it's important to the company so the entire team understands the direction of the change. Providing initial thoughts about what's in it for them kicks off the dialogue about the change. These initial WIIFMs could be based on employee survey information or other research gathered previously during benchmarking against other companies (see Chapter 6).

2. **Ask:** Ask about individual and team WIIFMs. Start with these two discussion questions: "Why are you here today? What do you want to get out of being part of this change?" Answers to these questions may range from being promoted in the next six months to learning new skills to getting a good recommendation at the end of the project. Everyone has different WIIFM goals; your job is to gather them. This step engages employees in exploring how the change will benefit them individually and as a team.

3. **Identify:** Identify ways that the project can motivate and reward employees according to their WIIFM goals while still meeting the project's overall goals. Although you can't promise employees that their WIIFM dreams will *all* be achieved, understanding and acknowledging different goals and helping employees achieve their personal goals goes a long way to motivating them to focus and commit to the project.

4. **Assess:** Assess whether or not the WIIFM goals you settled on are being achieved on a regular basis. This check-in may be in individual team-leader meetings or in casual one-on-one discussions. Your goal and role is to track the progress towards the WIIFM solution and make changes to the overall communication messaging as necessary.

We discuss how to incorporate the most important WIIFM goals into the overall communication plan later in this chapter.

As soon as your change project is identified, meet with groups of employees involved in the project to make sure everyone is clear about the overall goals, objectives, timeline, roles, and marketing plan — and make sure you are clear about what benefit will come for those employees. What people want and what benefits the change can provide may both be slightly different throughout your organization, so don't stop asking about the WIIFM goals after one or two meetings.

Not every group impacted by the change will share the same understanding of the sense of urgency or will find the vision or business case compelling. Some employees may not believe you can give them a good answer to WIIFM. Don't despair or waste precious time trying to appease these people; just jump right back to Chapter 4 to find ways to get these laggards to start embracing the change.

Question 3: How are we going to get there?

Although the change journey is like a trip in many ways, unlike a vacation, getting there is really not half the fun, but it *is* more than half the work. Going from the current state to the future state (also known as the *transition state*) takes effort, so you can help the cause by having a transparent and easily understood forecast of how the change will take place. Crafting this message helps you answer the third question employees have about the change: "How are we going to get there?"

Most change efforts have a project plan. (If you don't have one, plan on heading back to Chapter 6 for a refresher.) This plan is a good place to start the communication process about *how are we going to get to there?*

Project plans are great to keep project teams on task and are especially wonderful for the people who made them and people who love to have lots of information, but the general population can be overwhelmed by detailed project plans. (Remember, most people in your organization aren't going to be working on change as closely as you are during the project.) What's an expert change leader like you to do? Two things: Communicate the basic outline of the plan and provide enough information to keep everyone informed of what is happening in the short term.

A high-level project plan may look something like this:

- Stage 1: Creating the change team happens in Month 1.
- Stage 2: Providing training for the change happens in Month 2.
- Stage 3: Change happens in Month 3.
- Stage 4: Following-up on the change success happens in Month 4.

Simple. To the point. Just enough detail to help people understand what's going on during the entire change project.

Directly related to the question "How are we going to get there?" are three other questions that people are likely to ask:

✔ **What is going on now?** You may let employees know that a change team is being formed, leaders are creating a vision, or training is taking place for people in a certain department. If you have no significant reason to keep what's happening now secret, let people know and see the things that *are* happening! And remember, although some bad news may be associated with a change (perhaps a layoff or people being moved into new jobs), being honest with as much information as you can provide keeps the rumor mill at bay and makes your job easier in the future.

✔ **What will happen next?** People want to know what is happening next week, next month, and maybe even next year. Do you know why signs are posted for exits along highways? They're there to give you fair warning of what to expect *next*. If you were driving down the road and had to guess where the next exit or gas station would be, it would be pretty frustrating and stressful, right? The same is true in change projects. By providing a few key events or milestones in your communication plan, the level of anxiety will drop drastically in your organization.

✔ **What do I need to do?** Nothing is worse than missing out on something because you didn't know about it! As a change leader, don't assume people know what they need to do — tell them! If a department needs to take a training class, communicate it. If a manager needs to hold a meeting with her employees, make sure you let her know she is supposed to do it. Giving employees impacted by the change a specific action is the perfect way to involve them in the ongoing change process.

If you've ever been frustrated because you felt like you weren't getting enough information, you have probably been on the receiving end of change communication. Wanting to know everything *right now* is a natural reaction. But many times as a change leader you may be faced with not having the answer. In fact, sometimes the project team may not have the answer. Of course, as the project matures, many unknowns are defined and then can be communicated to the organization. Even if you don't have all the answers, by following the *What is happening now? What is happening next? What do I need to do?* mantra, you can provide a clear picture of how you're going to get to the future state to the entire organization, even if the plan is modified during the change.

The more unanswered questions out there, the higher the level of frustration is during the change project (and after). And the longer the questions remain unanswered, the tougher that frustration is to alleviate.

Developing an Ideal Communication Style during Change

Communicating during change is all about getting the message out in order to alleviate as much ambiguity and uncertainty as possible. Your job as a communicator of change is to encourage exploration and learning while maintaining productivity. It's a big task — but not an impossible one.

As a change leader, you have a choice about *how* you will communicate during change. Being inaccessible, telling only the partial truth, or ordering rather than seeking solutions may be effective in getting things checked off in the short term, but such actions taken together and repeated will not — we repeat, *will not* — lead to a sustainable change (and most likely your change will backfire on you fairly quickly). Providing a compelling reason to change, listening to concerns (really listening to them), and making sure people have the right level of information *will* lead to sustainable change. Which one do you want to choose to do?

In this section, we provide specific communication styles to emulate that will assist you while you communicate whatever changes you may be implementing.

Keeping it fresh, frequent, and flowing

While you're communicating with your employees, we recommend that you keep in mind the acronym KIF: keep it fresh, keep it frequent, and keep it flowing — to make your communication successful.

- ✔ **Keep it fresh.** Give new information often to prevent broken-record syndrome.

- ✔ **Keep it frequent and diverse.** Make your communication more than just a checkmark on the project plan. Do it again and again and again on a regular basis. Use a variety of communication tools to get the attention of employees. If you keep using the same two tools to communicate, people will eventually tune out.

- ✔ **Keep it flowing.** Nothing is worse than going out with a stellar communication plan, getting everyone excited about the change, and then hiding in a cave until the project is done. Employees must see, hear, and feel updated messages throughout the project. Otherwise, they'll assume the change has fizzled out like short fuse.

So how do you do it? Say, for example, executives at a large energy company are adding an entirely new service offering for customers. They launch their change efforts by broadcasting a company memo, holding an all-employees meeting, and starting an internal website to get the news to everyone in the company. However, these savvy executives know those techniques aren't enough to get the entire organization on board fast (they must have read this book!). The change team launches even more communication efforts, including a biweekly roundtable to answer any questions from the staff, a weekly webcast discussing what's happened that month with the change and what will happen in the next month, and site visits by the executives to really hear what the concerns are within each department.

Motivating and encouraging: Saying no to the status quo

The status quo is never a catalyst to change. Now is the time to remind your employees to leave the status quo and move to this wonderful new future. Here are some ways you can start challenging the existing situation and communicating why it's so important to "say no to the status quo":

- ✔ **Be the devil's advocate with a purpose:** Know the worst that could happen if you don't change, and be the spokesperson of those fears. What is the worst that can happen if you stay where you are? Could the market for your product or service go away? Could another company take over greater market share? All these possibilities are compelling reasons to move away from where you are today and can motivate your employees.

- ✔ **Know what everyone else is doing:** Be able to tell your employees why your company is changing to align with the competition or differentiate from the competition. Has the rest of your competition begun moving away from the same-old-same-old? You don't need to jump off a bridge because everyone else is doing it, but if you notice you're diverging from the pack, it may be a good time to reevaluate where you're going and why. Benchmarking is a helpful way to gather this information. (See Chapter 6.)

- ✔ **Keep up with customers who want something new:** Communicate to your employees that having customers isn't the same thing as keeping them. Even if your customers love you and your product, at some point in time, they will want to try something new. Wouldn't it be nice if you could give that new something to them?

- ✔ **Deal with other external factors:** Explain how regulatory change, pricing pressures driven by the market, or other external factors are driving you to change. Some changes are thrust upon us by the government or the global economy. Change may be required to meet the requirements of new laws.

✔ **Change in order to keep moving (even if everything seems great right now):** Convey to your employees that even if nothing is broken, you need to "fix" things to stay ahead. This point is a tricky one but important to communicate. Many people who will be changing created the status quo in the first place (and like it quite well, thank you very much). Your role is to acknowledge how the status quo has served its purpose and how now is the time to move on and move up!

Take it from the experts; many people can't bear to give up the status quo, because they think the fact that it worked in the past means it shouldn't change. Even if a process or product did *not* work in the past, you'll come into contract with a handful of people that won't admit it. By communicating the need to abandon the status quo and telling employees what's in it for them (see the earlier section "Question 2: WIIFM, or what's in it for me?"), you can offer a reason to change that's more compelling than their natural attachment to the status quo.

Listening

Are you a good listener? And a tougher question: Why would you want to listen? Listening is an important aspect of leading change successfully. When managing change, you need to channel your inner mom or wise old owl (take your pick) and start listening to your employees.

Two-way communication implies opportunities for people to give feedback, share ideas, voice their concerns, make suggestions, identify problems, and surface rumors. Effective communication plans build in those opportunities, so lend an ear and start listening by:

✔ **Creating buy-in:** Let employees (not just you or upper management) share why this change is important in their words.

✔ **Gleaning ideas you may not have thought of:** Ask employees what other ideas may move the change along.

✔ **Making course corrections:** Let an employee steering committee gather feedback from peers during the change; peers are more likely to talk with peers than feel they are squealing to management.

✔ **Letting concerns surface instead of suppressing them:** Let employees discuss their concerns without responding immediately. Ask for feedback, listen to it, and then go research the correct answer (not a talking point or canned answer)!

Doing a lot of talking isn't going to get you too far. In fact, the best approach looks more like this:

Talk, Listen, Listen, Talk, Listen, Listen

The ratio of at least two to one works well — which makes sense, because you have two ears and one mouth! When you listen carefully to another person's opinions, fears, ideas, or suggestions, you are able to understand their point of view and read between the lines of what they are REALLY saying.

The most effective tool in communication is the ear.

Sometimes when people say one thing, they actually mean another. As a leader, listen between the lines. For example, if an employee says, "I support this change 100 percent, but lots of people around here don't," you can probably infer that she doesn't fully support the idea. In this case, acknowledge the lack of support comment and engage her in further dialogue to better understand the concerns of the "other people."

Bringing It All Together: The Communication Plan

A communication plan creates a structured approach to meeting people's information needs. If you think you're ready to bring all your communication skills together with a rock-solid communication plan, you've come to the right place. (If you think you may need to brush up on some of the basics, flip back to the sections "Answering the Three Big Change Questions" and "Developing an Ideal Communication Style during Change" in this chapter.)

Another plan? Well, yes. Why? The information needs of everyone involved with your business change depend not only on the level of information you have available but also on the specific needs of the individual stakeholder groups (refer to Chapter 5 for info on stakeholders). During a large financial change, a marketer doesn't have the same information needs as the CFO or financial analyst.

By following a few simple steps, your communication strategy can focus on vital stakeholders and create awareness, interest, and involvement. So what are you waiting for? Read on and get to work!

Before moving any farther, don't forget to think about who you are talking to before you begin to talk. Communication is great, but the message will be different depending on whether you're talking to customers, employees, or senior leaders.

Deciding who is in your audience

Regardless of whether you're sending an early message indicating future change or a big mid-project update, you have to know who your target audience is: Who exactly needs to hear what you've got to say?

The *target audience* is a person or group of people who are the main recipients of your change. If you are changing the financial reporting system, the finance folks are one of your main target audiences. But don't limit yourself to just the bean counters (our deepest apologies to any bean counters out there). What about the people who use the reports finance produces? They have a vested interest in the change, too. What about administrators that run reports from the financial system? Your target-audience list may be 10 to 15 groups long depending on the type of change you're undertaking. A great way to compile your target audience list is to ask these questions:

✔ Who will be the main users of the changed product or service?

✔ Whose job/life/team will be different?

✔ Who is it essential that I talk about this change with before the change happens?

Those people are your target audience.

You may be saying, well, everyone should care about my change! I want to tell everyone about it! Ah, yes. You're now talking about the secondary audience members. These people are the groups who may find the change interesting but not life/job/career altering. Communicating with these people would be nice, but it's not necessary.

As tempting as it may be, *do not* run into your office or cubicle and start yelling out the news! Gather your trusty project team together and facilitate a session to identify all target audience members. We recommend identifying the target audience using the steps in the next section of this chapter. When you have your meeting to identify who is in your communication audience, it will go a little something like this:

> **Business-change guru (you):** "With this big project changing how we do business, who needs to know about this change? Can we list departments, specific individuals, or groups as our target audience?"
>
> **Everyone else:** "Yes, the marketing group needs to know so they can change our marketing materials; the engineers need to know so they can create the new product . . ." and so on and so on.
>
> **Business-change guru:** "Okay, let's look back at our list of events and times to communicate. [Bring out the list from your communication strategy.]

Are we missing anyone on our target audience list who may want to know about this information?"

Everyone else: "No, I think we have it all. This looks great! You deserve a raise."

Planning a communication strategy

A communication plan and strategy is not a onetime project or checklist. It is a continuous process that involves many audiences and that is both structured *and* flexible and spontaneous. Bottom line: Your communication strategy should be about getting the right people to learn about the right topics at the right time.

What does a thorough and deliberate communication strategy and plan achieve? Remember the vowels: A-E-I-O-U:

- ✔ Acceptance of the change
- ✔ Enhancement of morale during the change
- ✔ Increase of the openness and accuracy of the information out there
- ✔ Ownership of the change develops quickly
- ✔ Understanding of the what, when, why, and WIIFM (what's in it for me)

But successful change isn't going to happen until people accept it and commit to it themselves, and how you communicate has a direct and immediate impact on how likely people are to accept the change. Table 7-1 shows a few different communication strategies and their likely results.

Table 7-1	Communication Strategies	
Communication Strategy	*Example*	*Commitment and Acceptance Level*
Announcing/informing	"We are changing our marketing and sales strategy starting tomorrow. Check your e-mail for information."	People are aware of a change, but not really sure what to do with it. The rumor mill starts. Acceptance of the change is likely to be low, and commitment to taking action is not really possible because of lack of clarity about what to do.

Communication Strategy	Example	Commitment and Acceptance Level
Integrating/discussing	"We will be working with your department to help you adjust to the change as we combine our sales force across the country."	Change is being done *to* employees, not for or with them. People will adjust to change as necessary (perhaps even commit to it), but only as long as it's convenient.
Dialogue/partnering	"We will be working together to create the best sales department to support our growing business."	The strategy gives participation and ownership of the change to employees. They adopt the change and have positive perception of the impact because they are helping make it.

As you notice in Table 7-1, telling someone to do something doesn't create lasting change. Announcing big changes most likely only creates awareness that something is happening, and more likely causes significant confusion. The more you engage in partnership and dialogue, the more individuals will want to change and even take ownership of the change.

To use communication strategies well, you need a plan. Follow four steps to start planning your strategy:

1. **Research:** Find out what employees already know or think about the topic in question and the change. Find out what communication structures are already in place.

2. **Planning:** Identify the various audiences and communication goals and objectives to reach them. In this step, you also outline key messaging that would be used throughout the course of the change initiative. Such well-defined messaging will go a long way toward building repetition of consistent messaging.

3. **Implementation:** Decide the best way to keep you and your organization continually informed about the change project. Identify the many times and events where communication needs to occur during your project with your project team. Map out all communication tactics and have them connect back to the objective they support.

4. **Evaluation:** Evaluate the communications against the goals and objectives and make changes to the communications plan, as needed, for improvement. Also, remember to celebrate your success!

Step 1: Research

To find out what employees know and think about the change, what type of communication is already used in your organization, and how much of a communication structure you will have to create for your business change, answer these three questions:

- ✔ **What do employees know and think about the change?** Some employees will be forthcoming when asked what they think of the change; others may have difficulty giving frank and valuable information if this is the first time leaders are asking for feedback and options. Start small, perhaps using a representative group of employees who feel comfortable sharing this type of information and who can also gather the opinions of peers less open to sharing their ideas. Another way to elicit this feedback is through an anonymous employee survey. Regardless of the method, the goal of this research is to find out what information is out there so change leaders can fill the gaps and to determine initial opinions so leaders can leverage the positive perspectives, work to change the negative opinions, and quickly address any miscommunication or misinformation early in the process (stop the rumor mill).

- ✔ **Who communicates to employees in your organization?** Do executives trickle down messages to managers, or is most communication direct to employees and staff? We recommend that direct communication take place and be reinforced by line managers and supervisors.

- ✔ **What types of communication frequently take place?** Are most communications project presentations or informal communications? Are messages usually proactive or reactive? These answers give you a pretty good idea of whether or not you can use the communication channels in place and just beef them up a bit or whether you need to build communication from the ground up for your business change. A mix of both formal presentations supported by ongoing informal channels is ideal, as long as they are in alignment. Communication should also be as proactive as possible.

If you have a good amount of direct communication that's both informal and formal, you have a great starting point. If most communication is trickled down with little two-way discussion, you can use this change project to create a more effective communication environment.

Not sure of the types of communication your organization already has in place, or looking for more ideas? A comprehensive communication plan uses an abundance of methods to reach the target audience. Have you tried or seen any of these out in your workplace?

- ✔ One-on-one meetings
- ✔ All-employee meetings

✔ Presentations (live and online)

✔ E-mail

✔ Blogs, intranet postings, intranet Q&A forums

✔ Training classes, webinars, lunch-and-learns, and workshops

✔ Conference calls

✔ Scheduled voicemail messages

✔ Video messages from change sponsors; may be distributed via e-mail

 Use different methods to communicate the same message again and then the same methods to communicate new messages. You may communicate something five to seven times before everyone hears it! Don't take it personally; it's just the way people listen.

Step 2: Planning

In this step, you identify the various audiences and the necessary communication goals and objectives to reach them. You also go ahead and outline key messaging that would be used throughout the course of the change initiative so that your future communications are consistent (not the same thing as repetitive!).

✔ **Identify various audiences and the necessary communication goals to reach them.** When you begin identifying audiences for the change, you start with the basic question: Who are they? Audience groups should include anyone affected by the change, anyone needed to implement the change, and anyone who can block the change from happening. In this step, the change team is grouping the types of audiences out there into reasonable categories related to the change. For example, groups of audiences who may care about a change in the recruitment strategy for new employees can include the CEO, senior management, human-resource professionals, recruiters, newly promoted managers, managers who are hiring in the next year, and new employees.

Because the goal of the communication is to support a successful change, after brainstorming the audience groups (who should receive the communication), the next step is to find out what each audience needs to know and when. These groups are different, and they need different types of information. For example, managers need much more detailed information on how to recruit and hire new employees than the CEO does, who may just want to be aware of the changes.

✔ **Outline key messages that would be used throughout the course of change.** Even though the goals of the communication may be different for each audience, the key messages may be very similar, even though the specific messages will vary based on the audience and channel of communication.

Key messages may include

- **The project definition:** This message includes the vision, purpose, and goals of the change.

- **The importance to the company and employees:** Tailor the importance of the change to the WIIFM answers for each audience group.

- **Results of the change:** Share five key actions from the last month, what is currently happening, and what to expect next — and of course, the WIIFM answer!

- **Where employees can go for more information:** Include opportunities to voice concerns, give feedback, and volunteer ideas to make the change work for those impacted by the change.

- **A call to action:** Many employees will want to know what they can do to be part of the change. The call to action provides helpful information on the change project and how to get involved.

All communication tactics used at different times need to connect back to the objective they support, because communication must be tied to the project timeline, vision, goals, measurements, and objectives. Therefore, communicating must be seen as a process or series of events that are *linked* throughout the project, instead of a standalone e-mail or PowerPoint message.

Step 3: Implementation

In this step, you determine how you'll actually do the communicating. You decide on the best way to keep everyone continually informed about the project, you identify the many times and events when communication needs to occur during your project, and you map out the whole communication scheme.

Consider the best way to keep you and your organization continually informed about the change project. Regardless of what kind of communication structure you're starting with, when leading change you have a great opportunity to agree to a process for constant communication at all levels within your organization. Do people like message boards and blogs? Or do people in your organization still like face-to-face discussion? No communication plan should use just one medium to communicate, so work with your project team and employees to generate three or four main ways individuals can receive their information.

Need some ideas on how to communicate your message? Table 7-2 shows some of the most frequently used communication methods, how they are best used, and when *not* to use them.

Table 7-2   Methods of Communication and Their Uses

Type of Communication Method	Best When:	Not Appropriate When:
Face-to-face meetings (virtual or in-person)	You want to open up two-way communication channels. Messages are urgent and action items are expected after the session.	You don't want to establish two-way communication channels. You're in a rush. You aren't going to do anything with the information you collect from the dialogue.
Podcasts or webinars	You want to reach a large number of audience members who may work varied hours in multiple locations.	Employees don't have the technology to watch it. You expect employees to do something immediately.
Website or message board	Announcements do not require immediate action or input. Messages are not urgent. Everyone in audience has access to the Internet and uses it!	Messages are urgent. You're making the primary communication for large changes.
E-mail	The messages are pertinent to a small group of people.	Messages are urgent. You're making the primary communication for large changes.
Company or department newsletter	You're announcing the company picnic or the completion of the project.	You want your audience to know about the change *before* it happens.

Don't always jump to e-mail and web-based message boards or blogs. Although these mediums may be easy to send, you need to make sure people will actually take the time to read them. A number of unread messages are lost in e-mail-space, so try multiple methods, not just e-mail. And if something is urgent or requires feedback, try another method of communication altogether.

Don't try to change everything at once. If your company doesn't use message boards to communicate now, starting to use them as the main source of communication probably isn't a good idea. Introduce new methods, but make sure you keep the old ones, too, until you know the new methods work.

To link times and events when communication needs to occur, go back to your project plan with the project team and executive sponsors and identify when people need to know what is happening — either before, during, or after the change. If you need help with project planning, jump on over to Chapter 5 or pick up a copy of *Project Management For Dummies,* by Stanley E. Portny (Wiley).

To keep track of all your messages, strategize exactly when and where you're going to communicate what. Your communication plan in black and white will begin to look something like Table 7-3.

Table 7-3		Communication Plan		
When	*Who Communicates the Message*	*Who Receives the Message*	*Method/ Process*	*Message*
6 weeks before kick-off to the big change	CEO	Directors of the company	E-mail information and hold live meetings by call or face-to-face	The vision, purpose, and goals of the change — and the WIIFM answer
4–5 months before the big change and 1–2 months after the change happens	Employees impacted by the change	Leaders in the company	Face-to-face discussions	Concerns, feedback, and ideas to make the change work for people impacted by the change

When	Who Communi- cates the Message	Who Receives the Message	Method/ Process	Message
1 month before kick-off to the big change	Directors	All employees	Post infor- mative, 3-minute "Welcome to the change" podcasts or videos to company website	Helpful info on the change proj- ect, how to get involved, and the WIIFM answer
Ongoing during the big change	Managers	All employees	Hold regu- lar team/ depart- ment meetings	Share five key actions from the last month, what is currently happening, and what to expect next — and of course, the WIIFM answer

One of the biggest mistakes change teams make is to have most, if not all, the communication come from the project team or (gasp) the project-team leader! Please, don't make the same mistake. Employees want to hear from people they trust and have relationships with, so make sure your communication plan has messages from senior leaders, managers, direct supervisors, and maybe even fellow employees. The business owns the change, not the project leader. (Notice how in Table 7-3 the example communication plan has *no* infor- mation coming directly from the project leader to employee.)

Step 4: Evaluate

The last step is evaluating the communications. You need to follow up to find out whether they met your goals and objectives and then make changes to the communications plan if needed.

How do you know if your communication goals were met? You measure it! Evaluation and measurement of the communication can be done in two ways: random or structured. Random evaluation is more informal and includes follow-up phone calls and casual talks. More-formal structured evaluation can give measurements and unbiased information. A structured evaluation can be done via e-mail, web surveys, interviews, or focus groups.

Another great resource for evaluating communication is a team of communication agents. Similar to the idea of a front-line council or change ambassadors (see Chapter 12), these roles are appointed to individuals in each target audience who can spread the word formally and informally about the change. The communication agents would most naturally be the part of the change team, but they can also be regular employees who are excited about the change, who can facilitate positive discussions, and who are respected in their organization. These agents can be very helpful in giving honest feedback on how the communication has been received and what changes may need to take place in future communication efforts.

Although informal feedback is important and can provide relevant information, if data needs to be measured or analyzed, you need to take a structured approach.

Table 7-4 describes some methods you can use to gather more-formal, structured data to evaluate the effectiveness of your communication.

Table 7-4	Tools to Use in Evaluation
Tool	*When Should I Use This?*
E-mail	When reaching a large audience and you don't need more than 15 percent return on surveys
Web-based survey	When reaching a large audience with access to the web and you don't need more than 10 percent return on surveys
Interviews	When reaching a selected or moderate group of people and need a predetermined or high response rate
Focus groups	When reaching a moderate to large group of people and need a high response rate

Regardless of the feedback tool you use, try to obtain answers to the following questions and then check to see how the answers line up against the original intent of the message.

✔ What did you think was the purpose of the message? Does it match the goal of the communication?

✔ Did you receive the message in time? If not, when would you have liked to receive the message?

✔ Did the message communicate enough information? Did the message communicate too much information? This response can tell change teams whether or not they are hitting the mark with what employees need and want to hear.

✔ What additional information is needed or desired?

✔ Was the message easy to understand? Easy to understand should always be a goal of communicating during change. Make sure this goal is being met and adjust the type of message if needed.

✔ What would you change about the message? This question is the great catch-all. What you're really asking here is, what else do you want and need from the change team?

✔ Did you think the delivery method was appropriate? If not, what would have been better?

After you have feedback on how the communication is going, what do good change leaders do next? They use it. So often this information is just stuck on the back burner because people aren't sure what to do with it or see it as a one-time review of how a particular piece of information was shared. After the change team sees how the communication is working, it's time to communicate (yes, again) the results of the evaluation and put an action plan in place on how the communication can be more effective in the future. The change leader doesn't need to address every detail of the assessment; instead, you can mutually agree to work on specific communication concerns and ideas they want to improve.

Sending powerful messages

After your strategy for communicating is in place, you can start getting powerful messages out. If you have done all the planning up to this point, writing the message and getting it out is the easy part. All it takes is creating the message and continuing to shape it as events occur. As easy as pie.

Addressing the right needs in an initial message

To craft your first set of messages, take a few minutes to look back at your vision for change and the change road map from Chapter 5 (and you thought that was just a planning exercise). The answers and comments you and your project team came up with will be used to create those amazingly powerful messages that will make your change project a marvelous success.

Take a stab at your first message. With your very first message of change, you want to honestly and clearly answer the following questions for the message recipients:

- ✔ **What is happening now?** To thoroughly answer this question, you may need to break down answers for all the following questions: What is the change? Why are you sending/delivering this message? What information is going to be communicated? Why is this happening now? What is the business case for the change?

- ✔ **What will happen next?** Tell recipients what to expect. When will things start changing? What will people be doing differently? These answers should be directed at tangible items such as changes in personal schedules, meetings, and the way the audience will do things.

- ✔ **Why is this message important?** Tell your audience why it should care. Why is the individual(s) in the meeting, on the e-mail list, and so on? Communicate the WIIFM answer.

- ✔ **What do recipients need to do?** What actions do the employees need to take? (For example, should they sign up for a class, or wait for more information?) What should the employee expect in the next month, quarter, and year?

You can reuse this format again and again throughout your project — just remember to keep it fresh; no one likes a broken record.

Sufficient time is necessary if communicating an event. As a suggestion, when communicating an event, the first communication should go out six to eight weeks prior, with a follow-up message at three to four weeks prior, two weeks prior, and one week prior.

Keeping the communication going

You've started the initial communication, but don't stop there. Communicate project status and project awareness weekly or perhaps monthly. E-mail and websites work well for this type of documentation when followed-up with project-team conference calls or live meetings. Keep it simple, or people won't read it! Briefly (and we mean briefly!) point out the major accomplishments from the last week and the change goals for the following week/month — that's it. Short, simple, and to the point.

Say it with *gusto!* When you're creating these powerful messages, dig into your inner marketing genius and use this as an opportunity to positively sell the change. You can't just talk and expect things to happen — you have to deliver results — but making things interesting will make your messages a whole lot more exciting, and maybe people will even start looking forward to your fresh, frequent, flowing, and dare we say fabulous communication!

Information changes quickly. Keep project members up to date with the most current details with a repository to store communication, training, and information. SharePoint and other cloud software are tools that can keep everyone informed and avoid distribution of inaccurate information.

As you work through major milestones, people will believe you and want to help you if you are open and honest about what worked and what didn't. Think about answering questions like these:

- ✔ What worked? What didn't?
- ✔ What were the key successes?
- ✔ Which part of the project was most efficient?
- ✔ What is changing in the next phases?
- ✔ What can employees do differently to move the change forward?

Communicating across Differences

Wouldn't it be great if everyone thought like you and did everything like you? Well, maybe at first, but differences make the world go around. You can bet that you'll need to work through differences of opinions on teams and within your organizations, as well as personal differences like generational gaps. You can't avoid these differences when dealing with change, so start working on them.

Team and organizational opinions

When team members or people in an organization have differences of opinion, they usually stem from the receiver of the information not getting the same message as the sender of the information. As a change leader, your goal is to make sure that what you are sending is the same as what is received. In this section we help you do that by explaining how to get a firm handle on what you want to accomplish, mediate differences of opinion, come to agreement on specific points, and implement the agreement.

Now is a good time to pull out the resistance-dealing tools that we discuss in Chapter 4.

Knowing what you're trying to accomplish

When you're going to have a conversation with a dissenter, make a plan and know what you're trying to communicate to him. What is your objective when you are trying to overcome differences in opinion? Are you trying to gain agreement, change someone's point of view, or just make sure everyone can live with the outcome? Write down what your purpose is for working through differences of opinion before you open your mouth. Trust us; a little planning avoids a lot of disagreements.

When communicating with people of different viewpoints, consider why you *think* there is a difference of opinion (it may not really be as big as you may think), why it is important to understand the difference of opinions and work through them, when you need to communicate, and where you will do it. Most people don't like being taken by surprise when you ask for their opinion or ask why they disagree with yours, so think about when and where you can get your message across without barriers or disruptions.

Exploring differences of opinion and agreeing on facts

No one likes being accused of disagreeing or not playing nice with others. When using communication tools to address differences, start by exploring what's going on from the receiver's point of view. Inquire about the individual's perspective without accusing them, by stating something like, "When you walked out of the project team meeting, it seemed like you may disagree with our decision. Can I do anything to answer any questions you may have?" After you have asked for reasons for the receiver's opinion, you can then advocate your position and priorities (and the project's) and make the thoughts and facts behind your point of view clear (this is where planning the message is really important).

The point of exploring differences of opinions is not to argue; it's to get everything out in the open and have a rational discussion about the facts.

After everyone's laundry has been aired, you can come to agreement on the facts and overarching goals. Even if you can't agree on the direction of the project, use your communication and resistance-fighting skills (see Chapter 4) to agree on the facts. We recommend starting with small little facts first and then working your way up to bigger ones. Try something like this:

> **You:** "It seems like we have different points of view about the direction of the project. Can we try to agree on the facts of the project and then work through the best option?"
>
> **Person (or team) that disagrees with you (PTDY):** "I think the project is dumb."
>
> **You:** "Okay, you think the project is dumb. But do you agree with the main goal of the project: bringing in more revenue for the company?"

PTDY: "Yes, that is a good goal. But I don't like the project."

You: "Okay. Well I am glad we agree on the big goal for the project. Do you have a different idea on how we can reach our goal of bringing in more revenue?"

This brief dialogue just moved the conversation from a hotbed of opinion to fact. But think of an onion and keep peeling back the differences in opinion until you get to the real reason for the disagreement. The conversation probably won't be easy, but nothing worthwhile is, right? Let people vent about the differences; then bring them back to the facts.

Deciding on specific commitments

After opinions have been given and you have been able to come up with a few facts everyone agrees with, now is the time to decide on specific commitments. Don't worry about getting everything agreed on upfront; some people and teams just need more time to adjust to the change than others. Your role is to get specific commitments from the dissenter so the change project doesn't come to a complete halt.

Although getting the commitments may not be easy, how you ask for them is. Try these questions for starters:

- ✔ What are you going to do?
- ✔ When are you going to do it?
- ✔ What may stop you from doing it?
- ✔ What support do you need from me?
- ✔ On a scale of one to ten, how likely are you to follow through on your commitment?

Now you and your disagreeing team or individual can work together to come up with an action plan that specifically lists what you both have agreed to do and when you are going to do it.

When you are coming up with agreements, think of the agreements as anchors in mountain climbing. When you make an agreement, you are putting an anchor in place so you don't fall back to square one again. This process helps prevent many repeat disagreements and keeps your change project on track.

Remember that at this point you aren't trying to get people with differences of opinion to agree on everything, just on some things.

Implementing your agreement and follow up

At this point, everyone is in agreement and happy! Well, something like that. With your action plan in place, after you are absolutely sure you have agreements (no matter how small) in place, make sure you let your supporter of the project know you would like to follow up with him and how and when you will do so. This meeting isn't to check up on him or spy; it is merely to make sure everyone continues to agree on what's happening. This type of follow up helps the entire team address any problems that may have come up or further questions about the change or change communication.

Generation gaps

Another giant barrier to communication in the workforce is the generation gap. In your office, you may have someone who remembers life before e-mail and Internet, whereas others can't even dream of living without constant news updates, texting, and telling friends what they did last night with the touch of a screen. But generation gaps can be great to spur change, because they help us think of new ideas to problems and perhaps apply old solutions to new challenges.

When communicating across generations, make sure you don't change the meaning of the message. The best way to avoid generation differences is to involve people and ask for their opinion and ideas about the change.

When working across generations, keep these things in mind:

- **Remember that "What's in it for me" is number one:** Whether you are working with the Me, Y, X, or Z generation, people value different things. Sure, studies show younger generations value happiness and life balance more than money and success, but that's not always the case. Don't assume that those "kids" in your office don't care about success, and don't assume that older workers just want to sit back and wait for their retirement day! Be honest about what's in it for the organization, team, and person, and don't just say what you assume the generation wants to know.

- **Don't feel your generation is superior:** Just because one generation invented the phone and the other created the smartphone doesn't make any generation smarter.

- **Perception is reality, but don't perceive everything too fast:** Even if a person is talking too fast, using slang, and dressing a way you hardly believe, try not to dismiss him or her. You may be able to instantly perceive what generation someone is from based on behavior or appearance, but don't let it affect your ability to listen. Focus on the facts, not the outfit.

Part III
Making Change Stick through Thick and Thin

"Helen—I think I need to fine tune the concept of 'change in the workplace' for you."

In this part . . .

Welcome to the reality of change: getting through the change when obstacles are in the way and making the change last long after the project is complete. Now that you know where you want to go and how to make the change process happen, you need to know how to break through resistance from employees, manage stress levels, and make midcourse corrections if necessary. Of course, the human side of change is not all bad. You also find out in this part how to celebrate success and use lessons learned for future change projects.

Chapter 8

Getting Employees on Board and Keeping Them Motivated

In This Chapter

▶ Creating an atmosphere of trust

▶ Helping team members work through conflict

▶ Shedding the baggage of past failed changes

▶ Giving employees the power to participate in change

All the work you have done to this point in your change project has set a perfect stage for change success: You have a vision, a need, a plan with appropriate measures, and a great communication approach to getting the entire change moving in the right direction. In this chapter we examine the importance of stepping away from the computer and planning and cultivating relationships with your employees to motivate them and make change last. You can't have change without cooperation, and no one likes to cooperate with people they disagree with or don't trust!

In this chapter you gain the tools necessary to build trust and cultivate relationships with peers, employees, and leaders to get work done more quickly. You find out how to handle conflict when it invariably arises. We also provide you with tips on how to help teams and organizations let go of past change baggage that may be halting the progress of your change project. Finally, you discover how to engage employees through delegation, problem solving, listening, and rewarding positive behavior. By the end of the chapter, you'll be able to make almost any change happen in the blink of an eye (well, maybe not that fast or easy, but pretty close!).

Building Trust

Trust is one of those words everyone uses but rarely defines. *Trust* means belief and confidence in another person that he or she is presenting facts and circumstances entirely and being open and honest with emotions and feelings. It is your job as a change leader to build trust with your employees, peers, and team as well as throughout the entire organization. Without trust, you cannot cooperate, and without cooperation, no change can happen.

Cultivating relationships through trust is the building block for change that many leaders forget. Trust propels your vision of two-way communication into a reality because people will want to talk with you about the project, not feel that they are forced to speak with you. Although cultivating relationships and building trust takes time, here are some things you can do to make it happen:

- ✔ **Actively listen.** Open your ears, make eye contact, and have empathy. If as change leader you want to build trust, first listen to understand the other person's perspectives and opinions, and then focus on leading change, not the other way around. You can practice being all ears when we discuss listening skills in more depth later in the section "Listening."

- ✔ **Be credible.** Change leaders back up the vision for change with resources and action. This means setting targets that the organization can achieve and being genuine when talking about the vision. Then walk the talk and make sure resources are dedicated to the change to make it happen. Don't exaggerate the scope of change or the expected results.

- ✔ **Be open.** Be open and cooperative with information. When employees ask questions about the future of the change, don't misrepresent the facts to make things sound better. Instead, be compassionate and offer what information you can. If you don't have the information an employee is asking for or can't share it with her for regulatory, financial, or other reasons, say so. Be honest (did we say that already?).

- ✔ **Create an environment of mutual respect through solutions that suit both you and your employees.** Leaders often make the mistake of believing everyone has or should have the same motives as they do. Find out what your employees' motives are and tell them that you want the change to meet their goals, too. Your employees will trust you more readily if they know you respect them and you're on their side. Check your ego at the door unless you want to go it alone.

- ✔ **Help employees resolve conflict.** One of the best ways to build trust is through effectively resolving conflict. We cover this strategy in more depth in the next section, "Resolving Conflict among Employees."

Building trust is not just a one-time deal, as you probably can imagine. You have to prove yourself worthy of your employees' trust over and over again. But the upshot of having motivated, hardworking employees is worth the effort.

Over the course of the change, you need to build trust not only between yourself and your employees but also between members of the change team. Building trust on the team is a significant hurdle to overcome, and when you do, you will see the payoff in the form of an aligned and energized team. Here is what you should do as your team evolves:

✔ In the beginning of the change, build trust by answering as many questions as possible to offer consistent support. Check out Chapter 7 for tips on communicating about the change.

✔ When you team begins to have conflict (and it will), whether the conflict is based on personality issues, political power, or any other reason you never imagined, build trust by staying level-headed and focusing on the goals and objectives as you coach team members on how to resolve conflict on their own. The later section "Resolving Conflict among Employees" helps you deal with this process.

✔ When the team is up and running and has gotten over the conflict hump, continue to build trust by letting the team develop its own plan for how to work together. The best change leaders allow the team members to find their own roles while providing just enough guidance on how to keep the project moving in the right direction.

✔ Provide the right recognition for a job well done and ensure that any unforeseen obstacles are dealt with efficiently. We think of this step as letting others shine. Trust is built when you have the confidence to step back, help where necessary, and let the work happen.

If a group has been working together for a while, make sure any new team members don't feel excluded. If leaders set an exclusive tone, others can and will follow suit. Build trust with new members by individually reaching out to them and following the same steps of building trust you may have already done with the team.

Resolving Conflict among Employees

Change is a journey, not a destination, and conflict is just one of those things you come across during the ride. Instead of letting conflict stop change (or you), use conflict to discover the real obstacles and perhaps identify some alternative solutions. Often, resolving conflict involves the simple tools of communication: Listening and giving feedback.

Resolving conflict has three basic steps:

1. **Let the other person know you want to resolve the issue in the best interest of the organization.** Acknowledge reality. You know that differences exist and the other person, unless completely clueless, probably knows that conflict exists as well. Beginning to fix the problem is sometimes as easy as saying, "I know we have conflict, but let's try to resolve it." Then open your ears and listen in order to better understand the other person's point of view.

2. **If possible, show support for the other person's goals, feelings, and ideas.** Disagreeing on the means to get to the finish line is a lot less problematic if you at least all agree on where the finish line is!

3. **Show the individual how conflicting action will lead to unintended consequences or will negatively impact the overarching goals (which you just agreed to).** Don't do this step like a nagging school teacher; just outline how the process will flow if the conflict continues.

By this time, your amazing conflict-resolution skills have gotten everyone on board and ready to move forward. What's that you say? Some people are still stuck in the mud? If casually approaching the problem by listening and keeping an open line of communication doesn't seem to work, or if you're in the middle of significant conflict, a more formal conflict-resolution technique may be needed.

Your goal as a change leader is to bring awareness of the behavior causing the conflict to attention, help the two sides of the conflict agree on and accept the consequences of continuing to harbor the conflict, and then create specific actions to resolve the conflict. We now dive into these steps a bit further with the four As of conflict resolution: awareness, agreement and acceptance, and action.

Creating awareness

When beginning the process of conflict resolution, we recommend talking with each of the two parties separately. Having one-on-one meetings allows you to build rapport, trust, and respect while also learning about the individual's level of motivation. Ask if each person has any concerns or barriers to change, and ask if you can help resolve the conflict in the best interest of the organization and the change. As you help bring awareness to the conflict, try using these techniques to get results:

✔ **Ask what happened; don't tell people what you think happened.** If people or departments are butting heads over a process, you may probe for more information by asking: "How did we get to this point and what do we have to do differently to move forward?" These questions do not place blame; they focus the discussion on the future but still get all the facts straight.

✔ **Focus on reality, facts, and awareness of behavior.** For example, you may ask, "Can you think of an instance when you may have displayed this sort of behavior? Walk me through the facts of what happened."

✔ **Use interrogative words: what, when, who, how much, how many.**

✔ **Avoid analysis early in the process if you're trying to get someone to recognize behavior.** Analysis comes after awareness.

Coming to agreement and acceptance

After meeting and listening to both sides of the conflict, you're ready to bring the two sides together. Now isn't the time to pretend you're setting people up on a blind date — tell both people outright that you're asking them to come to the meeting to resolve conflict and make the change move forward. If the conflict is small or perhaps just a misunderstanding, this process should be fast and efficient. However, if the conflict has been festering for a while, bringing up all the emotions, opinions, and perspectives may be overwhelming in volume and impact, so be willing to hold this meeting over a few sessions. If the conflict has been occurring for a long time or is highly emotional, your role as a change leader is to judge how much everyone can absorb and accept. The first goal may then be to strive to arrive at a common understanding of the problem — not to generate solutions just yet! The second goal of a later session may then be to resolve conflict to move forward.

Use these tips to facilitate the conversation:

- ✔ **Move from broad-scope questions to increasingly narrower ones, getting right into the observation.** For example, "So, we've agreed that one of the things you do, regardless of your intent, is to be tough and critical with your people when they misspeak in project team meetings. What is an example of that behavior?" If you work in an organization that does not always discuss conflict, this type of open and genuine question can open the door to opinions being shared respectfully.

- ✔ **Always give people the option to say that something is not correct.** Everyone should feel free to say what they think, albeit politely if possible. For example, "I don't want to be too pushy here, so please tell me if this is incorrect. I think we have agreement that the problem is that HR sends out e-mails with urgent information, and the finance department would prefer urgent information to be shared on a phone call."

- ✔ **Make sure you ask open-ended questions, not closed-ended questions.** For example, toward the end of a meeting, ask "What can I do to help with the items we talked about?" rather than "Do you need help with any of the items we talked about?"

Taking action

Successful conflict resolution comes about when the target audience receives the exact information the sender intended to send and both parties agree to move forward to the future state. After the problem (or a subset of the problem) is agreed on, you're ready to discuss specific actions that everyone can take. To formalize the conflict-resolution process, create an action plan that identifies behaviors to maintain and behaviors to develop as the change moves forward. As the change leader, you can take an active role in assisting the two sides to review the actions planned by asking the following questions:

✓ **Are the actions doable, and do they achieve the goals of the project?** If individuals feel the action plan is too difficult or doesn't meet the agreed-on goals of the project, people may just nod their heads throughout the conflict-resolution process and then do nothing (you do not want this to happen!).

✓ **Do they have the necessary skills, resources, budget, and so on to carry out the plan?** You may not ask the individuals directly if they have the right skills, but you can ask them if the team has the right resources and skills to move forward. If the answer is no, go back to the actions and make them doable within these constraints.

✓ **What does the leader need to do to keep the plan on track?** Although you may be on your way to being the best change leader in the world, asking other people for their opinion does wonders to solidify a new direction (without conflict) as you build and cultivate relationships. People like being asked their opinions, and if you do so, you will be seen as a great change leader (and we're not just saying that because you bought this book!).

Sometimes you need someone higher up in the organization, with hefty conflict-resolution experience, to step in and bring about a solution. If this situation happens, make sure you maintain confidentiality throughout the process, because when the conflict is resolved (and it will be), you want to walk away with a positive relationship so you don't have as many conflicts in the future.

As you cultivate relationships throughout the change, remember that resolving conflict is neither a one-size-fits-all intervention nor a single event.

Even if you think a conflict has been resolved, make sure your team feels the same way. Resolving conflict positively continues to build trust within the team. But conflict resolved in a way that individuals don't want can lead to judgment of the leader or judgment of the change (two things you want to try to avoid).

Letting Go of Baggage: Resolving the Negative Impact of Past Change Efforts

Sometimes change projects face extra resistance due to past change failures. For example, perhaps the company attempted a big systems change that didn't deliver the expected results. Employees tried to make the change work, but their workload just got bigger, and now they're reluctant to commit to another large scale "improvement." Or if a company has something of a revolving door for senior leaders (they come in for a few years and then leave), some employees may have change baggage around accepting any new initiative or "this time it is different" speech from a new leader, because their experience is the leader will be out the door as soon as the change is done.

You probably already can guess that no book, no matter how wonderfully written, can get rid of old behaviors and usher in a new era in a few easy steps. Letting go of past baggage is not a quick fix that instantly turns around old and sometimes reinforced behaviors. Letting go of past behaviors is like resolving conflict and building trust: It just takes time and follow-up. It requires the change leader to provide ongoing support, observe the teams in action when they're trying to move to a new type of behavior, debrief the teams, reinforce the desired/modified behavior, and push for continuous improvement in areas that still need it.

You may choose to approach past-change baggage just like you did conflict resolution in the previous section. The conflict is: You (and the organization) want to move to a new and better way of doing business; the other person does not, because a previous attempt to change failed. But if conflict resolution doesn't have the effect you want, you can try our six steps to getting over the past and the tips later in this section on dealing with cynicism.

Getting over it in six steps

Getting over change baggage is important. Really important. If you tried the conflict-resolution tips earlier in this chapter and they didn't work, you may need to use the root-cause information you gathered to break through the change baggage.

Following are six steps to collaboration, key tools and techniques that leaders can use to facilitate a group through collaboration:

1. **Raise the change-baggage issue.** Although this step may seem obvious, in reality the first move is owning up to the fact that a disagreement is happening. If you haven't already clearly done it, surface and name the issue now. You're then able to move to the next step.

2. **Get curious.** Holding an attitude of curiosity enables you to move away from defending your own position to explore other people's perspectives with an open mind. Balance advocacy (presenting your own views) with inquiry (seeking to understand others' views through questioning).

3. **Identify underlying concerns.** One of the biggest challenges with conflict is a lack of understanding or appreciation of others' perspectives. Although you may think that you understand the root of the issue, you may be incorrect or have only partial understanding.

Getting to the root cause of the problem helps people toss that old baggage that makes them reluctant to change and move to the bright future. A few questions to ask to get to the root cause may be:

- Why did these past changes not deliver the results you were expecting?

- What would you recommend doing differently with this change?

- How can this change avoid the same mistakes as the past changes in the organization?

- What was successful about the changes in the past? (There are probably a few things that worked well.) How can this change duplicate these successes?

4. **Develop a shared-purpose statement.** This step is the essence of collaboration: The group moves from having *my* concerns and *your* concerns to *our* concerns. In developing a shared purpose, include the concerns, interests, and needs of all parties. Look for and document areas of common ground. Deeper values are often a rich source of commonality. Creating common goals to rally around sets the stage for creative brainstorming.

5. **Generate solutions.** Now you get to the fun part. All parties work together to brainstorm solutions that can meet all the needs, address the concerns, and reach the goals defined in the shared-purpose statement. Be sure to use brainstorming rules (see the "Brainy brainstorming rules" sidebar) to avoid premature judgment of ideas. You have the potential to create a holistic solution that's greater than the sum of the parts. By collaborating, you can develop novel and creative proposals that go beyond the original positions that created the conflict.

6. **Devise a plan for implementation and evaluation.** This step is where project management takes over. The hard work of collaboration can really pay off at this step because you have strong alignment and support for the plan of action. Take advantage of the momentum from the collaborative exercise to quickly develop an implementation plan to see the fruit of your labor!

Dealing with cynicism toward future change

One of the not-so-pretty outcomes of having past changes fail is the amount of cynicism that develops toward any future change. If you are staring cynicism in the face every day, you can do a couple things to improve the situation. First of all, don't take it personally. Change is hard (we've said that before, right?). What may seem like the best idea for the future for you may be really hard for others. Although we walk through how to deal with these common reactions to change in Chapter 9, here we tell you some things to keep in mind as you try to toss the baggage of change on your first-class flight to the change vision.

Brainy brainstorming rules

When you pull the team together to brainstorm solutions, before diving into ideas, make sure everyone understands the common ground rules of brainstorming:

✔ Let the ideas flow. Just call out ideas or give opinions. Don't discuss or evaluate them yet.

✔ Show respect by listening to others when they're talking. Then build on other people's ideas.

✔ Collect as many ideas as possible.

✔ Allow silent time if it happens. This is thinking time.

✔ Document the ideas.

When the brainstorming session is complete, you can then have everyone clarify ideas and begin to evaluate which ones to implement.

Allow employees to express some doubts. Go back to the conflict-resolution skills and gain acceptance in baby steps. This process may take more time, but it will be worth it if you want everyone to move forward together.

Those basic steps may not work for everyone, though. You may find complete resistance to change or encounter someone who, no matter how well you cultivate relationships or resolve conflict, goes along with the process but doesn't actually participate in the change (or actively tries to derail it). This person says, "Oh yes, I'm so happy with the new change," but then he either tries to sabotage it or just does nothing to help the process. The problematic behaviors may take the form of being really, really, late for meetings, canceling or ignoring any formal or informal activities that are part of the change plan, or participating by simply saying "yes" and "no" with absolutely no added value to the process.

Here's our best advice: After going through the conflict-resolution process and digging into root causes, prepare a script to deal with situations of complete resistance and be prepared to call out the nonparticipation either over the phone or face to face. An example of what you can say is, "I sense a reluctance to continue with this change process. Can we set aside some time to resolve your concerns, or should we try to pull in other leaders to help move this forward?" Be careful to be genuine and respectful with this type of statement. You want to convey not a thinly veiled threat but an opportunity for the person to get on board on his own or to ask a more senior lead to help resolve differences. This point is really your last straw, but when all else fails, getting back to honest, straightforward communication is your best bet.

Sometimes, just making reluctant or unhelpful employees aware of how their attitude and behavior impacts others is enough to prompt them to let go of past beliefs and behaviors and become more cooperative. Your job as a change leader and change coach is to get them there.

A stressed-out person looking for a place to vent will look everywhere for the perfect target, and change baggage is a great venting platform for these individuals. Someone may have significant frustrations at home, on other projects, and in life, and because the change is an easy target, you get to be the punching bag (lucky you). The best solution is to listen and ask how you can support the person most effectively. But some people are never happy, and setting limits on the number of punches you're willing to take is perfectly acceptable. Bottom line: Be empathetic, but don't let one person's issues put the brakes on your change.

Empowering Employees to Change

The advice in this section helps you empower your employees so they'll be inspired to perpetuate the change in their own ways. By delegating authority, offering feedback, problem solving together, listening, and rewarding positive behavior, you'll end up with employees who are on board with your ideas and are motivated to work hard to help you.

Delegating authority

So many leaders we work with have a fear of delegating work to their employees. They either don't know how to do it or are afraid of being seen as handing off work to their already-busy teams. However, if delegation is done correctly, it can be both empowering to employees and engaging. Here we look at three different ways of delegating.

- ✔ **One-way:** Delegation down the pecking order is largely one-way. The leader chooses the change project, identifies the way to make the change project work, and then tells employees to go and do it. Forcing someone to sit, listen, and then go do something rarely gets any results unless you're managing a group of well-behaved dogs. Sadly, this type of delegating is what most leaders do. The leader does all the planning, makes all the decisions, and just needs people to go and implement. Use this type of delegation only when employees have no idea what to do next and are asking for specific steps to follow.

- ✔ **Coaching and cooperation:** When leaders coach and cooperate with employees in delegation, two-way communication takes place, and often times employees are the ones who come up with the best ideas on how to move forward with a plan. As a leader, you can ask questions, listen, share ideas, and guide the task at hand. Although this method of delegation does take a good amount of prep work, if done correctly employees feel a good balance of support and freedom to take on tasks throughout the change project. After the team identifies how to solve the problem and next steps (with reasonable explanation), a leader can then delegate tasks that the entire team agrees are important.

✔ **Independent delegation:** When a change leader chooses to delegate the problem and all decision making, the leader briefly establishes any guidelines or boundaries and lets employees get to work. This type of delegation requires the most trust in employees to do the right thing, but if done correctly, employees have tremendous potential to build confidence in their own ability by doing the work.

If you hand over the task, take care not to check up on it frequently. Independent work must be just that, so give employees the flexibility and freedom to get the job done. If you need frequent updates on the project, try the coaching-and-cooperation mode instead.

Delegation is rarely successful if a change leader holds on to the most important and glamorous aspects of change and delegates the seemingly trivial items to employees.

Offering feedback

By offering honest feedback, leaders can give employees the opportunity to change and learn on their own. This is empowering for many employees because feedback is really just an opportunity to give an opinion or idea so employees can make more informed choices. When dealing with conflict, the intent of feedback is not to criticize but to widen the repertoire of choices the other person has available in his or her toolbox.

To give effective feedback, you must do the following things:

✔ Listen, observe the specific behaviors that the person displayed, and document everything.

✔ Check to see whether the person or group wants feedback. You may also want to ask what kind of feedback the other person wants. Providing unsolicited feedback — positive or negative — is a risk you should only take when you absolutely need to.

✔ Offer a few suggestions of how the other person can improve his performance or continue to give a positive performance. Check for understanding and ask whether the feedback was useful.

How effectively you motivate other employees depends on your ability to provide direct, candid, and supportive feedback. If feedback is wanted, focus on results versus expectations and follow these feedback best practices:

✔ **Gather feedback continuously.** Part of your job as a change leader is to monitor performance (good and bad) throughout the project. This monitoring goes much deeper than an annual review and allows you to coach employees on a timely basis.

✔ **Focus on what matters.** We discussed in previous chapters the ideas of critical paths and critical milestones. The same concept of focusing on the most important points holds true for providing feedback. Giving feedback on everything the employee does is cumbersome and takes up your entire life. Instead, try to focus feedback on the areas that have the most significant and strategic impact.

✔ **Include the results and the way they were achieved.** By giving feedback that focuses on the results you saw (or expected to see) and the level of professionalism expected on the change project, you enforce the importance of doing the right thing the right way.

✔ **Use your leadership judgment, not just cookie-cutter feedback.** As a change leader, your employees want to know what you think. Effectively motivating employees is not a scientific formula or prescription (if only it were that easy!), so make sure you keep the people element present in your positive and not-so-positive feedback.

✔ **Be candid; don't sugarcoat.** As a change leader, you are uniquely qualified to deliver feedback with empathy and respect, especially when it is negative, but don't sugarcoat or exaggerate the message. Be clear, concise, and honest (there's that word again!), and you will help employees be the best they can be, achieve the goals of the change, and continue to drive positive change in the company in the future.

Problem solving

Problem solving together with your employees helps them recognize their important role in seeing the change through. If they're able to help you solve whatever issues arise, they're more likely to stay engaged with the change. How you think about the process of problem solving and how you relate to others can have a dramatic effect on the outcome. At the risk of stating the obvious, problem solving, planning, conflict resolution, and even coaching change are all based on your ability to work with others.

We suggest clearly defining the term *problem* before considering problem-solving strategies and tactics. For many people, that term has a negative connotation (for example, problem children, a problem with my computer, and so on). Leaders have come up with something of a workaround to address problems, sometimes calling them *challenges* or *opportunities*. But instead of playing wordsmith (which many people will see straight through), a more direct approach is to define *problem* in a way that focuses on the intent of what you are trying to solve or accomplish. If you define it as a situation you want to change, people tend to not take it personally, and they relax and get to work. And getting work done is exactly what you want and is what motivates most employees!

A number of problem-solving techniques and methods are out there, but in this section we discuss a unique way to think about problem solving to engage and empower employees. These steps focus on uniting everyone before any solution is proposed:

1. **Agree together that a problem exists, define what the problem is, and agree that the problem needs to be solved.** This beginning may seem unusual, but leaders often jump into action too quickly. Rarely are people asked if everyone agrees that a problem really exists. By making this small adjustment to the problem-solving method, you get the team to its first milestone — the definition of the problem and everyone being on board with working on the problem.

2. **Ask the team to identify what is causing the problem.** This step may take five minutes or five weeks, depending on how easy pinning down the cause is. Until the real problem is uncovered, the team may be chasing after something that is not going to solve the problem at hand.

3. **Identify solutions to solve the real problem.** Have the group brainstorm ideas for fixing the problem.

4. **Decide and agree on the solution to the problem and steps to take.** Be sure to include the timing, milestones, roles, and what the solution looks like.

5. **Consider how the team will work together and what you'll do if the solution doesn't work.** After such hard work at getting to the solution, admitting that the solution may not work is hard sometimes. As a change leader, make sure the team knows that problem solving doesn't end when the meeting is over. Get agreement from your change team to work together until the problem is solved.

This approach to problem solving is focused on building agreements and creating small wins through small milestones throughout the process of problem solving. This momentum-generating approach to problems engages employees and teams to want to do more and continue with the change; much more so than telling people that there is a problem and having them go off in a corner to solve it.

The great news: People are generally problem solvers. The bad news: People rarely talk about the problem-solving process a team will use, an oversight that causes confusion and little motivation. Therefore, your first step in motivating employees is to define the problem, analyze the cause, generate solutions, and then make sure the solutions work.

As a change leader, encourage your teams to come to agreement on the way problems will be solved and then let your top-notch team go to work. If you see teams derailed by coming up with solutions before addressing the root of the problem, step in and make sure they agree on the problem first. This simple strategy does wonders for motivating your team, because most people (even those who may seemingly be the most unmotivated of the bunch) want to solve problems; they just may not agree on what problems they're solving or on how the problem can be solved.

Listening

Have you ever been at a dinner party and thought the person you were talking to was only listening so he could decide when to chime in and give his own opinion? Often in a conversation, people listen to determine whether they agree with a point, what they're going to say next, and when they can say it. Your goal is to not use listening as a tool to help you and your fellow change leaders disagree or agree with a problem but rather to accept a different point of view and legitimize that point of view.

Listening to employees in order to ask better questions and guide more effectively is a well-known change leadership skill that involves compatible body language, repetition of the speaker's words, and summarizing for understanding. As change leaders, you listen not only to get ideas on how to make change happen as an organization but also to help your employees move forward as you embark and continue on the change journey.

When people say they have trouble communicating (which we discuss in Chapter 6), they're really talking about not feeling that their voice, motivations, or point of view is heard. Because people often don't say what they really mean the first time around, an expert change coach like yourself has to listen, understand, and then utilize the message.

Here are some ways you can try to listen a little better. Engage the speaker by

- **Using open-ended questions rather than those that require a one or two word answer:** Don't ask "Do you think we are measuring the right thing in our change project?" Instead, ask "What are your ideas for measuring our change?"

- **Having appropriate body language:** Yes, body language is important, but few people really like it when someone leans in and looks deeply into your eyes after she gets back from an active-listening class. Instead, focus on having appropriate body language that's in line with your topic. Whether you're conducting an employee meeting, speaking in front of a crowd, or having to deliver bad news, focus on your hands first. Unless you are a cheerleader or a personal trainer trying to get everyone up and running, make sure your hands are either placed lightly on the desk in front of you or in your lap. This little trick automatically helps you avoid flapping bird arms and hands and allows you to center your thoughts on what is being said. Your eyes and the rest of your body language will follow.

✔ **Clarifying perceptions, rather than parroting:** If you have ever been to a communication class, you have probably been told to paraphrase what you hear to make you listen better. Although checking for clarity and understanding is important, paraphrasing (or "parroting," as we call it) does little to prove you are anything but a tape recorder and can abruptly end the conversation. A 3-year-old can parrot everything back to you, but he probably doesn't understand your change. Instead, try to add depth to the conversation by listening to what the person has to say and then using your own words to confirm and clarify. Here is an example of traditional paraphrasing and parroting:

> Speaker: "I think the best raisins come from Fresno."
>
> Listener: "So, what you're saying is that Fresno raisins are the best in the world."
>
> Speaker: "Yes."

The listener has effectively ended the conversation by stating what is already obvious to the speaker; probably not his ultimate goal.

Here is a new way to look at paraphrasing to add depth to the conversation by clarifying perceptions:

> Speaker: "I think the best raisins come from Fresno."
>
> Listener: "It sounds like you really like Fresno raisins. Why do you think they taste so good?"
>
> Speaker: "Well, I am so glad you asked. See, my family grew up on a raisin farm in California and . . ."

See the difference? By adding inquiry, you keep the conversation going, learn more about the topic, and allow the speaker's true feelings to surface.

Rewarding and recognizing positive behavior

As the saying goes, you attract many more bears with honey than with vinegar. The same is true when changing business. Rewarding and recognizing positive behavior gets you much further than simply punishing or ignoring poor behavior does.

Focusing on results and execution rather than activities and effort ensures that you reach your business objectives as a company, challenges you to constantly improve performance, and provides employees with the latitude to innovate and develop dramatically improved solutions. Yet because swinging and missing is okay sometimes, you can also find and acknowledge value in employees' calculated efforts that don't achieve expected results but still lead to significant learning.

A mistake we often see in new change leaders (and leaders in general) is tying rewards and recognition to money. Yes, money is a very nice reward, but it is not the only reward. Additionally, in an environment where money and promotions may have slowed down due to economic or market conditions, change leaders need to be a little more creative in recognizing and rewarding their team.

Here are some great examples of rewards for teams and individuals that don't break the bank and still keep employees motivated throughout the change project (and most likely jumping up and down to be part of the next one):

- ✔ **Informal reward and recognition:** Even in our world of nonstop e-mail, texting, and cellphones, nothing conveys appreciation like slowing down, walking over to an employee's desk, and giving a sincere thanks. Informal rewards are spontaneous. Other leaders write hand-written thank you cards (no typing — pick up the pen and paper!) to employees when they feel a job was done incredibly well.

- ✔ **Formal financial and nonfinancial rewards:** Financial rewards are great and can do a good amount to maintain motivation. You may provide a bonus to team members at the end of the project, or even a promotion. On a smaller scale, some change leaders hand out $5 coffee-shop gift cards when someone goes above and beyond the call of duty. However, other "financial" rewards can be a few extra days off or flexible hours during slower times on the project. Time is one of the most valuable rewards out there.

- ✔ **Formal company-wide awards:** The difference between a bonus, raise, or time off for work well done and a more formal company-wide reward is simply the level and awareness the rest of the company has for the accomplishment. A formal recognition during an all-employees meeting may be a wonderful motivator for some team members. Others may want to have the opportunity to be part of a leadership group within the company (status) or be asked to present the results of the project to senior leaders (recognition).

Finally, you may be wondering when the right time to reward employees is. Well, we can't tell you an exact formula to follow, but here are some times that tend to work during change projects:

✔ When a change team delivers results with significant time and cost savings, and with greater than expected results

✔ When a spontaneous act of leadership on the team takes place that wasn't asked for and that made a great difference in the direction of the change

✔ When someone is a consistent role model for the values of the change

Regardless of the type of recognition you choose, make sure the reward for good work is seen as valuable to the individual and is specific. Just handing out certificates to everyone at the end of the project is a nice idea but not personal. Put some time and effort into finding out what motivates your employees and then use that to recognize them throughout the change project.

Chapter 9

Dealing with the Challenges of and Reactions to Change

*T*oo often, wonderfully planned and needed changes fall short because change leaders don't recognize and deal with common challenges and reactions during the transition period. This time is exciting, but it can also be filled with ambiguity and uncertainty. Your goal as a change leader is to help move ambiguity and uncertainty to a place of exploration and learning.

In this chapter you find out about the challenges and reactions you may encounter during the change period. You also gain skills that help to minimize the depth and breadth of these reactions so you can close the common temporary productivity dip associated with change.

Reacting Effectively to Common People Problems

Your change project is focused on making organizational change happen. At its most basic level, change is experienced by individuals, and therefore individual experiences and reactions must be addressed in order for change to happen and stick. Similarly, because change is experienced by individual people, people problems are likely to be your most common challenges to change.

As a change leader, have you heard or seen any of the following reactions?

- ✔ People are talking about why the change won't work and why things won't be better in the future.

- ✔ Emotions are at an all-time high — anger, fear, resentment, apathy, depression, and so on.

- ✔ Employees are procrastinating or just not showing up to get the work done.

- ✔ The rumor mill is running at full speed.

Yes, some people move through the negative sides of change as smoothly as a hot knife through soft butter, but others seem to think that they can avoid the change, no matter how many times you tell them the change will affect them. (This is the bad side of change.) Other individuals do everything is in their power to resist the change, even though they know deep down it will come sooner or later — they hope much later. (This is the ugly side of change.)

People resist change for a number of reasons. They may feel a loss of control, a fear for their own job security, or confusion about their career path, status, or future workload. Some of these fears are rational; others may simply be based on habit, skepticism, or a short-term focus rather than focus on what is best for the organization (and their job!) in the long term. Some people have negative reactions to change because doing things the old way was wildly successful for them and they're not sure if the new way will generate the same results.

The good news is that large-scale changes tend to share some fairly common people problems, so if you can recognize them, you can do something about them before they get out of control. Common people-focused challenges to change include depression and withdrawal, apathy, fear, decreased productivity, and general negativity. In the following sections we explain how to deal with each problem.

Just because you're encountering some less-than-favorable reactions doesn't mean your change is doomed. If you take care of your people by paying attention to how they're adjusting to the change, establish open two-way communication, and treat them with dignity and respect, you will very likely have a successful transition process.

Countering depression and withdrawal

People may not be crying on your office doorstep, but some employees may be crying on the inside, feeling depressed as a result of the forthcoming change. These folks may be continually missing meetings or withdrawing from the conversations about the change. They're afraid that the business or their jobs are doomed because of the change, so they're feeling down in the dumps.

People have to give up the old way of doing things in order to accept and perform new processes, new methods and procedures, and new skills, and letting go can be tough. Great change leaders visibly acknowledge the positives of the past while communicating the great things the future holds. If a co-worker seems depressed because of the change, encourage him to talk about his concerns and feelings. You may want to set up office hours so that people can talk to you one-on-one and ask any questions or express any concerns they may have.

For employees who still don't open up, perhaps your company can offer employee-assistance programs as part of the benefits package. These programs can come in the form of individual counseling by a professional or facilitated workshops that give employees a chance to work through the emotional aspects of transition. You may want to set up these sessions during working hours to encourage employees to attend.

Approaching apathy

You may encounter employees who seem to just not care about the change. Their apathy may manifest as a general lack of interest or by their pretending that the change just doesn't affect them in any significant way. Apathy can be a psychological defense mechanism that employees use to avoid having to directly deal with their own emotional reactions to change.

We encourage you to test whether an employee truly doesn't care or is using apathy as a cover for something else, which is typically fear. One way to do so is to ask probing questions such as, "How do you see this change impacting your job?" If the employee says, "Not at all," you may want to help him more clearly understand how the change will directly impact him. If, on the other hand, the employees are able to articulate their concerns about the change, you have likely discovered that fear is the root issue — not apathy.

Facing fear

Even people who believe in change can become scared of the personal cost of having to learn how to do things differently. This fear shows up in a number of ways, represented by the handy acronym SCARED. SCARED people engage in sabotage, conflict, absenteeism, rumors, exasperation, and distraction. To deal with these issues, consult some of the conflict-resolution and problem-solving techniques in Chapter 8. If someone's really acting malevolently, you may have to state the obvious: "You have not shown up to work in ten days," or "I feel you may be sharing incorrect information about the project." When these challenges surface, some change leaders may be tempted to just tell employees to get over it and move on. This approach does little to engage the workforce or bring about lasting change (but you know that!). Instead of telling fearful employees to just get over it, a savvy change leader helps employees move from fear to confidence.

We encourage you to talk to employees to understand what is driving their fear. Often fear is created by a lack of information, and you can address that problem through better communication, as discussed in Chapter 7. Another cause of fear may be a lack of confidence in one's ability to learn the required skills to be effective. Managers and supervisors should work with each employee to create a personal development plan to outline the steps to gain the required skills.

Battling decreased productivity

When employees aren't sure what to expect next or are unclear of how the change personally affects them (either negatively or positively), they may start to miss deadlines and turn in less-than-quality work. These people are doubtful, anxious, and distracted, and that's normal.

A learning curve is required to learn and excel at new processes; a loss of productivity is to be expected. Productivity suffers during your transition period, but by the time your change is complete and you've arrived at the desired state, your productivity is (hopefully) higher than ever before.

Your goal is to move people to the positive as quickly as possible so you can see and feel the desired results of the change. Be clear and honest about how and when individuals will learn the new skills needed and when they will get more information to help mitigate the time spent worrying. They'll be back up to their usual productivity soon.

Fielding a general vibe of negativity

The people who think the change will negatively impact them are usually the ones who move more slowly or back away. These individuals may be confused about the purpose of the change and its implications for them, no matter how well planned the vision may be.

How do you balance getting the work done while acknowledging and helping people move out of this stage of change? First, know that each person will see the effect of change differently, and therefore they will move to the acceptance of change at different speeds. Here are a few tips to help you field the negative responses to change related to denial or resistance:

- ✔ **Communicate once again.** Although you probably have discussed the value and expectations of the change until you're blue in the face, you should make sure you also talk specifically about what is changing and what is not changing. Make sure you are communicating many different ways so that employees are hit from all sides and are informed in at least one way that's meaningful to them. Putting this structure around uncertainty can help people realize that their world is not going to turn upside down overnight.

✔ **Give people time to absorb the change.** Although the business may want the change to move at the speed of light, take a step back to listen (see Chapter 8), and then be as patient as possible. Be realistic about what absolutely needs to happen right now and what can move a little slower until more people get on board with the future state. You may want to ask your team to not react to the change immediately. Instead, ask them to think about it and then come back in one week with a list of what challenges and opportunities the change is presenting. This request moves the reaction away from a gut instinct to a more thoughtful inquiry.

✔ **Look in the mirror (and ask other leaders to do the same).** The way people respond to change has a lot to do with how people around them are acting. Sometimes people who are not willing or able to jump on board with change are doing so because they perceive senior management's attitude toward the change to be less than stellar. When you see a number of people reacting negatively to change, do a change assessment of your own leadership attitude and the attitude of others. Are you feeling overwhelmed with the change, and is it visibly showing? Do you or other leaders seem to be on a short fuse because of the workload?

✔ **Encourage constructive discussion.** Although asking people what they fear or don't like about the change may feel natural, this type of discussion can turn ugly very quickly. Instead, ask people to express what they think should be done to achieve the future and make change happen.

✔ **Stay calm and carry on.** Take a lesson from the Brits — when you feel in the line of fire from employees who are upset, keep a stiff upper lip and don't take it personally. They may appear mad at you, but they are probably just using you as the outlet for fear or frustration. Don't overreact. If an employee needs to vent, cry, or express his anger, let him do it, but then ask him what he would recommend doing differently. Move the negative conversation to the positive.

Embracing the Positive Reactions

Although you will face challenges to change that aren't so fun to deal with, remember that not all reactions are negative. Some people hear your message loud and clear and sincerely support you in your quest for change. During the phases of exploration and engagement, your task as a change leader is to use this positive energy to drive results.

As a leader and manager, you can help the excited and change-ready individuals reach higher levels of productivity as quickly as possible by:

✔ **Providing as much flexibility and as many learning opportunities as possible:** Although some individuals may love just "playing" with the new system, try to direct the play instead. Encourage experimentation and creativity, but ask employees to try something new with a purpose. For example, ask individuals to try out the new way of doing business and then provide input and feedback on how the system may need to be adjusted.

✔ **Setting focused short-term goals aligned with the change priorities:** If employees have moved from being against the change to exploring the environment, some managers are just grateful that employees have made the jump. But now you need to take it to the next level and reiterate the short-term objectives that need to still be achieved before the future state is completely realized. For example, you may be implementing a new HR system and structure, but paychecks still need to get out. Put together objectives that allow time for exploration of the new while still keeping the business operating.

✔ **Clarifying the details and team roles:** You want to make sure that all employees are clear on the specifics of who is doing what in the new environment. Lay out the details so the team knows exactly what it will take to make the future a reality and be more productive overall.

✔ **Matching up the positive people with the ones still dragging their feet:** By now you have done such a good amount of planning, envisioning, and people management that even those employees who seem stuck in the mud at least have heard the message about change (even though they may not be embracing it just yet). Encourage the people who have accepted the change to help get those still questioning it to realize the benefits of the future state. This pairing provides the positive people with a leadership opportunity to show their knowledge and be recognized for their contribution to the team. As employees embrace change, they have an overwhelming willingness to learn from one another, which also can translate into teaching one another.

✔ **Don't take your change cheerleaders for granted.** Even if people were initially excited about the change or the vision of the future, they can slide back to resisting the change if they begin feeling overwhelmed or stressed. Giving employees space to explore with the structure of specific outcomes helps to limit the feeling of having so much to do they can barely keep their heads afloat. This space helps in managing stress levels too, but we talk more about that later in this chapter.

Being a Change Facilitator

In this section we tell you about one more tool you can add to your change toolkit: becoming a facilitator of change to overcome resistance. Most of the industry terminology out there is focused on how to manage change (hence the popularity of "change management" in big consulting firms). As a change leader, why not try to look at the change process as one you can facilitate, not manage? By being a facilitator, you share change ownership with your employees, which better prepares them to work under the new conditions. As you help other people overcome resistance, your goal then is to provide the opportunity to change but not necessarily make the change happen.

Seeing the purpose behind facilitation

For some people, change is second nature; for others, it is not. The change may seem straightforward to you, but not everyone sees it the same way. Realize that some people may have competing priorities that may surface as resistance. However, the real problem behind a competing priority is just the perception of having way too much to do. Instead of being a taskmaster who pushes everyone to see the way you do, facilitation helps people see your point of view so that you don't have to be so bossy or pushy. Instead, people naturally start accepting the change and acting accordingly.

Changing isn't just imparting information; it's giving employees the chance to learn, grow, and enhance new skills. When facing resistance, give employees a number of chances to reflect and respond, not just listen and do.

Everyone brings different skills to the table. As a facilitator of change, you help employees use their skills to get to the future state. This way, it's not all up to you. Most likely your employees are not newbies, and this change is one of many steps in their careers.

Encouraging self-direction and problem solving

Although you may need to face some resistance head on, other resistance is the perfect stage for facilitating creative problem solving. In this section we discuss some ways to encourage self-direction.

The most straightforward approach you can take is to move from asking employees to do something else to asking them to *recommend* something else. If people feel that their ideas are heard and used, they're more likely to accept them.

If the change has little room for discussion (the end state may have been decided a long time ago by people way up on the pay scale), let employees know. Then as you use problem solving to navigate the change, be present to answer questions and present the change but still try to allow some movement in how to get to the end state. You can provide the structure and end goal, but let employees have input on the way to get there.

Look at change like learning: Change is really just learning to do something different and then doing it. When asking employees (even resistant ones) to change, make sure they have the opportunity to learn through problem solving. Help employees balance listening, speaking, seeing, experimenting, and doing throughout the change:

- ✔ **Listening:** For example, you may present a problem by sharing the change need and vision and answering questions verbally.

- ✔ **Speaking:** Allow employees to have their say. Ask for their input and ideas. Let them share their own stories.

- ✔ **Seeing:** Balance out the verbal side of learning with more visual and experience-based change. Present an inspiring slideshow and ask employees to read more about change.

- ✔ **Experimenting and doing:** Ask individuals to create connections between the future state and their current way of doing business.

This cycle of learning involves employees at all levels and helps you move them from resistance to change with positive problem-solving skills.

To really facilitate self-direction, stop talking. Change leaders get excited about change, but a time comes when leaders need to let employees do the talking. Yes, we have said over and over again how important communication is and how you should make sure the vision, goals, and plan for the future state are said again and again and again. But now is the time to step back a little bit and slow down (we know from way too much personal experience how hard this is to do, but bear with us for a moment). We like that great saying, "The more you say, the less I learn," but you don't want people thinking that about you. Make sure the project plan includes time to allow people who resist change the opportunity to work it out themselves.

If all else fails, make sure employees know the exact expectations of the change and when it needs to happen, and then step back. You may be surprised to see leaders emerging from those change resisters when you give them space to do it themselves.

Working through Disruption Problems

Workflow disruptions happen for a number of reasons. You may face technical problems, political issues, or cultural norms that prevent the change from moving full-speed ahead. Even in the most change-excited and change-ready organizations, the road to change will have a few bumps.

None of our vacations have ever gone off without at least one little hiccup along the way, and honestly, few of our change projects have been absolutely perfect (we would say none, but then you might stop reading the book). So in this section we take a look at how to resolve technical, political, and cultural issues quickly to make sure the change doesn't get derailed before you get to your final destination of the future state.

Managing technical ills

We love technology just as much as anyone holding a little device starting with *i* or ending in *-berry* does, but technology can fail. Whether the technology failure is a sad little face on your computer screen or your payroll system crashing just as paychecks are ready to go out the door, technology can create a number of issues in the change journey.

In order to manage technology ills, you need to pinpoint where they are coming from in the business. Following are the four primary suspects:

- ✔ **Has insufficient end-user input been received?** No one likes to come into work one day and find out she's expected to use an entirely new technology system, and oh, by the way, it doesn't run any reports she's used to running. The best way to run change (as you know by now) is to educate and communicate that a change is happening and involve the people who do the work in creating the solution. If you were handed a change midstream and didn't have the chance to communicate from the beginning, don't go back to the drawing board. Instead, ask end-users what can be done better and where the gap between what they need and what they have exists with the new system. Most likely, the technology can do what they need it to (otherwise the change wouldn't have been implemented); it just looks different or needs a few different key strokes. Giving end-users a voice in the creation of the new system (the earlier the better) helps you manage technology change issues.

- ✔ **Was the system designed using incomplete or changing requirements and specifications?** During technology changes (or any changes, for that matter), deciding what is needed and designing the system both occur early in the process. But business happens, and change happens even when you're already undergoing change. Therefore, requirements and specifications may change along the way, too. If you have problems in this area, revisit what was planned and designed and compare that info with what is needed today. If something doesn't fit, change it. Technology is only as good as how it is used.

- ✔ **Does the team expect world peace from technology?** No system is going to solve every problem, but for some reason if someone mentions three initials like CRM (customer-relationship management) or ERP (enterprise resource planning), people think all the business problems they are facing will go away. Unrealistic expectations are one of the top reasons for technology not being used to its full potential, because when the technology goes live and fails to solve everything in the world, people become resistant to the change and tend to toss out the baby with the bath water. By managing expectations with technology, you can remind people that although technology can make the world faster, better, and more efficient, it will not make the world perfect.

✔ **Do technology users have an unspoken (or spoken) lack of technical skill?** In our world of touch screens, smartphones, and every other gadget out there, admitting you don't have the skills to work with changing technology can be really hard. We have seen individuals create more work-around solutions to technology ills than we care to admit. Don't let this problem happen to you! Provide education and support for learning everything employees need to know about the technology in question.

Getting through political problems

Politics are not just for politicians anymore! Office politics are nothing new, but they can create new reactions to change — often reactions you don't want to see. Although we can't help you solve office politics, we can help you work through the political problems associated with change. Two main factors are the reasons for political problems when it comes to change: self-interest and misunderstanding or disagreement about what the real problem/solution/change is.

Office politics usually boil down to people being afraid that their status/pay/team/responsibilities are threatened. Although this view tends to ignore the future of the business, it is real and you do need to deal with it if the politician in the office has the power to make the change come to a screeching (or perhaps slow and steady) halt. As a change leader, you can negotiate how to work together, give the politico an opportunity to save face, or go through the conflict-resolution and trust-building process.

Negotiation usually doesn't bring about the fastest or best change (negotiation is often the preferred option in politics, so that gives you an indication of how fast it works!), but it sometimes is your only option to move forward. If office politicians have the power to stop change, allowing them to have control over parts of the change may be a great incentive for them to give their support.

Saving face is a big change tool (if used wisely and sparingly) when it comes to politics. If you can agree to the end goal and the most critical aspects of the change, go ahead and allow political powerhouses in your company to make other visible, meaningful decisions that still keep the change on track. A possible strategy for you may be offering the political resister the opportunity to co-create a new organizational chart or have co-signing power on any major milestones (as long as you have the time to negotiate each one). Be careful to not use this method to just give the impression of having power, though, because it will cause leaders that are beginning to resist to move even further away from the change.

Sometimes a lack of information and communication issues can lead to a misunderstanding of why the change needs to happen. This issue can spiral into political problems quickly. Nothing can take the place of conflict resolution and problem solving to clear up disagreements, which we discuss in Chapter 8. However, if you feel the situation has gotten out of hand and power struggles are raging, you may need to confront the situation head on.

State your opinion of the situation, and then ask for agreement and ideas. Start by stating a fact. For example, "Hey Mr. Misunderstanding, I see that you have been pulling your resources off the project. Do you agree?" Because this first statement is factual and therefore hard to disagree with, after Mr. Misunderstanding answers, you can follow up with, "How can I help clarify the importance of this project?" Now you have the perfect opportunity to clear up any misunderstanding about the project and then allow Mr. Misunderstanding to save face and lead part of the change.

Facing up to cultural issues

Like it or not, in addition to your organizational culture's wonderful aspects that have made it successful, it also has some not-too-wonderful aspects that need to, well, change. Some organizations are very determined to maintain security and stability. Things may have been done a certain way for decades, and that seems to be just fine with everyone (and is probably one of the reasons why change needs to happen, but we get to that in Chapter 16). If you are facing a resistant organization, try these cues to get the group moving:

- ✔ **Introduce ways to take alternate opinions into consideration in group meetings.** Don't stop at "Are there any other ideas?" Instead, tell employees that ten minutes of every meeting will be devoted to brainstorming alternatives or asking specifically for arguments against doing things the same way (the chance to play devil's advocate).

- ✔ **Ask the change team members how they learned from mistakes and disappointments when they did not change quickly, and then seek out examples.** You may also ask what the advantages are for changing proactively rather than just learning from mistakes.

- ✔ **Provide an opportunity for teams to jump into the unknown.** Taking risks can be a learned skill. If a culture is resisting change, let employees practice change by participating in a competitive activity in a safe environment (such as paintball, trust exercises, or beating each other up in those sumo-wrestling suits) that can help teach people the value of unpredictability and quick thinking.

Managing Stress Levels

If change leaders don't feel some sort of stress during the change process, they probably aren't really leading change. When stress hits, projects often start moving a little more slowly, and decisions are made out of exhaustion. By managing your own stress and helping your MVPs deal with their stresses during the change, you are able to get projects moving back on track and get anxieties back to workable levels.

Dealing with your own stress

Stress can come in all forms, but it frequently ends up with late nights at the office, a poor diet, and your family and friends not recognizing you anymore. Try a combination of these strategies to reduce your stress level:

- **Schedule time for family and relaxation.** We know you're busy, but setting some personal boundaries around your work schedule to spend time with family or friends will enable you to maintain your support network. By taking a little time for relaxation and recreation, you maintain your mental sharpness and are more ready to handle the stress that is inevitable in leading change.

- **Slow down to consider all the options rather than making snap decisions.** Take time to consider the impact of the change to others. Although slowing down seems like a bad way to get you through change more quickly, if you take the time to think how others will react before acting and you listen to what people have to say before commenting, change happens more quickly because you're allowing people the time they need to get on board with the change. In the long run, that time will reduce your workload and stress.

- **Let go of being a perfectionist.** This goal won't happen overnight, but you can try to release your perfectionist impulses one project at a time.

- **Cut back on multitasking and prioritize instead.** If stress comes from multitasking too much, take time to prioritize your list of jobs and tasks. Don't stop at working the biggest priority first. Look at your list and determine how much of your time is spent on the change strategy, how much of your day is spent keeping the lights on (just doing the business of change), and how much of your time is spent running to put out fires. If you find yourself spending time on things that don't add value, reevaluate how you can align your time to the change goals of the project. By spending time on things that make a difference, your energy (and stress) focuses on the positive.

- **Try a two-minute relaxation exercise.** Take one minute to get comfortable and allow your body to relax. Close the door to your office or room, turn off your phone and computer monitor, and then for the next minute pay attention to your breathing. Close your eyes and breathe slowly and deeply. Let the day's worries escape you for just two minutes. Just listening to your own breathing reminds you that even though change can get hectic and overwhelming, focusing on the basics conquers stress.

✔ **Exercise, even if it's just walking up and down the stairs at the office.** A regular exercise routine, two to three times a week, produces endorphins in the body that maintain not only physical health but also mental agility. If you can't get to the gym, try walking up and down the stairs in the office or walking a few laps around the building. We also recommend you consider having walking meetings with colleagues to get some exercise and get some work done at the same time.

✔ **If overtime is necessary, get to work early in the morning.** Your brain works better when it's refreshed in the morning instead of when it's fried after a full day of work. If you're not a morning person, at least schedule the complex activities that require a lot of concentration during the time of day when you are at your best and schedule less-complex tasks when you tend to have less energy.

✔ **Take short visual breaks from the computer screen every hour.** Eyestrain can contribute to feelings of tiredness. Getting up and walking around to give your eyes a break from the computer screen, as well as your body a chance to stretch and move, will keep you more refreshed throughout the day.

Helping your employees cope with stress

To get your team's stress level under control, the most important thing you can do is manage your own reactions to change. If you aren't taking time to see your family, go to the gym, or relax, neither will your team. Employees often imitate their leaders, and you need your most valuable players to be at their best, so begin by setting a good example.

Another tried and true technique is recognizing that not everyone on your team, even your star players, is stimulated by arguing or confrontations. When leaders are under stress, they can act overbearing, causing unnecessary stress on the team. As a change leader, make sure to stop and listen to other people's ideas and opinions before moving ahead with the plan. This practice helps create a culture of flexibility and open-mindedness.

It may sound a bit cheeky, but one of the best ways to help your MVPs cope with stress is to be a great leader. Thousands and thousands of leadership books are out there (for obvious reasons, we love *Leadership For Dummies,* by John Marrin [Wiley]), but most of the leadership techniques to help others cope with stress come down to these simple principles:

✔ **Clearly communicate directions but allow people to do their own work.** Having someone looking over their shoulder is really stressful for employees, so get the team going with a great vision and mission (have you heard that before?) and then let people do their work.

✔ **Delegate effectively.** Delegation is tough, but not doing it and taking everything on yourself is tougher. You'll get stressed, your employees will feel you don't trust them to do the work, and things will begin to spiral out of control. Ask others to take on work, give them the support they need, and share the workload associated with change.

✔ **Provide a motivating atmosphere that encourages everyone to perform successfully.** Motivating people to do their best doesn't mean yelling GO TEAM! Your role as a change leader is to make sure the culture of change is supported by encouraging and rewarding positive behavior and helping to get rid of any negative behavior.

✔ **Don't avoid necessary unpleasant discussions and actions.** Everyone makes mistakes, even your MVPs. Your MVPs are probably smart enough to realize this — so don't let mistakes, misunderstandings, or bad situations fester. Talk about them and then move on.

Managing corporate stress

When lots of little stresses come together in a big office space, corporate stress is bound to happen. Deadlines, financial reports, and customer interests can turn even the best-intentioned change leader into a high-stress corporate monster. When change is happening, corporate stress can be at a record high. Sometimes change breeds other change, and people begin to change or rock the boat just because change is in the air. Embracing change is great, but make sure the change is aligned with the vision and strategy.

Corporate stress can also lead to corporate silos. When a change need arises, certain leaders are willing to make the change happen, even if it means going it alone. High achievement and early adoption are wonderful traits, but having a group of people saying, "Wow, let's get moving," while another group says, "Whoa, slow down," is bound to create stress. To manage this problem, stick with the project plan and critical milestones. Keep marching forward, but remind people that the best change is change everyone is willing to take on.

Managing stress is all about keeping things in perspective. If something does go wrong (as it probably will), stop and evaluate what the real impact is. If it merely means you missed a deadline but didn't blow the project, let it go. Measure reactions to change and setbacks on the scale of big deal, medium deal, or small deal. If your vision is solid, the need for change is understood, and your plan is well designed, very few things in your change project will be make-or-break. A small derailing of the project can quickly be fixed with conflict resolution, listening, and taking a minute to evaluate the real impact.

Chapter 10

In Transition: Assessing Your Progress and Acting Accordingly

. . . .

In This Chapter

▶ Tracking how the project is going

▶ Rewarding jobs well done

▶ Keeping momentum going in the midst of change

▶ Applying what you've learned to future projects

▶ Making corrections when things go wrong

. . . .

*Y*our change project is well underway. However, you can't just get the ball rolling and take a break. You have work to do while the change is happening and your organization is in transition. Your role as a change leader now moves out of the "planning and envisioning the change" stage to overseeing the changes and supporting the team and organization while the change is in motion.

In this chapter we introduce a transition model checklist with steps that exponentially increase the likeliness of success in your change project. We then walk you through the celebration of change and help you not only designate markers for success but also positively recognize individuals and groups for their efforts along the way and build confidence in the future. Because all changes need a little boost during the change lifecycle, we also give you essential tips on how to maintain energy when interest in the change starts to wane. And finally, you find out about a word no one likes to talk about during change: failure. We walk you through what to do if you fail, how to make midcourse adjustments if the change gets derailed, and most importantly, how to do everything in your power to increase the probability of success.

Checking Your Progress: The Transition Model Checklist

If you planned and organized your change effectively (see Parts I and II), delivering on the change should be the easy part of your project. Basically, you're just doing what you said you would do. In this section we take a look at a *transition model checklist,* a simple tool to make sure your project is set to deliver the results you want. The list is broken up into five categories of accomplishments that you and your team will reach as you successfully complete the change project. You'll probably want to review the checklist on your own (something of a self-assessment) and with your core team.

Most likely, you probably are already delivering on some of your critical milestones. Even though your change project may be moving at full speed, run through the checklist to make sure you aren't forgetting anything.

Vision:

✔ You've created an energizing and bold sense of the future and articulated this vision to others in the company.

✔ Other people are asking lots of questions and beginning to embrace the idea of change.

✔ You know your key allies and you've reached out to them, building vital networks to launch and support your change initiative.

Road map:

✔ You have a plan in place to get you from the current to future state.

✔ You're comfortable with what's coming up next (for both you and your team) to move the change forward.

✔ You've created a training plan to give people the skills they need in the new environment. (You may not have the training content in place just yet, but making sure this step is on your plan ensures they know that they will learn everything they need to about the change.)

Team:

✔ You have a team of at least three to five energized change agents with clear roles and responsibilities — plus all the skills needed to make the change happen.

✔ Your team has a strong connection to the executive level to help drive the change.

✔ Leaders are walking the talk and modeling the new behaviors within the organization.

✔ The core team has minimal conflicts of interests. If your core team is beginning to fight and disagree early on, you need to resolve these conflicts before moving forward with the change.

✔ Your team leads by example and challenges the status quo.

✔ You've instilled a sense of cooperation on the team, giving everyone a chance to problem solve instead of merely following orders.

Measurements:

✔ You have visible, practical ways of tracking progress, and you know your objectives (see Chapter 6 for more on measurement development).

✔ You hold people accountable for these milestones.

✔ You've scheduled frequent ways to track results of the change effort and communicated the results as the change progresses.

Communication:

✔ You regularly update your team, organization, and leadership on the change journey.

✔ You engage in frequent feedback sessions with the organization, key employees, and leaders in the company to make sure the pulse of the organization is heard loud and clear.

The checklist is not a pass or fail list; it is simply a guide to keep you on track. If you find yourself checking off all the items, move on to the section "Celebrating Milestones" to give yourself the proper pat on the back. If your transition phase isn't going so well, flip to the section "Bouncing Back from Failure: What to Do When You Come Up Short" to get back on your feet.

Celebrating Milestones

Celebrating milestones is something you have been doing since you had your first birthday. Celebrating milestones during a change effort is really no different; unfortunately, noticing the milestones isn't as easy as putting a date on the calendar. You defined your milestones in Chapter 5; if you look back on them and feel that you've met them successfully, read this section to figure out how to celebrate them appropriately and identify what type of rewards fit the performance. This process may appear to be a little harder than making a birthday cake and lighting candles, but with our help it's as easy as pie!

Even when you hit a marker of success, retain your focus and energy. The markers of success are *indicators* that you're moving in the right direction, not guarantees. Just because you hit one marker doesn't mean all the others will fall perfectly into line — you have to keep your eye on the end goal until the change is complete.

Everyone likes to be thanked and rewarded for hard work and commitment. Celebrating and rewarding success improves morale and acknowledges the behaviors or actions that help drive the success forward. Recognizing individuals and groups is a terrific way to maintain positive momentum for the change. Recognition for individuals' contribution to the success of the project or the achievement of critical success markers falls into three basic categories: economic, public recognition, and job satisfaction.

When it comes down to it, recognizing employees and motivating employees are very similar. Chapter 8 discussed great ways to motivate employees throughout your change project, and Chapter 9 mentioned ways of rewarding your MVPs and helping them cope with stress. Don't forget to use those methods to help propel your recognition for all individuals and groups during the change effort.

Giving economic rewards (Money!)

Money is a great motivator for some people (okay, a lot of people). But remember, it isn't the only motivator, and you need to be sure to tie it to the behavior you are rewarding. A $10 gift card is probably not a great reward for someone who led a change that saved millions of dollars for the company, but neither is a 10 percent raise for someone who simply did his job. Don't throw those gift cards to the coffee shop in the trash just yet: Small rewards are appropriate for attaining smaller goals (like finishing a project plan), saying thanks to a particular unexpected effort (catching typos on a corporate message before it was sent out or helping another team member), or just to keep the motivation going when the change seems a bit overwhelming.

Publicly recognizing accomplishments

If your company has a recognition program for high performers, use it to distinguish key players throughout and after the change. When individuals or teams have done a great job, make sure you mention them in newsletters, on the internal website, or in e-mails. If significant work has been done, consider having an organization-wide meeting to update everyone on the progress of the change effort and publicly recognize the key groups and individuals that have played noteworthy roles in the success. You can also allow individuals to share their personal experiences through stories of how the change effort has benefited them to date (we talk more about storytelling later in this chapter). You can also bring in key customers or leaders to share their appreciation.

Lots of managers want to recognize individuals and groups with team luncheons or dinners, and although this type of gathering is a great team-building activity, it may not be fully appreciated by the team. If team members has been working 24/7 to get the change implemented, they may appreciate a catered lunch in the office or you picking up the tab on a dinner with their families instead of spending three more hours with their lovely co-workers.

Counting on increased job satisfaction

As simple as it sounds, most people want to do a good job and be happy in their job. Use this simple fact to reward employees and teams for a job well done. You can give them the great assignments, allow freedom to do what they want (within limits), ask for their feedback into even bigger changes or strategies for the organization, or invite the team to participate in key business-planning sessions. At the end of the day, if employees are happy in their jobs, they will deliver results, which is exactly what you want: Happy employees delivering results to drive the change forward.

To find out what rewards may be most appreciated by groups or individuals, ask the employees for their WIIFM (what's in it for me?) requests. Go back to Chapter 7 for a WIIFM refresher if you need one.

Maintaining Mid-Change Interest

Maintaining interest in your project may not seem like a big problem to worry about, but it deserves some discussion. If the interest begins to lag, so will the momentum. Then you may have to go back and redo most of the planning for the change to pick up the pieces and get it moving again (something no one wants to do, no matter how much they love planning, visioning, and the initial communicating!).

Mid-change interest dropping is usually not caused by a malicious plot to stall the change project (really, it is not). Often, the reason it occurs is often just because people have no idea what is happening and begin to assume that *nothing* is happening. While the core change team may be working along very smoothly, employees may wonder what is happening behind the scenes. As we emphasize throughout this book, communication with everyone in the organization is critical to keep the change effort in the front of everyone's mind.

Now is a good time not only to reflect on your accomplishments so far but also to paint a clear picture of what the second half of the journey will look like. Now is also a good time to revisit your vision and remind people of the benefits the change will provide to the organization, employees, and customers. Let employees know that they need to pace themselves for what lies ahead. As everyone knows, success breeds success, so build on what you have been able to accomplish so far and use your knowledge and skills gained along the way to propel you into success for the rest of the change journey.

The best way to maintain mid-change energy is to walk the talk — you need to keep your energy up. The general mid-change attitude is kind of how marathoners feel around mile 22 of the 26.2 mile run (that would be kilometer 35 out of 42 for those of you on the metric system). *Hitting the wall* is runner speak for the feeling that you can go no further, and change projects can hit a wall, too. One of the biggest reasons for failure in change is that leaders declare victory too early or assume that when the change is 80 percent done it will continue on without the leader's dedication and interest. Don't fall into this trap! When you see interest fading or feel like you have hit your own change wall, take a deep breath, gather the team together, and push through to the finish line.

If you have done a good job celebrating your successes and recognizing and rewarding key personnel and teams, you should already be in a good position to maintain the organization's interests in your change project.

Building Confidence in Future Successes

Successful change can do wonders to build confidence in employees, and that confidence can be used immediately to create future success. We have seen many successful changes springboard an organization to a new playing field in their industry, but you can't just move on to the next project and expect the change to be a springboard without planning (you knew we would say that, right?).

After a major change, employees (and you) need a break. Major-league sports stars need an off-season to recover from the big game, and employees and organizations need time to recover from the big change. The trick is maintaining momentum and confidence during the off-season.

When successfully executing a change, reflect and re-think your methods to make the next change or next big project be an even bigger success without reinventing the wheel. Two ways to build confidence in future successes are to maintain the organizational knowledge about how the change is happening (not just what's changing) and make the change a living, breathing story to inspire others to want to do it again.

Maintaining organizational knowledge

Before the change is complete, devote energy to how your organization can transfer what everyone has learned to future projects. To get the most from your experience, you want to evaluate not only how well the change is occurring but also how you can improve the way things are done in the future.

Although we love (and recommend) documenting how processes are done, that is a very small piece of the puzzle when it comes to organizational knowledge. We tap into how and what to document in Chapter 11 when we discuss closing the project, but you can do many other things to maintain organizational knowledge that doesn't involve process maps, flow charts, or an elaborate system to capture all of these great pieces of work.

To help maintain organizational knowledge, we recommend creating communities of practice, asking employees to train others, and developing coaching and mentoring programs. In the following sections, we explain how.

Creating communities to practice new skills and knowledge

Frequently called *communities of practice* or *centers of excellence,* these groups are teams of employees that meet to share best practices, ask the group for ideas on how to solve problems, and leverage their joint knowledge to work on day-to-day and strategic issues. During your change, this group may be part of the change team; after the change, ask the group members if they would be open to meeting on a monthly or quarterly basis to talk about how they continue to use the change tools in their new jobs and perhaps even learn new ones. An added bonus to creating communities that practice new skills and knowledge: This type of a forum allows people to ask one another for some of the heaps of information on each other's work computers — which can reduce the need to reinvent the wheel every time a change comes up.

These teams may not be part of the same group within the organization, so the communities tend to have a less formal feel to them. These communities can meet face-to-face or on conference calls, and some communities simply use a blogging website to post questions and provide user-generated answers to challenging problems.

Asking employees to train other employees

Training is a wonderful tool, but it can be expensive and is frequently only focused on classroom learning with little follow-up after students complete the course. You can change this practice to make sure knowledge is captured and maintained by training employees on how to provide training to other employees. If one person goes to training, she learns how to do things a different way; if one person goes to training and then shares her knowledge with the entire team, the entire team learns the new way of doing things. The trained employee doesn't need to give the entire course to others; she can simply share documents and tools or provide a forum for the entire team to acquire and maintain knowledge.

Developing coaching and mentoring programs

In most organizations, mentoring and coaching programs, whether informal or formal, are a "we-have-one-but-are-not-really-using-it-well" tool. Ask your change team to take the lead in coaching others on how to lead change or even one aspect of change. This coaching does two things: It provides a certain level of prestige to your high performers (they are now mentors) and it helps transfer and maintain knowledge, even in the most complex environment. If you need help starting the mentoring and coaching process, pick up a copy of *Coaching & Mentoring For Dummies* (written by Marty Brounstein and published by Wiley) and starting coaching away.

Creating your change story

Stories are powerful tools for change and for future change. You created a story of the future state when you began to plan your change, and now it is time to create your story of what happened and how it happened and make sure it is now part of the culture of the organization. Think back to your favorite childhood story and how you were completely engaged in every word, every picture — you could probably repeat most of the story today even if it has been years (decades) since you last read it. To create that same type of story for change, you can follow these seven principles:

- ✔ **Have a clear purpose for the story.** Decide if the goal of the story is to give people a can-do attitude or to show how the change made the company and employees' lives better. Then write down the purpose of the story in one sentence. You may have a few stories for a big change, each with a different purpose.

- ✔ **Pick a vivid example of change.** If the goal of the story is to build confidence in future success, find a vivid example of how the team overcame obstacles to achieve a significant milestone during the project. If the goal of the story is how the organization operates differently in the new environment, pick an example of how your customers, employees, and management are all doing better, bigger things because of the change.

- ✔ **Tell the truth.** We hate to have to say it, but make sure the story is true, not just corporate folklore.

- ✔ **Keep it simple.** We aren't asking for a novel here. Keep the story to 90 seconds or so. Tell what happened, who was involved, where it happened, and what the result was.

- ✔ **Link the story to results.** One of the goals of change is to accomplish some metric or milestone, so try to incorporate reaching this achievement in the story.

✔ **Link the story to future success.** Remind your audience to imagine how great all projects and changes can be if they are able to capture the same energy and focus of the change you just went through.

✔ **Re-tell the story to further institutionalize it.** Find other ways to re-tell or share the story (such as through employee newsletters, company intranet, or whatever else you use for company-wide communication).

You don't need to wait for everything to be said and done to create a story about change. A story that inspires teams to keep moving forward when interest wanes (which we discuss in a previous section) or when you have to make midcourse adjustments (which we get to in the next section) is one of the most powerful tools a change leader can have.

Bouncing Back from Failure: What to Do When You Come Up Short

You did everything you could do. You planned, you communicated, you created a great team. But when you assessed your progress with the transition model checklist (see the corresponding section in this chapter), you realize the project has gone splat! Even though you may be tempted to bang your head against the desk, don't. Now is a great chance for you and your organization to learn from the change and maybe even get the project back on the right track.

As you lift your head up from your desk, you can start planning a "what now" session (sometimes called *lessons learned* or *after-action review*), but first remember that no one really is to blame. The company's goals may have changed, the market or economy may have given the company surprises, or some other unforeseen event may have taken place. So don't blame yourself, or others, for where the project is — that practice will lead you down the wrong path. No one likes to be blamed; it shuts people down and can make people defensive. Instead, focus instead on what happened and why and what the company can do differently going forward. As a change leader, you need to create an atmosphere of curiosity that helps others understand what happened and what the company can learn from the experiences.

Now that you have your pep talk, in the following sections we tell you what you can do to get your change back on track. First, we discuss what to do if your change has failed or stalled, and then we cover actions you can take if your change is on a slippery slope downhill but hasn't yet failed.

Was the change a bad decision?

What happens when the change was just not right for the company? If you and other leaders are realizing that the time has come to stop throwing good resources after bad, we recommend that leaders take responsibility for their actions (not blaming anyone else) and say what is happening next. Just like with any other misstep, a leader (or multiple people) who made the initial decision to start the change must step up and admit that, in hindsight, it wasn't the best decision, and that now the company must move forward. This open communication establishes integrity and credibility for future decisions.

We know that admitting you've made a bad decision is hard, but it can be as simple as this: "Six months ago, I made a decision to turn all our customer-service centers into virtual service centers to reduce costs. Based on the data I had, I thought directing everyone to the website was a good idea at the time. However, it was a bad decision, I take responsibility for it, and I am also taking responsibility for the future. Here is how we are going to fix it and move forward. . . ." This simple statement includes three vital elements for admitting failure: stating what went wrong, taking personal accountability, and outlining the next steps.

Figuring out how to start over

A "what now" session can helps teams brainstorm new ideas to get a failed or stalled change back on track. Before the meeting, ask team members to think about what happened to stop the change and why. Remind the team to not place blame (give that little pep talk we just shared with you!). This preparation before the meeting will give the team time to think about what they learned from the change and start to diffuse any emotions that may be out there because of the failure. A great way to phrase this pre-work is, "What do we need to start doing (something different), what does the team need to stop (what didn't go well or was not necessary), and what does the team need to continue (what went well)?"

At the meeting, ask team members to think through the following five key steps for each area of the project that either stalled or didn't work out as planned:

- ✔ **What area failed?** In other words, what didn't work as planned? This area of failure can be anything from the project plan not being followed (time delay) to the supplier of a new information system not being able to deliver software that worked (we know this never, ever happens by the way; it is merely an example).

- ✔ **Why did this happen, and what are the implications?** Now you can get down to the root cause of the failure. For example, if the information system wasn't delivered on time or it wasn't the quality you expected, was it because the project plan wasn't clear, or were these expectations not communicated? Often, the root causes of failure can be boiled down to resources (not having the right skills, not having enough money), expectations not being clear, or the scope of the project changing.

✔ **What are the lessons learned?** A failure on the project does not need to stop the project cold. If team members didn't have the knowledge on how to hold meetings, then teach them, and make sure the lesson learned is captured as something like, "Did not provide adequate training" or "Assumed individuals already had skills needed." Again, you're not placing blame; you're just trying to make sure the problem doesn't reoccur.

✔ **What's next?** This "fork in the road" question covers: What is the next step, who is going to do what to fix this area, and does it need to be fixed or can we just move on? (We help you answer this question more fully in the next section: "Making midcourse adjustments.")

✔ **Who needs to know?** After a failure happens, you need to go back and communicate what happened and what is happening next to fix the problem.

When you kick off the meeting, make sure you lay some ground rules. Here are four critical ones to get the after-action discussion going:

✔ Trust that your colleagues want(ed) to do the best job.

✔ Avoid blaming anyone. Focus on what the team can do differently next time.

✔ Avoid "shoulda, woulda, coulda" language. Instead, talk about impact and learning.

✔ Identify areas where the organization still needs change or improvement, but focus on learning right now and not on inventing new solutions.

Making midcourse adjustments

Sometimes you see trouble coming before it arrives. Just as you may experience delays, road construction, or bad weather on a long cross-country road trip, you may spot problem areas up ahead and have to rechart your path on the change effort as well. This turn requires all the stakeholders to be creative, flexible, and willing to let go of prior plans and to think about new strategies to reach the destination. You may have to tweak (or rethink) previous plans and reengage the organization. Don't worry; all your previous work was not in vain, and with some small adjustments you can most likely get back on the path to the future vision.

Here are some points to consider when revising plans:

✔ **Timing:** Did we choose the wrong time to initiate the change project? Would postponing it to another time ensure greater success of the project?

✔ **Resources:** Are changes needed in resources or funding for the plan? If money has stopped the change from happening, decide whether you can be creative with funding, move around resources, or modify the project to fit the budget.

✔ **Knowledge:** Did a gap exist between critical knowledge and technical expertise? If the team didn't have the skills or knowledge to do something, identify ways to get the team the training and then continue on the path.

✔ **Duration:** Did the team underestimate the amount of time required for a particular step? This problem happens quite frequently — even with the best plans, things can take longer than expected. Your best move is to be open about this misjudgment, reassess the amount of time the task will take, and then get right back to work.

✔ **Retention:** Did key players on the team leave? If you lose key resources to another company, you will have no choice but to backfill the position or move work to others on the team (which is why maintaining organizational knowledge is important). If a key team member is moved off the project, your job as a change leader is to voice this concern to leaders and help the entire organization know what the move means for the project. You may not get the team member back, but at least the consequences will be heard.

✔ **Commitment:** Has commitment dwindled? See how to maintain interest (check out "Maintaining Mid-Change Interest" earlier in this chapter) and how to motivate employees and then make sure you don't jump on the dwindling-commitment boat.

✔ **External forces:** Has the external environment (customers, suppliers, or competitors) shifted the landscape? You can't do much about external forces during change — they happen. You probably planned how to minimize this risk in Chapter 6, so if external forces are your problem, gather your change leaders together and change or adapt the assumptions and goals of the project as needed.

Increasing the probability of success going forward

The best way to increase the probably of success after you begin fresh or make a mid-change evaluation is to make sure you have a plan in place for things outside your control, have clear and realistic expectations, and maintain confidence when challenging times arise. This advice applies for any stage in the change game, but especially after you've noticed problems, tried to fix them, and want to see success for the rest of the change project.

Some things are always beyond your control, but contingency planning enables you to brainstorm and anticipate possible issues so they aren't unpleasant surprises if they surface. Have a plan in place and ready to go in the event one of your obstacles shows up.

You also want to set expectations with your team and within the organization that more challenges may need to be dealt with along the journey. Even the best-planned journeys run into issues. Set expectations with employees that these surprises should be expected and not feared, and just because you've solved a few problems now doesn't mean that more, different problems won't arise.

Finally, maintain confidence in your own ability both to get things back on track and to encourage your team. Don't be discouraged when faced with obstacles. Babe Ruth struck out 1,330 times in his career and 30 times in the World Series, and the man didn't give up (yeah, it's another sports analogy; we can't help ourselves). See challenges as mere obstacles to overcome as opposed to roadblocks that cause you to give up and go home. This attitude gives your team the confidence to make necessary course corrections along the way.

Chapter 11

What Happens Next? Keeping the Change Ball Rolling

In This Chapter

▶ Building for lasting change

▶ Managing change advocates and barriers

▶ Driving a successful after-change review

*W*ell done. You made it through the good times and the tough times; now your change is implemented, your boss is thrilled with the initial results, and you're ready for your next big move . . . to that corner office. But before you shut the door on this change, you should do a few things to make sure the change doesn't unravel the second you and your team move on to bigger and better things.

Keeping the ball rolling is often perceived as a footnote to the overall change project, yet it can be the difference between people saying "Wow, that change was great, we're really doing things differently around here!" and "Wow, we're glad that change leader is gone; now things can go back to normal." Ensuring that your change retains momentum does more for your organization's future than anything else you do in the project. You owe it to yourself and your organization to make sure the change sticks — even if means postponing that celebratory vacation to St. Bart's for a few weeks.

This chapter describes how to develop the structures to make change last, including processes to redesign performance measurements and align resources to the new way the company operates. You can also find out how to communicate your change structures and how to manage the change helpers and hindrances within your organization. Then get ready to head up the after-change review, the final step in leading business change.

Developing the Structures to Make Change Last

Back in 1904, a famous psychologist named B. F. Skinner proved that if you reward a mouse with cheese when it presses a button, the mouse will continue pressing the same button to get more cheese. (For all those psych students out there, we know Skinner's work was a little more complicated, but that's the gist of the psychology behind rewarding a specific action.) Well, people are really no different from mice in this case. People repeat actions they are rewarded for, so it makes sense to establish a reward structure if you want a change to stick. Rocket science, we know.

In many cases of business changes, the change takes place and everyone is happy, and a new report may come out with metrics that show the change happened. But little if any change to the structure of the organization occurs to establish the change for years to come. As a result, things sometimes come unraveled rather quickly; other times the change remains on the surface of the organization, ready to be blown away in the winds of the next big thing.

To avoid this problem, you can develop organizational structures to make change last. This sustainability is not really that hard to tackle, as long as you know what you want to achieve. In the previous chapter we provide a checklist for getting through the change process. Well, you can use a similar list after the change happens to increase the likeliness that it sticks. This new checklist can be broken down into two categories: redesigning performance measures and aligning resources to the new way of doing things.

Developing useful performance measures

Carefully considering how people are rewarded for performance in your organization can help you anticipate their eagerness to embrace or abandon your change. Individuals and teams will simply go back to the old way of doing things if they are paid or otherwise rewarded for doing so. The most long-lasting changes within a business are accompanied by changes in how the organization measures the new desired performance or behavior and how individuals are rewarded for their performance. Both of these transitions require two things:

- **Ongoing evaluation and measurement:** You cannot stop at measuring how successful the initial change is. By helping your team evaluate and design how the new way of doing business is assessed — on a continuing basis — you can keep the change implementation rolling long after the change has happened.

✔ **Clear policies and guidelines:** At this point, even you may be overwhelmed by the volume of your own communications about organizational change. Well, to make sure change sticks, assure everyone that the new way of business is official by establishing — and clearly explaining — policies and guidelines. This step ensures that the new way of doing business is locked into daily operations.

With those steps in mind, you're ready to identify what the new organization should be measuring and how to tie these metrics to individual employee performance.

Measuring team and organizational processes

In Chapter 6 we discuss the importance of balanced measurements in defining the success of change, and the same principles hold true for determining how successful the change is long term. The first step in developing (or redesigning) new measurements for your organization is aligning them to the new way of doing business. You may be able to continue using the same measurements you used throughout the change, but some may need minor tweaks. If you're struggling to develop meaningful metrics for the organization — or if you need some creative juice to take a few metrics to the next level — you may want to ask your project team for new ideas.

For instance, you can ask the team, "What are you learning from the metrics we're using?" Often, measurements have been in place for as long as the company has been around. Use the change as an opportunity to refine measurements to best track current operations and how the company is meeting its future goals. If the measurements the team or organization had in the past are still the right measurements in the future state, the targets for these measurements may simply have to change. For example, if the change is focused on improving customer satisfaction and the organization was measuring customer satisfaction before, you probably want to keep measuring it but the target may move from 80 percent of the customers being satisfied to 95 percent. If the team seems happy with the current metrics and the old targets, something may be amiss and you may want to revisit the purpose of the change.

Try to balance leading and lagging measures in the new measurement system. Here's what these terms mean:

✔ **Lagging indicators:** Response measurements, such as customer complaints or monthly sales, come after the fact. Lagging indicators can prompt change in the way you conduct future processes.

✔ **Leading indicators:** Forward metrics may include such things as attendance in a call center on busy call days (which may contribute to the wait time for callers) or the number of sales positions opened in a current month (which may indicate sales growth in a territory).

The second step in developing (or redesigning) new measurements for the organization is identifying the target or goal for the measurement. If your measurements are staying the same, your targets probably have to change to show that you changed for a reason (not just for the fun of change!). Targets can be set based on industry performance, best practices in other departments, or company goals. In the end, your new performance measurements will be aligned to strategic goals and have clear targets like the ones shown in Table 11-1.

Table 11-1   Example Performance-Measurements Chart

Strategic Goal	Measurement(s)	Target
Improve use of technology	Percentage of clients using Web customer service	70% of sales
Stay on top of industry knowledge	Number of hours of professional development for employees	12 hours a year

Evaluating individual performance

After you refine your organizational metrics to support the change, you can adapt them to monitor the performance of individual employees. Organizational metrics are great at keeping the company on track, but the people make the metrics move. The closer you tie organizational metrics to individual metrics, the better your chances of individuals working to make the change last.

For example, say your change focuses on creating an organizational culture that runs the business more efficiently, resulting in higher profits. You may have a metric like profit growth to gauge this goal for the entire organization. Executives and investors will love this metric — it looks great on a spreadsheet — but the average employee may have a hard time tying it to his day-to-day work. So make that metric more meaningful at the individual level by asking an individual to make an improvement that maximizes company profit, such as finding three areas to cut costs in your daily job or identifying one process improvement to impact product quality. The key is to make metrics meaningful and actionable to individuals. When employees can tie what they're doing to the new way the business is operating, they often become more invested in the change.

When creating individual metrics, focus on the critical few and include the details. Here's what we mean by this advice:

✔ **Focus on the critical few:** Don't try to accommodate every goal or performance metric that could possibly influence the survival of the change. In addition to being cumbersome and time consuming for managers, overly ambitious measurement systems for individuals lead to resentment of the new way of doing business. Instead, focus on initiatives that are most strategic to the business. Try to keep individual assessments to three or five metrics.

✔ **Include details:** Include both what needs to get done (the results you expect) and how it needs to happen (living up to the new company culture) in individual metrics to reinforce that you can't just get something done for the sake of accomplishing it; you have to get it done right.

Performance measurements and momentum are closely related, so track the progress of change regularly (at least each month or quarter) to make sure the change continues to reach organizational and individual goals.

Monitoring change over time

With measurements in place, the project team can implement a plan for collecting data. In some circles, this plan is known as a *control plan,* and we like to compare it to dieting: If you spend a year losing weight, how do you know you're keeping it off? You can step on the scale every day or just see how your clothes are fitting; either method works, but you need to do it on a regular basis to make sure you're staying on track. So find a way to measure the progress of your change, and make sure that the measurement method works for your team.

The purpose of a control plan is to make sure that the impact of the change is trending as expected and desired. A practical control plan includes the following information:

✔ **Metric:** Describe the measurement with a straightforward two- to four-word definition of what you are measuring. Think: cost of goods sold, new jobs created, customer-satisfaction ratings, and so forth.

✔ **Goal:** Simply state the objective in a way that can be measured. What do you want to accomplish? Some examples of goals may be to reduce caller wait time to less than three minutes or to increase the online help-desk support by 50 percent.

✔ **Data source:** A clear guideline on where the data comes from ensures consistency and accuracy of findings. In our experience, asking people to tell others where the data comes from helps make collecting the data a little easier. If someone can explain where the data came from in less than a few words, it most likely is easily accessible. If someone has to write a novel on how to collect the data or where is comes from and who has to do what to it before it is used, the data may be a bit difficult to collect (and may slow down the process).

✔ **Review frequency:** Make sure the frequency of data collection is suitable for your information needs and not overused. If your objective is to create 25 new jobs over five years, for example, then a daily count of new positions is not likely to be helpful. A quarterly collection may be more suitable. There is no sense in collecting lots of daily data points if they will just sit alone in a database somewhere.

If your change potentially has daily results, then you may want to display daily reports in the early stages of implementation to encourage employees to embrace the change; after the change is securely in place, your reports may be more effective as weekly accounts. We like the motto of quality over quantity. Bottom line: Make sure your control plan works for the project team and other stakeholders.

Just as the change plan focused on different stakeholders at different times in the process, the measurement system must address the information needs of people on different levels of the organization. Check out Chapter 6 for more ideas on creating a meaningful change scorecard.

Aligning resources to the new way

With the change in place and the project team disbanded, sufficient resource support for the new way of doing business is critical. To support resources most effectively, make sure the change is reinforced through training, documenting info, integrating changes into daily operations, and clearly assigning process owners to champion the change for the long term.

Training

One of the most important aspects of implementing change that sticks is relevant and ongoing training to individuals and teams. Employees with the skill set and ability to perform according to the change are the best resources. Use this training opportunity to ensure that people know what to do and how to do it the right way to support the change for years to come.

Be on the lookout for unspoken confusion. People don't always know what they don't know. If people have been doing a particular process before the change, they may have trouble recognizing — let alone communicating — that they don't know or understand how to behave or perform a task differently in the new environment. Make sure you provide ample training and mentoring for everyone; don't assume people know what to do or how to do it.

To hire or train — that is the question

As you go through the change process, you may find that an entirely new set of skills is required for the new way of doing business. At this point, you must decide whether to hire new people with the desired skill set or to train current employees in order to develop the skill set internally. Neither the task nor the decision is easy.

To guide this decision-making process, a *needs assessment* of current and desired skills can help you assess the feasibility of your options.

Take the time to carefully consider what resources you have and what you need.

If you find that an individual or team is lacking the skill set *and* the potential (based on interest, competency, or other factor) to be trained, then hiring resources to do the job may be a strong option. However, if existing employees have some of the skills and can be trained on the others to do a new job, then your best bet may be to train or redistribute work.

Documenting the details of change

You, the change team, and perhaps the entire organization may think the change is obvious, but that doesn't mean it shouldn't be documented somewhere. The change should become part of the knowledge-management process in the organization so that as time passes and memories blur, people in the business can refer to it for reminders of who is supposed to do what. Following are a few aspects to document:

✔ New organizational charts

✔ Job roles and responsibilities

✔ Process maps and instructional guides

✔ Budgets and strategic-planning tools

✔ Action plan for what to do if the change reverts back to the old way it was done

Integrating change

Incorporating changes into daily operations takes much more than writing up procedures and policies (although you need to make sure that is done, too). An organization implementing change benefits tremendously by leveraging *formal and informal influencers* in daily operations. Here's what we mean by these terms:

✔ **Formal influencers** include the organization's top leadership, who must advocate the change and be role models for it. But formal influencers are more than people; they include clear responsibilities, new job descriptions, updated reward systems, and perhaps even new technology to support the change.

New procedures are great, but if the team only follows the procedures when you're looking over people's shoulders, the changes aren't sustainable. That is where informal influencers can make a big impact.

✔ **Informal influencers** are people in the organization who may not have a leadership title but are trusted sources of information. These people often have been around the organization for a long time, have political savvy, and have a strong commitment to the success of the organization.

A great example of an informal influencer was a long-term mechanic at a manufacturing company going through significant cost-cutting changes. The manager at the facility was the official change leader, but nothing got done until the mechanic said it was the right thing to do. People trusted his opinion, even though he had no direct management responsibility. Informal influences can make things happen if you give them access to senior leadership and allow them the opportunity to voice their opinion.

Designating process owners

Until now, you (or a team member) may have been driving the change and owning (or co-owning) the improvements. But now you need to designate a clear owner for the change in the long term, and that person may or may not be you. If you have been in charge of revamping how new employees are recruited and oriented in the company, you have probably been working with the human resources, recruiting, and training teams. You may also have been working with hiring managers and new employees to get their feedback and buy-in for the change. As a change leader, it is time to make sure someone owns the new process. Ideally, the process owner has been part of the change all along and has authority to make modifications to the process as necessary to meet the organization's new challenges.

Top leadership can make this choice, but sometimes the process owner will step up and take ownership because it is a natural fit. If you are still looking for someone to own the process in the long term, consider finding someone who has these traits:

✔ **Making the change stick is her priority.** The process owner must be accountable for continued results, so now is not the time to drop the ball.

✔ **She has enough influence to make adjustments to the change, if necessary.** Influence often means strong leadership skills in the areas of continuous process improvement and coaching others.

✔ **She understands metrics.** The process owner will need to explain and review how the process is going, so she should be comfortable and perhaps even excited by numbers and metrics.

You can't give someone a process without power. Process owners should have access to senior leaders, be involved (perhaps even lead) review meetings, have control of the budget, and be rewarded for making the results stick.

Communicating for Lasting Change

As we describe in Chapter 7, a strong communication plan can do wonders to help you implement business change. As you move from implementing the change to making it part of day-to-day business, communication messages should continue to go out to the organization. Although not necessarily as elaborate as the messages sent during the development and initial implementation stages of the change, these communications are no less important. Following are some key questions you may consider answering as the change process becomes the new normal:

✔ **What were the results of the change?** Use stories (like the ones described in Chapter 10), case studies, and metrics to show how the change happened and why things are better now that the change is in place.

✔ **Where can people get more information?** While you have been living and breathing the change, other people may have been going about business as usual or just hiding out in their office (or perhaps someone was recently hired and knows nothing about the change!). Make sure you provide ample opportunities for employees to learn more about the elements of the change, including online resources, information on the company intranet, education and training programs, and perhaps even coaching or mentoring opportunities.

✔ **What can people do now?** Although the change has been implemented, let people know if there things they can do to get more involved in the new way of doing business. From self-directed training related to daily tasks to a systematic review of how they do business, give people a way to ensure that they're supporting the change and new company goals through their day-to-day performance.

As part of your assessments related to the lasting impact of the change, monitor the impact of your communications. Were any specific communications especially helpful? Did any create disruptions and controversy? This information can feed into your after-change review (which we describe in the later section "Leading the After-Change Review") and help you identify the best practices for future communications regarding this change and others.

Managing Helpers and Hindrances to Change

Difficulties, annoyances, hindrances. Call them what you want, but obstacles to success are probably still lurking around your change somewhere. Whether your hindrances are people in power positions not willing to fully embrace the change, dwindling budgets, or resourcing constraints, you need to overcome the major obstacles in order to bring the project to a close and make the changes stick.

But before you start letting all those obstacles get you down, remember that you have helpers on your side, too. Helpers are those informal influencers, employees with political savvy, and people who really want the change to happen. Manage those correctly — as well as the hindrances — and you'll be well on your way to mixing up a successful change cocktail. Cheers!

Minimizing the impact of hindrances

Basically, a hindrance is anything stopping the change from being 100 percent successful in the long term. If you put on your optimist hat and approach your hindrances with a determination, you can turn them into helpers, and you just may gain important new support for the effort. Following are the three primary competencies you'll want to tap into to engage your to-be helpers (current hindrances):

- **Patience:** The change needs time to succeed, and sometimes hindrances just require a little patience. If the change plan had any setbacks or if the entire strategic goal was not immediately achieved, people in the hindrances camp are perhaps overly focused on those elements of the change. As a change leader, stay positive about the big picture; business change will succeed if you have the right performance measurements in place and resources are adequately aligned.

- **Effort:** Converting hindrances to helpers requires effort. If specific people or processes continue to impede the progress of change despite the time and energy you've allotted to date, then you may need to align more resources to further investigate the obstacle or just continue to chip away at the problem.

- **Consistency:** Consistency is paramount. When faced with a hindrance in the organization, consistently respond to questions and address negative behaviors. Although you would probably like nothing better than to just ignore a specific hindrance and hope it goes away, consistency improves the likelihood that things will change.

Now that you know what you need to bring to the table, you're ready to delve into some common hindrances to change projects.

Handling common hindrances

The following list describes some hindrances you may come across — but don't worry; we also provide some advice for how to turn them into helpers for lasting change:

- **Lack of high-level buy-in:** If executives are feeling burdened by the amount of work related to the change or have lost interest in it, you can be sure some employees have, too. Use this opportunity to clarify the vision or objectives of the change. Consider asking executives to speak honestly to other employees about their concerns and challenges with the change and find specific ways for people to re-engage.

- **Inconsistent communication:** Communication is a big part of change. If you worry that the communication you're sending isn't doing its job, then take a closer look at what's working and what's not. Go back and evaluate the value of communication efforts; determine which ones led to greater attention and action and which ones fell into a black hole. Do more of what works.

- **Scope creep:** An expanding field of change can slow down the completion of your project. Especially if you do a wonderful job on the change project, the unintended consequence may be an expanded scope. This is the case when every change seems to bleed into another one. Use this hindrance to acknowledge all the great work to date, complete the after-change review (more on that later), and recruit a new team to take on the next phase of work with the benefit of lessons learned from the current change.

- **Inadequate training/resources:** Insufficient preparation for change can often lead to a slow adoption. If the training you've provided seems to be falling flat or if you can't seem to get the right resources (financial or people) to make the change happen, speak up and revisit your risk mitigation strategy (see Chapter 6). You may need to break down the project into manageable segments or step back to recognize and better address cultural impact.

Of course, these examples are just a few of many possible deterrents you may face when change is underway. But no matter what is stopping the success (or slowing it down), you can convert the hindrance to an element of support for the change (and future changes). Here are some ideas:

- **Seek help from a real live person.** You can easily blame technology, communication, or a process for being a hindrance to change, but those factors alone cannot stop change. People who make decisions about these possible deterrents matter. So identify the obstacle and then reach out to the person responsible for it and ask for help.

✔ **Learn why hindrances still exist.** Avoid the mistake of believing everyone shares your motives. Talk with people, especially those who may be hindering the change, and ask them about their ideal outcomes. Just keep in mind that people rarely express their true motivations the first time around, so exercise that consistency and patience we mention earlier in this chapter.

✔ **Request specific action.** Leave no room for misunderstanding. Explicitly state the goals of the change (again) and be clear about what specific action(s) the individual needs to do (or stop doing) to get on board.

✔ **Lead with a stronger hand.** After you've worked at facilitating the change with process suggestions, inviting ideas, and encouraging discussion with hindrances, establish a more concrete plan. Show empathy for the opposing position and then agree on specific actions that will happen according to a timeline. Leading with a strong hand also means explicitly rewarding positive behavior and being consistent with the consequences of poor behavior towards the change.

Roadblocks to change usually boil down to a lack of knowledge, insufficient resources, or fear of what will happen if change is successful. With this in mind, be sure to show empathy when addressing hindrances. Take a look at the ideas on conflict resolution in Chapter 9 for help with expressing an understanding of another person's point of view.

Coaching stragglers and naysayers

During change, there are always stragglers (people who will eventually come along but seem to take pride in dragging their feet) and naysayers (people who never have uttered a positive word about the change). No matter what you do, some people just do not want to jump on board with the change. Employee attitudes affect the sustainability of a change, so if these stragglers and naysayers have strong influence in the organization, you and your team may have some coaching work to do.

As a coach, be ready to dig into your toolkit for communication (remember listening and addressing conflict in Chapter 8). Also prepare to take your conflict-resolution skills to an entirely new level.

The game plan with the naysayers is to dig out the roots of resistance. What is holding these people so tightly in the old way of doing business? Allow objections to air and listen to opinions that may differ from yours. The dialogue — getting to the core of the disagreement — may require every one of your conflict-resolution skills, but only after you get to the real issue(s) can you address them and get everyone on board.

Here are some ideas to help motivate naysayers and stragglers:

✔ **Identify short-term and long-term issues.** Although your change likely focuses on strategic, long-term goals of the company, naysayers and stragglers may be facing some very real short-term issues. For example, your change may be merging two cultures after an acquisition or merger, but some day-to-day problems (like integrating two payroll systems or combining different ways of launching new products) do not have clear or immediate solutions. You can alleviate some of the pain points by revisiting the stated goals in context of individual situations.

✔ **Be honest about intentions.** You may be the most honest and open-book person in the history of world, but some people out there may doubt the change (and you) because they don't trust your intentions. Respond with a two-step process:

   1. Take a deep look at your real intentions for the change.

   2. Communicate your intentions in a genuine way. Hopefully your message is something along the lines of wanting the change for the improvement of the company with no hidden agenda.

✔ **Listen.** When someone has an idea, part of his ego is attached to that idea. People tend to disengage if their ideas aren't accepted or taken seriously. So make sure that you take time to listen to people. Every idea won't be implemented in the current change, but people want to know their solutions and opinions may be considered for future changes. Therefore, you may want to document stakeholder ideas and concerns in the after-change review to formally validate this input to the group.

✔ **Escalate issues with respect.** Sometimes issues are brought to your attention that you simply do not have the authority to address. When a former boss got an uncomfortable question, he'd say, "Oh, that decision is above my pay grade" (chuckle, chuckle). We do not encourage readers to use that excuse, but if you do need to escalate issues to someone above your pay grade, do so with respect toward all the parties involved. You can do this by getting the two sides to agree on how you will escalate the process through other channels, documenting what has been done already, and maintaining confidentiality throughout the process.

See if you can task the naysayers with addressing their own concerns. For instance, if someone is concerned that a new report will not give her the information she needs, ask her to create a new one that can potentially be used. Or, if the naysayer does not like a new information system, ask him to list some ideas for what can be done to fix the problems. Putting naysayers to work in support of the change can help solve persistent issues and convert them to helpers.

At some point in time, people who don't get on board with the change may have to make a decision to either get on the change bus or leave the company. This choice isn't the first step in minimizing the impact of people in the hindrance camp, but it may be the end result. Work with your human resources department to help manage these negative performers, and read up on how to give performance evaluations and terminate employees in *Managing For Dummies,* by Bob Nelson and Peter Economy (Wiley).

Leveraging your helpers

Individuals who embrace change and business processes that complement a specific change can make your life as a change leader much simpler. Harness these gifts and allow them to move your change project forward. Often, other employees are your best motivational experts for future change. If employees have been exposed to change and have had a positive reaction, having them talk to other people about the change can help less-eager employees embrace the new way of business as well. Enlist these helpers as part of the success story and encourage them to communicate what happened and how life is better now that the change is complete. You may even give these helpers the title of change ambassador to recognize the value these employees bring to the organization.

Here are some other ways to keep your new change ambassadors (the helpers) energized and moving the organization forward:

- ✔ **Make them trainers.** Let these employees show other employees first-hand how the change will make life and the company better.

- ✔ **Give them the stage.** Let change ambassadors speak to the entire company with how the change has helped them and film it. Post these videos on the company intranet.

- ✔ **Provide visibility.** Giving them the stage is a great way to have the entire organization see their support, and giving helpers visibility and exposure to top decision makers can help cement their role in making change last.

- ✔ **Promote them.** Are you still looking for that process owner we talked about earlier in the chapter? Helpers may be willing to step up to the plate and take ownership for the change in the long run.

- ✔ **Tell them they're special.** No, you do not need to give them a dozen roses, but simply letting people know you appreciate their positive attitude goes a long way.

For more ideas on how to motivate your helpers (who may also be your MVPs), check out Chapter 20.

Leading the After-Change Review

Before you ride off into the sunset, be sure to deliver a meaningful after-change review. Great changes provide ample ideas to leverage during future changes; changes that hit a few potholes along the way can show you what to do differently in later projects. The process of the after-change review is much more than a one-hour meeting to say "thanks and good-bye." As you finalize the change, think of this review as a cycle that begins as soon as the initial changes start happening and continues until you integrate the learnings into the way of doing business. The after-change review process is outlined in Figure 11-1.

Figure 11-1:
Keeping the ball rolling with an after-change review.

So now the change has begun to happen, and you are seeing results. The new way of doing business is understood, adopted, and in full swing. Using some of the ideas outlined in Chapter 10, you may have also begun to recognize and reward the team for desired behaviors and outcomes. Seeing these changes happening is a good indicator that the time is right to begin formally closing your change project. Here are the steps you can use to make the change review be part of integrating all the lessons learned into the new way of doing business.

1. **Conduct the after-change review:** Invite people who had direct experience with the change successes and failures to an after-change review session. At this meeting, lead the team in discovering what worked and what did not during the process of developing and implementing the change, plan out what to do with this information, and then decide how and when the change may need to be adapted.

   We recommend that you use an experienced facilitator to manage the meeting. Otherwise, if politics come into play or if naysayers are in the room, an after-change review can devolve into a complaining session or finger-pointing activity.

Questioning change

To help your after-change review team uncover the things the change team did right and where it lagged, answer these questions in your change-review session:

✔ **What were the key successes?** Don't stop at "The project was a success because everyone did their job." Dig deeper. Why did everyone do their job? Was it a result of clear roles and responsibilities? Was it due to well-communicated expectations? If things went well, go ahead and brag. This meeting is your chance to create organizational best practices to follow for years to come.

✔ **What where some unexpected barriers?** Even with the best planning, there are challenges with change. Maybe getting the executive team to approve a change took a month longer than planned because of schedules. Document barriers for the benefit of the next change team.

✔ **What would you do differently if you had to do it over again? What would you want to do exactly the same?** There are probably things you'd like to do over. By documenting them, you can avoid making the same mistakes again. On the other hand, pat yourself on the back for things you did well. Make sure these successes are documented and shared throughout the organization.

The review session is a good opportunity to offer recognition to employees who helped make the change successful. Use some ideas outlined in Chapter 10 to recognize and reward the team for desired behaviors and outcomes.

2. **Discover, plan, and decide:** During the after-change review, analyze where you've been and where you're going with your team of stakeholders. Here's what we mean by this:

   a. **Discover:** Take some time to document what parts of the change process worked and what parts didn't. See the "Questioning change" sidebar for ideas on how to draw out relevant information about the change process.

   b. **Plan:** Focus on how to solve the project's problems and how to leverage its strengths. Many kinds of business change apply to more than one area of the organization, so identify small modifications that can help the change benefit the larger organization.

   c. **Decide:** Figure out what to do with the recommendations to make the change even better. Some ideas may need to be postponed; others need to happen right away. Break down your list of modifications into time-based categories: short term (under 90 days), long term (over 90 days), and future (not applicable to current change but helpful for how change happens in the future).

3. **Revise, focus, and identify future change goals:** After the change review is complete, the ongoing process owners have an opportunity to step up and revise the changes as needed to keep the change alive. This part can be difficult for the change team because many team members have moved on from implementing the change and are busy with exciting new projects.

4. **Identify additional/new team members:** Selecting new team members is all about aligning resources to make the change sustainable. While you and your project team may always be living and breathing the change (and moving on to new projects), new individuals can help make practical modifications with new energy and perspective.

5. **Integrate learning into the way of doing business:** The real benefit of the after-change review is sharing it with others in the organization. Don't keep those lessons locked up! Communicate what you learned from the process and share information openly and honestly. A change leader never really stops communicating, but you knew that already, right?

Change takes time, so be sure to not skip over some of the more important parts of change: reflecting on the results (through an after-change review) and then integrating these results as the organization continually refines strategic objectives, metrics, and initiatives. Successful change projects can help an organization grow into a more adaptable organization if they end by reflecting on what went well and where they need to focus more energy.

Three principles of sustainable change

Wouldn't you like to have a perfect formula to know if your change is sustainable? Well, if you can answer yes to the following questions, you know that the change has a high chance of sticking:

✔ **If people move in and out of the organization, will the change last?** Although talented people certainly impact the strength and longevity of certain changes, change should be based on the organization and its processes, not just on a really great person or team.

✔ **Is the change adaptable?** If the change can endure shifts in the market, the economy, or even organizational structure, then it has a good chance of lasting long term.

✔ **Is sustaining the change pretty easy (or at least not overly difficult)?** Considering the effort required to develop control plans, establish measures, and align resources, there should be no major setbacks in the short term. Just make sure that the training and tools are easy to access and easy to use. Aside from that, if the change requires much work to sustain, then you can probably guess what will happen.

Part IV
Leading Change in Specialized Circumstances

The 5th Wave   By Rich Tennant

@RICHTENNANT

"Bob, I want to tap into that part of your brain that wants to change, that wants to promote the change, that wants to stop leaning on my desk..."

In this part . . .

Change is often the only constant in business, mainly because so many things can cause a business to change. Sticking with the status quo leaves a business in its competitors' dust. In this part, we show you what to focus on during different types of change. From how to make teams work more effectively to how to leverage organizational redesigns, from mergers and acquisitions to changing cultures and technology, we have you covered. We also give you some pointers on how to lead change when everything in the business is changing and how to keep your sanity when it feels like you're in the midst of chaos.

Chapter 12

Creating Meaningful Team Change

. . . .

. . . .

*H*ighly effective teams strengthen the organization overall. Getting the right people to work as a team and do the right thing at the right time is the definition of teamwork. If you have the right team, then work runs smoothly, even in the midst of change or uncertainty. When you have the wrong team, work (and results) can be pretty miserable.

Organizations are just groups of smaller teams all pulled into one big team, so when changing a team and changing an organization, the same principles apply but on a different scale. Some of the changes are minor adjustments, but some changes systematically change how work is done and who does it. In this chapter we focus on those meaningful, sizeable changes to teams within your organization. Teams, regardless of their size or scope, operate most efficiently when the best people have the resources to get the job done.

In this chapter you find out when team change is needed. You also dive into the importance of a well-functioning team and consider the wide array of teams within organizations. You then look into how to improve team effectiveness, both during and after change, and specific issues related to team leadership and team dynamics. Then we help you create and enable teams to lead their own change in the future.

Understanding the Importance of Teamwork

You've heard that two is better than one; a cord of three can't be broken; there's no "I" in "team." A team working together well is a beautiful thing. Here are a few of the best aspects of teamwork:

✔ **Teams accomplish more than individuals.** We're sure that someone reading this is rolling their eyes right now and saying, "I can do so much more when I don't have to work with others." But although an individual may be able to get a lot of work done, it is quite unrealistic to expect a single person to know enough and have enough time to get *everything* done. Teams can help get work done more quickly and meet cross-functional challenges.

Some research suggests that introverts, who are able to give a lot when working individually, do not contribute as much when forced to work in team environments all the time. Make sure introverts are provided an opportunity to contribute in other ways. An organization must recognize personality differences to be successful.

✔ **Teamwork helps to retain the best people.** Effective teams do more than just get the work done. Think about a time in your career when you were incredibly energized to come to work in the morning and felt you were really delivering results. You were probably surrounded by some high-performing people you could rely on to help get the job done. Teams, when working well, have the ability to engage some of your brightest stars.

✔ **Teams contribute to the whole organization's success.** A team can only be fully understood in terms of its relation to the other parts of the organization. The interrelatedness of teams is important because it contributes to the overall functioning of the organization. Think of the change team like a baseball team: You may have a great pitcher and catcher on the field, but if the first baseman doesn't know what's going on, the team will not be wining any World Series titles anytime soon. During business change, you may have a great leader in one part of the organization, but if he or she has no technical or functional support, the change may not be successful. Teamwork across teams sets up the whole organization to win.

We use the word *team* throughout this section, but remember that an organization is just a bigger team often made up of smaller teams. So the meaningful change can be driven from the organizational level or project, process, or department level. A team is a team, no matter how big or small.

Checking Out Types of Teams

In practically every organization, a variety of tasks are best tackled by working together in groups or teams. The type of challenge varies, and so does the type of team best suited to it, drawing from a range of informal and formal types of teams for all different circumstances. In this section we check out what types of teams you may see out there in world (or at least in your workplace) and their purposes.

For an in-depth dive into every type of team you may encounter, check out *Managing Teams For Dummies,* by Marty Brounstein (Wiley).

Project teams

Project teams are temporary, have a special focus, and often have both core and secondary members. Core members contribute throughout the project to get the job done. They are the ones with their names next to various deliverables or tasks on the project plan. Although not always the case, on bigger projects, the project is the core team member's full-time (or close to full-time) job. On the other hand, a number of secondary or resource team members come and go throughout the project. They may have a specialty in one area and help the core team and then go back to their day-to-day job. Following are some examples of project teams:

- ✔ Change teams
- ✔ Problem-solving teams
- ✔ Process-improvement teams
- ✔ Product-development teams

Some types of project teams are temporary. The members come together for a specific project (the change) and then go back to their normal jobs after the change is implemented and is part of the new way of doing business.

Organizational work teams

Organizational work teams are long-lasting, and they're often the teams you see on organizational charts. Organizational teams can either be functional or cross-functional and co-located or virtual (more on virtual teams in a minute). Organizational work teams are often the ones that benefit most from meaningful change because they'll be around long enough to reap many of the long-term benefits (but project teams can benefit from all the tools of change, too).

Work teams come in a variety of structures, but the two most common are traditional work teams and self-directed work teams. The most *traditional* work team is one in which every individual has her own job, one person is the leader of the team, and the team is focused on completing a bigger goal through individual work. Sometimes managers direct the specific work, others delegate decision making but maintain responsibility for the final decision, and still others do a little of both.

Self-directed teams also work towards completing a bigger goal for the organization, but the management responsibilities tend to be shared within the group. One team member may work with budgets, another with performance management, and another with scheduling work. Although moving to self-directed teams can take a good amount of effort and learning, employees often have higher satisfaction with their work and commitment to the organization because they have more responsibility.

The types of work teams don't stop there. We don't claim to know every type of team out there, but following are a few others that are popular out in Corporate America and are worth mentioning:

- ✔ **Agile work teams:** Popular after their success in the software-development field, agile teams are self-directed teams that look something like an accordion. The come together nearly every morning for 10 to 15 minutes, discuss issues, ideas, and needs, and then go out to conquer their work. This cycle is repeated once or twice a day.

- ✔ **Kaizen work teams:** Kaizen teams are one type of process-improvement team that continually works together to make "a change for the better" (that's a somewhat Americanized translation from the original Japanese concept). Kaizen teams are often part of a long-lasting organizational work team and come together on a continuous basis to make job and work processes more efficient.

- ✔ **Fantasy football teams:** Okay, just checking to see if you were paying attention. But for the record, fantasy football teams are run by the guy in the cube next to you who spends his Friday morning trading players for free agents instead of working on the project you asked him to complete.

Recognizing the Need for Team Change

Some teams are so broken that you know the team needs to change in order for the business to survive and grow. Maybe you know that something is wrong with the team or organizational structure but you aren't exactly sure what's wrong or how to fix it. Your role is to diagnose what is not working (and what is) so you can recognize what you need to repair.

If you diagnose the real reason for team change, it will cost you a whole lot less in the end. Think about recognizing the need for team and organizational change like a doctor diagnosing what is wrong with you if you don't feel well. The doctor will probably ask you what is bothering you and then with some tests and some questions will begin diagnosing and treating your specific health concern. A good doctor would never start running multiple tests and treating an ear infection if you came in and said your knee hurt. This would be a waste of time and resources. If you have a specific ailment, the doctor does not treat the entire body, but rather diagnoses the specific issue and treats that issue. The same is true in organization change: Find out what the specific problem is and change that problem.

In order to recognize whether or not your team needs to change, diagnose how well your team is performing against the four dynamics of team development:

- Strategy
- Capability
- Development and building
- Motivating

First and foremost, the strategy for the change needs to be in place. After the strategy is set, then you can determine if the team has the capabilities and skills to get the job done. If the team has these skills, move straight ahead to defining the new performance expected of the team and get moving with the change. If not, identify ways to help build or acquire the skills. You can't do one before the other, so make sure the elements of team performance are in place before rushing ahead to the next step. Figure 12-1 outlines these and their core components.

Babe Ruth once said, "The way a team plays as a whole determines its success. You may have the greatest bunch of individual stars in the world, but if they don't play together, the club won't be worth a dime." The four dynamics of team development determine how your team plays as a whole. If your team or organization is not hitting it out of the park in any of these four dynamics of team development, the time has come to consider making meaningful change.

Teams are everywhere. Some teams are focused on survival or the maintenance of the existing order, while other teams are more dynamic and focus on change and improvement. Regardless of the type of team you are working with, the four dynamics of team development need to be part of the day-to-day activities and strategic team goals in order for the team to be effective.

Virtual teams

Because many organizations are moving toward more virtual work teams, a group of individuals may work together (either on a project or on an organizational work team) but either not go into the office every day or work in different locations. Because these virtual teams don't have many face-to-face interactions, creating meaningful change through the four key dynamics we discuss earlier in this chapter (strategy, capability, development and building, and motivating) can do tremendous good toward improving how the team works. When teams operate across time zones, geography, and organizational units, having shared goals, a place for shared knowledge, and strong leadership helps build trust and mutual respect — something that's harder to do on the phone or through e-mail than when simply spending time together face-to-face.

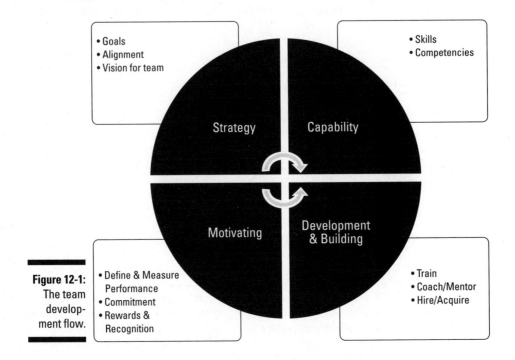

Figure 12-1: The team development flow.

- Goals
- Alignment
- Vision for team

Strategy

- Skills
- Competencies

Capability

- Define & Measure Performance
- Commitment
- Rewards & Recognition

Motivating

- Train
- Coach/Mentor
- Hire/Acquire

Development & Building

Working together with strategy

When looking at whether or not meaningful change is needed, you should ask two questions: Does the team have a clear purpose and direction? Does the team work together? Having a clear team *vision and goal* is not just something fancy that first-year MBAs like to talk about; it really does set the direction for the team. Each team, whether project based or long term, should have a clear goal and vision that directs the work. (If you don't have one, refer back to Chapter 4 for how to build one for your team.) Everyone has seen many teams fail, but the failure usually isn't caused by the people but by the direction of the team. If the people know what to do, who is doing it, and how they will be measured for the team's success, the team will usually operate extremely well. A great team strategy means having a clear purpose and direction aligned to each person's work.

A team that works together is able to leverage everyone's strengths. If the members of a change team do not trust one another or if mutual respect is absent, meaningful change can be hard to accomplish. On the other hand, when people operate as a team, almost anything is possible. The two most important skill sets for team members are conflict resolution and facilitation. When a team can work together to solve conflict and facilitate ideas, rather than shut them down, the change team will be off to a running start.

A bunch of superstars do not make a great team. Having a team goal and vision is great, but they need to be aligned to each person's day-to-day job, and the team needs to agree to work together. If stakeholder groups or team members are not working together (commonly referred to as *working in silos*), even if they are on different teams, the organization may need to undertake meaningful change to overcome teams being too detached from the bigger picture of the organization.

Organizations are big teams. Whether you are making meaningful change at the team level or at the organizational level, you will still be working with teams of people focused on a common goal.

Checking out capability

Do you have capable people on the team? The capability of a team must reflect both the competencies and skills the team needs to grow. Without sounding too "HR," *skills* are things someone can learn (writing code, using a spreadsheet, or building a machine). *Competencies* are a little fluffier and often refer to whether or not someone can effectively apply these skills. Someone can go to a training class to learn the skill of singing, but he may never have the capability to be a soloist at the Sydney Opera House. Don't get too caught up on skills versus competencies (and don't get us started talking about attitude), but just know that capability is a mix of someone knowing how to do a certain task and having the abilities to do it. And if the people on your team do not have the capability to do the work, you may need to make meaningful change.

Capability is very important, but it isn't the *only* important aspect of a team and team performance. Yes, you need competent people who can do work, but even the star players can't be successful without good communication within the organization. Star players may be able to do a lot of work, but they can't do it all. Capability only goes so far, and you can do many things as a leader to develop, assess, and improve the capability of the team.

Don't confuse capability and resources. Many companies are doing more work with fewer resources, but to make change happen, resources have to be devoted to the change. Without adequate staffing to make change happen, there will be frustration on the team and a high potential for employee burnout. To determine the right staffing levels needed for the change project, fine tune your project plan and resourcing needs with the help of Chapter 5.

Assessing development and building

Successful teams are always looking for better ways of doing things and stretching themselves to make improvements for their customers and the organization. *Training* is one aspect of development but not the only one. If a team has a culture of improvement, then training is a medium to get to a goal, not the end-all solution. Sometimes the need for team change happens not because something is wrong or broken but rather because the team is just not moving forward.

Besides training in relevant areas, teams can make meaningful improvements by *mentoring and coaching* one another or hiring and acquiring knowledge. But don't stop there: Effective teams build knowledge and pool it together by working with one another on a continuous basis. If just one person has all the information on how to complete a process within your team, you probably have a good indication that the team isn't functioning as efficiently as it could. Although team members should have their own roles, highly functional and sustainable teams have the ability to draw on others' knowledge easily and efficiently. One of the benefits of great teams is a pool of collective knowledge that drives a team forward.

If you look at the team and realize some critical skills are missing, it may be time to *hire or acquire* other team members to help make meaningful change. This solution is not always easy, but if a skill can't be taught, or if a team member has a skill but isn't capable of applying it after he's been coached and mentored and trained, then hiring in new talent may be the best option.

Motivating

Teams must be motivated in order to work well within the organization. If teams are giving lackluster performance, stop and evaluate what kind of stimulation and incentives they're getting for their work.

Motivating employees is not just about being a cheerleader or paying them more. Meaningful teamwork can happen when motivation in the workplace includes defining measurements and performance, gaining commitment, and having the right rewards and recognition.

1. **Defining measures and performance:** This first step ties straight back to the vision and alignment of the team. Letting the team know what is expected of it and how it will be measured helps elevate an average team to an extraordinary one. Although the team may have a great goal, when it comes down to motivating individuals on a team, what is specifically expected of the individual has to be clearly defined and then tracked, just like you may do for a bigger project or team goal.

2. **Gaining commitment:** Two tangible ways of getting meaningful change on a team through commitment is to make sure the work is distributed evenly and communication is free flowing (you didn't think we would let a chapter go without talking about communication, did you?).

   • **Distributing work:** Leaders often make the mistakes of wanting to do everything on their own (because they believe that delegating work takes too much effort and time) and spending more time doing the work than being an advisor and leader to the team. These tendencies do not gain commitment. Ownership of change happens when people do the work, so no matter how much time it may seem to take to delegate the work, it will be worth it in the end. If you think you are spending too much time doing and not enough time delegating and distributing the work, think about making meaningful team changes.

   • **Communicating:** Commitment also comes when communication flows with ease. If communication within a team isn't smooth, look at how the organization is structured and where the barriers to effective communication lie.

3. **Rewarding and recognizing teams for what they do:** In Chapter 8 we discuss the importance of motivating employees during change, but sometimes the rewards need to change in order to make a team more effective.

By aligning rewards to desired behaviors, the team members want to work toward the common goal of the team and organization. Don't forget that different employees prefer to be rewarded based on different needs (getting back to the WIIFM we discussed in Chapter 7). Some employees are motivated by money, others by flexible work schedules, and still others by promotions and recognition in the company.

Changing Teams for the Better

Even if you're thinking that all four of the areas of team and organization effectiveness (see the preceding sections) are in need of a tune-up, you want to focus on the one or two areas of most importance first. Trying to change everything at once can work (and we talk about changing everything at once in Chapter 17), but most of the four dynamics of team development are closely related to one another, so if you change one or two, the others most likely will follow suit.

The same principles for leading business change apply to leading team change: Be specific about what you want to change and have a clear vision of what the team should look like at the end of the change.

In this section, we introduce you to the tools and techniques to help you make meaningful change on the team level. The change methods we cover include team charters, the three Cs of team change, and leadership and individual skills needed to make meaningful change.

Developing clear team charters

A team charter designates the expected results, measurement methods, vision, and resources the team has to accomplish its goals. Just like a change charter (see Chapter 4), a team charter is simply a document used to track these areas in a common place. Although most project teams have charters (or at least most high-performing project teams have them), often organizational work teams don't think to create one even though an organizational work team probably has a greater need to make sure everyone continues to stay on track in the long term. A team charter for a long-standing work team can be a source of knowledge for new members on the team and a reference guide to make sure team members are always aligned to the bigger team goal. Here are a few things a charter can include:

✔ **Who are the team's customers, and what problems do they face?** Why does this team exist? Every team has a customer and a problem they are addressing, even if that customer is an internal one (bosses, executive leaders). Think about the pain the team is training to solve or the innovation the team is training to achieve.

✔ **What are the team's goals, and how does the team define the specific deliverables they are continually working toward?** This explanation doesn't have to be a lengthy report, just a concise description of what the team does. Describe these goals using the SMART methodology for goal setting (specific, measurable, action oriented and agreed on, realistic, and time bound).

✔ **Who is on the project team, and what are the roles on the team?** You don't need anything fancy here. A listing of who does what is a great central repository to share with people who work with the team.

✔ **How will the team work together to solve problems?** Teams sometimes can incorrectly assume that conflict is bad and they have to reinvent the wheel whenever a problem crops up. Instead, ask the team to decide how problems should be solved (which may include having a senior manager help resolve conflict or coming together for input as a team, making a decision, and then going out and getting the work done). This area is also a great place to write down how and when brainstorming may occur on the team for new goals or ideas, and how and when the team will meet to share information and concerns on a regular basis. For more on how the team will work together, check out the discussion of the GRPI model in Chapter 5. For a team charter, check out Chapter 4.

When team members and other change agents are moving in and out of change initiatives and projects, or when disagreements crop up about how a change should proceed, a charter can get everyone focused on what was originally agreed on when the team came together. By eliminating confusion when times get tough or conflict arises, a charter can be a powerful tool for a productive team.

Taking steps toward a productive team

Some team members may intuitively recognize their role on the team and have been on enough teams to know that teams evolve and find their groove over time. Others may be shocked to know that a team doesn't function perfectly and collaborate with ease on day one. What many people tend to forget is that even if a team has been around for a long time, making the move from working in silos or without a clear strategy to having a perfectly functional team can be hard. Great teams collaborate, but you can't command collaboration — it takes time. Here are three tips for making your team (or organization) more productive during change:

✔ **Let team members get to know one another first.** When the team or organization has a new strategy, new expectations, or new members, allow time to let individuals process the changes without expecting everyone to jump in with both feet. Team members need to get their feet wet with meaningful change.

During this time, a team leader can reach out to individual team members and listen openly to their concerns. Team leaders may also want to work in smaller groups to help team players work out issues they may be facing as the team evolves.

✔ **Let some conflict happen.** When conflict arises, a change leader may feel the need to step in and solve it in order to keep the change on track. The team may even argue with the team leader when emotions are high. Now is not the time to get defensive; instead, be a positive force for change. By keeping the overall goal in mind and allowing teams to collaborate and discuss issues without being pressured, you create solid ground for future success. During conflict, some team members may want to go back to the old way of doing things because they perceive it as easier. Others may not want to collaborate at all because they realize things will be different and change can be scary. A strong facilitator can help break through these conflicts and emotions (check out Chapter 8 for more on resolving conflict). Keep in mind all the tips, principles, and tools you have gained about how to lead business change to work through this part of the new team creation.

✔ **Encourage skill building through mentoring and trust.** Although many changes have some element of training, when teams are working together, classroom training is not what makes the biggest impact. Instead, mentor people about how they can develop skills by working with one another. This may include best-practice sharing between team members, partnering individuals with different skill sets to coach one another, or job shadowing to allow team members to have hands-on experience with a different skill. Working together builds trust, a fundamental building block for lasting change.

If your team has been around for a while, don't expect trust and cohesion to be built immediately when a new strategy, skill, or motivational tool is introduced. The team may have to work through conflict and get to know one another again to start performing at the expected level necessary for the change.

Aligning teams to the three Cs

Teams don't operate in a vacuum; they operate within a bigger organization or are part of a larger environment. Successful teams not only achieve the goals of the team but also continually make sure the goals are meaningful to the bigger picture of the organization. Making changes on a team can come from aligning teams to the three Cs: focusing on the *content* of what needs to be accomplished, the *context* of why objectives need to be accomplished (how the goal is accomplished in relation to the social or organizational cir-cumstances), and the *community* that will be impacted by the purpose and mission of the team (how the goal impacts other stakeholders).

✔ **Content:** *Content* refers to what's going to be accomplished at a tangible level. It addresses the alignment of specific activities, problems, or solu-tions that need to be accomplished, and it's one of the easiest places to make meaningful change on teams. The content may be the implementa-tion of a new technology system, creating a new product line, or devel-oping a new training program.

✔ **Context:** The *context* of the team change can be impacted by social, organizational, and technological environment considerations that can enable or inhibit the team from accomplishing its goals. Context may include economic conditions that are encouraging team change, poli-cies or procedures the organization has asked for that are driving team change, or changing technology demands from customers (for example, all customers are expecting an application from your company for their smartphones). Context can often be related to why the team needs to make meaningful change.

✔ **Community:** *Community* can be any group impacted by the team's goals, from customers to other teams with competing or complementing goals. This part of making meaningful team and organizational change is all about who the change will impact. While customer-service representa-tives and salespeople are in close contact with clients on a daily basis, not everyone within an organizational team has the opportunity to work closely with customers. A good way to align with the community is to give other teams within the organization an opportunity to talk with cus-tomers. Some organizations hold quarterly customer-advocate sessions in which employees across different teams get to hear the compliments and concerns from customers. Other organizations let change team members do job shadowing with client-facing positions so they can see and hear how the changes will impact their customers.

By aligning (or realigning) your team to these three Cs, goals can become clearer and give everyone in the organization a better understanding of the team's purpose.

Being a leader who inspires team change

Leaders have many responsibilities during change. They help to set the vision, remove barriers and obstacles, and make people and human resources dedicated to making the change happen. Another change-leader responsibility is to inspire teams during the entire process. Yes, some work will be done individually, but even individual work is part of the bigger team goal. Whether leadership is distributed among many members or concen-trated in one person, teams and organizations make the most meaningful change when leaders face concerns and issues head on during team change. Here are six ways a leader can inspire team change:

✔ **Develop a habit of self-awareness.** Many leaders joke by saying that their weakness is being a perfectionist, but this "weakness" is just plain weak. If a leader didn't want to deliver a perfect product or service, she probably wouldn't have a job. But overconfidence on the way to perfection really can be a weakness. A leader's confidence can sometimes be seen by others as crudeness and may alienate the very people they need on their team. Fast-paced leaders may see themselves as goal oriented, but if they don't slow down and ask "what if" (even if it doesn't come naturally), they may miss possible negative implications down the road.

✔ **Be a role model for balancing short-term wins with long-term goals.** Winning new clients, successfully completing a project, or simply getting praise for a job well done raises your confidence and team spirit. But don't allow yourself to get so caught up in the details of change that you forget to look at the future. As a leader, remember to keep your eye on the bigger picture, both in the organization and professionally. Where do you want to be in three years? What job do you have, and what have you accomplished? If the answer is "I don't know" or "I don't have time to think about that," you can't fairly expect anything to happen differently.

If you want to accomplish something, the first step is envisioning yourself there, and the second step is identifying what needs to change to get you there. Being a role model is often referred to as leading by example. And don't forget to lead by example through your values and principles. Individuals and teams are inspired by ethical leaders, not dishonest ones.

✔ **Delegate, delegate, delegate (and then repeat).** What, delegating can be inspiring? Yes, if done correctly it can inspire others to take on leadership roles during the change. Continually being overwhelmed with unfinished items does not make a good leader. But don't just hand over projects you have no interest in completing. Identify employees with a desire to be part of the change and ask them to cover a specific area or topic. This gives the employee the opportunity to own parts of the change and be rewarded for their involvement.

Although it may seem like too much of an investment to spend time getting other people up to speed on how to do things, after they're trained, your day is left wide open to spend on things you want to focus on. We often hear that delegation and asking others to do something takes much more time than doing it yourself. Yes, maybe initially. But if someone is competent and committed, he usually picks up things rather quickly. If delegation is done properly, you free up time to do the next inspiring act for leaders.

✔ **Be clear on what problem you are solving and do it really well.**
Leaders solve problems. Whether you are a small-business owner
or a CEO of a large corporation, solving problems is what keeps you
employed. The easy answer is "Well, I solve everything." But very few
leaders can do everything perfectly well. In ten words or less, write
down the problems you solve. For example, do you help people with
money or career issues? Are you focused on making your clients health-
ier? This clarity helps to keep teams focused on the bigger picture, even
in the mist of change.

✔ **Be humble and adaptable.** One of the biggest reasons for failure in
companies with huge potential is the inability of a leader to know when
the time has come to step down from leading the day-to-day operations
and let someone else guide the organization to success. A leader may
be great at creating and launching a successful product or service, but
another leader may be the best to make the team (or company) grow
and innovate in the future. Inspiring leaders are also adaptable. They
recognize when Plan A isn't working, learn from what happened, and
make significant corrections or move on to Plan B. Sharing success with
peers and employees, admitting failures, and adapting when needed are
all ways humble leaders inspire others to do the same.

✔ **Be ethical.** It should go without saying that being honest, trustworthy,
and genuine are important leadership traits to inspire lasting change.
Being respectful of others' opinions during change, especially when
there are conflicting opinions, goes a long way in inspiring an organization or team to do the same. A strong work ethic during change is important too. Successful companies don't "just happen" to people. Landing
clients doesn't just happen. You have to get up, work hard, and then see
the rewards of your labor.

Summing Up Traits of an A-Team

A team is greater than the sum of its parts. When all the team members come
together, their skills and capabilities work together and multiply what can
be accomplished as a whole. After all, a championship sports team isn't just
a bunch of superstar players doing their own thing; the group has to play
together to be champions. However, when making meaningful change by creating an A-Team, individuals can positively (or negatively) impact the team
dynamics and ultimate success in a number of ways.

Many superstar athletes just don't play well with others. In the workplace,
for meaningful change to happen, a team needs to be ready to come to the
table with all the traits that make up a successful team. Here's our A-Team
A-trait list:

✔ **Awareness:** The first step to being part of a team is to be aware of your team style, how you communicate, and how others see you. Awareness can come through 360-degree feedback or assessment tests like DiSC, Thomas Kilmann Conflict Mode Assessment, and Myers-Briggs. These assessments are not meant to just give you a score and color code your work style; they're meant to provide insight into how an individual operates and how others see your behaviors. Knowing this can be the baseline for altering a team member's style to improve team dynamics.

✔ **Adaption:** You already know that people are different. Team members can learn through practice and training how to adapt personal styles to make the team operate more effectively and efficiently.

Another piece of the adaption puzzle that doesn't come from a training classroom is having a forum to openly discuss issues and concerns and for team members to provide and receive constructive feedback. Great team players are open to seeing others' opinions and adapting their own way of doing work if others' opinions and ideas are the better answers.

✔ **Attitude:** Urgency, passion, and attitude are part of team effectiveness, and they all boil down to having individuals see themselves as team players not just team members. Team players are actively engaged in problem solving, creative thinking, and innovation.

✔ **Accountability and accomplishment:** Having clear, objective performance expectations and clarity about what each individual is responsible for helps all the A-Team members know how their roles fit with others and how the team will accomplish its goals.

✔ **Action:** Having a personal action plan tied to what is expected is equivalent to watering a seed and giving it sunlight in order grow something. Wishing, wanting, and dreaming are essential parts of being wildly successful. But if team players don't do something, nothing will happen. Olympic runner Bernard Lagat could wish on every star to run faster in his next race, but without stepping on a track or putting on running shoes, it's not going to happen. A-Team players create an action plan and stick to it to get things done.

Enabling Teams to Address Organizational Change

When a team is enabled to address organizational change, it is like hitting the jackpot. A team that can drive change on its own is a place where customers, team players, co-workers, leaders, and information come together. Throw in quality, customer satisfaction, employee morale, and efficiency, and you have a team that can do anything it sets its collective mind to.

If you take all the traits of leadership that inspired others and all the positive work traits of an A-Team, combined with the right content, context, and community, you have a group of team players that continually are learning how to become more capable professionals and how to keep improving the work outcome over time.

But of course these things do not happen overnight, and, in addition to pulling together an A-Team and having inspired leadership, enabled teams have the following characteristics:

- ✔ **Team players regard each other as peers and professionals.** Trust and respect for one another can't be created in a rope-building course or training room; they develop when team players and leadership do what they say they are going to do and support one another in the process.

- ✔ **They are empowered to make changes.** We would like to think this one is obvious, but if leaders don't provide teams the space to change and the authority to change, no amount of inspiration or volume of action plans can create an enabled team. Teams must be given the permission and expectation to change and improve the way business is done in order for change to happen. Leaders can explicitly tell teams they are responsible for making changes and have the authority to do so.

- ✔ **They have time set aside to change.** Look around and you'll see that almost everyone is busy. Many people are busy, active, perhaps frantically trying to do more, be more, see more. Enabling teams to think strategically about what needs to get done and balancing short-term success with long-lasting change takes skills and time, but in the end, team members get a sense of calm that's needed to make lasting change, not just change in the face of chaos and panic. Change leaders and team leaders can set aside time for thinking and strategically changing and can reward this new behavior.

One enabling team philosophy is to set aside an hour a week (yes, an entire hour) to brainstorm new ideas to problems. If teams don't have time to think and innovate, they don't have time to change.

- ✔ **They work in a collaborative environment supported by leadership.** Collaboration, change, and empowerment cannot be mandated by senior management and expected to last in the long term. Senior leaders can provide a platform for discussion and ideas, and they can ask what is happening and if the organization is getting the results desired, rather than simply chase after the next greatest invention. Opening the floor to questions and encouraging discussion instead of just results pays off in the long term when employees have opportunities to guide qualities in the workplace they may otherwise not be able to impact.

Chapter 13

Leveraging Restructuring Changes

· ·

In This Chapter

▶ Evaluating the pros and cons of restructuring

▶ Making changes in staffing

▶ Letting the human resources department handle tricky areas

▶ Getting an overview of how restructuring happens

▶ Remembering to always communicate

· ·

*I*n this chapter we talk about the "R" word: restructuring. Few words in corporate-speak can compare to this baffling word, which means to change the way an organization looks and operates. In some executives' minds, restructuring is the solution to all evils in the world and the only thing that is holding them back from making huge profits. We're here to tell you the truth about restructuring — the good, the bad, and the ugly.

In this chapter we explore the benefits and drawbacks of restructuring and give you a bird's eye view into what employees and managers may be thinking and feeling during the restructuring. We then walk through staffing concerns and our recommendations regarding when to involve the human resources (HR) department. Finally, we map out the restructuring process and explore communication issues (and answers) you may face along the way. So before anyone in your organization starts deciding who is dotted-lined and solid-lined to new boxes on a piece of paper, jump in and get an understanding of restructuring from A to Z.

Weighing the Benefits and Drawbacks of Organizational Restructuring

If you have been in an organization long enough, you probably have been through some form of restructuring (or downsizing, rightsizing, or just plain old lay-offs). The problem with all these organizational changes is that just moving people around rarely solves the real issue. A 2005 study conducted by the Oxford School of Business and CIPD (Chartered Institute of Personnel and Development) found that only a third of restructuring initiatives in major companies achieve their productivity and change objectives. You have better odds in Las Vegas! Want more reasons to question the traditional approach to restructuring? Forty percent of the initiatives were over their budget, and 60 percent were not on schedule. With these findings, restructuring, rightsizing, and downsizing seem like pretty uncertain approaches to change.

We are not going as far as saying that reorganization is a risky task, but we do say that the benefits and drawbacks must be weighed very carefully and other change options should be explored before the organizational charts are haphazardly thrown together.

First, take a look at the benefits of restructuring:

- **Creating a more flexible organization:** In today's global marketplace, having a number of approval and management tiers in an organization is a strong indicator that innovation and progress will move slowly. Restructuring a highly hierarchical organization (many management layers) into a more horizontal organization (fewer management layers) can help to physically and mentally break down barriers that prevent rapid innovation and sharing of ideas.

- **Focusing on what the company does best (and makes money from):** Many organizations have outsourced something that is not their core competency — whether that's benefits administration, information technology support, or functions like billing and travel. Restructuring departments, if done correctly, can free up company resources and brain power to focus on core competencies, or whatever else makes them most competitive in the marketplace. Although outsourcing these services may save some money in the long run, the first goal of outsourcing should be to allow your best and brightest employees to focus their skills and capabilities on profitable growth and competitiveness.

- **Complying with new government regulations:** As companies expand their markets, some restructuring may be necessary to be in compliance with various government regulations and international trade and taxation requirements. For example, some countries require foreign companies to have specific legal structures when doing business in them. We are not legal, taxation, or international business experts, so if this is a hot topic in your area and a key reason for your business change, we recommend speaking with an international tax or financial expert first.

When considering restructuring within the organization, you want to weigh the opportunities against the risk, so we now turn our focus to some of the downsides of restructuring to give the whole picture of what you can expect when an organizational chart starts moving. Here are some of the downsides of restructuring:

✓ **Off-the-shelf organizational models rarely work.** Inevitably, when a company is in the news with all the wonderful results it achieved after moving one department from the next, some other CEO reads this and says, "We should do that, too!" They say that imitation is the best form of flattery, but trying to copy another company's or consulting firm's process does not take into account the nuances, strengths, and differences of your own company. A big downside to mimicking others' structures is that people get tired of changing for the sake of change or trying another approach without a clear reason.

✓ **Large-scale restructuring is often out of date by the time it's implemented.** With products, services, and customers changing at the speed of light, by the time a company undergoes a significant structure change, it may already need to change again to meet new demands. This problem can be avoided by creating dynamic teams that can change quickly without changing reporting structures. Agile teams that have talented players with the capability to change to meet new company goals or product demands always win against functional teams that change based on who signs off on their expense account. Think of an agile team like a basketball team: Five players are always on the court, and they play defense and offense, depending on who has the ball.

✓ **Moving pieces masks the real issues.** We have heard CEOs say they want to restructure because a particular department is not performing at its best, or because a leader is complaining that he doesn't have the right people on his team. These complaints are valid, but shuffling people and teams around just means the problem is relocated, not solved. You're better off focusing on developing new capabilities to handle significant challenges than on pawning off problems on someone down the hall.

With these benefits and downsides laid out, you are better able to make an informed decision regarding whether or not restructuring is right for you and your company. If restructuring seems like it could be the solution, read on to find out how to mitigate any concerns and make your new team structure a powerhouse capable of fielding any issues, concerns, and opportunities that may come your way.

Looking at restructuring from an employee's point of view

Say *restructuring* and a number of thoughts can come to mind for employees, ranging from comic-strip satire to the possibility of being "restructured" out of a job. As with all change, these emotions and thoughts are valid and expected and should be addressed quickly and honestly to replace the rumor mill with facts about what employees will really see on the horizon. Every restructuring change is different, so employees' points of view vary, but in this section we discuss the most common concerns during organizational structure changes and what you can do about them. Although some changes are mainly greeted with negative concerns, you will also have some employees thrilled with the change. So we include a few of the more optimistic reactions you may see as well, because we hate being downers!

Restructuring changes are often the most difficult for employees because they physically see a change (people moving to another department or being laid off). To add to the complexity, most restructurings are initiated by financial savings or larger corporate goals. Remember to tie corporate goals to the employee WIIFM. For example, instead of focusing on the cost savings from de-layering the organization, let employees know they'll have greater opportunities to learn new skills and more chances to interact and gain recognition from senior staff.

Centralizing or outsourcing administrative/support functions

A possible business change involves centralizing or outsourcing administrative or support functions such as payroll, employee-benefits administration, information technology, or security. Centralizing is commonly done to gain economies of scale and efficiencies by standardizing processes. Outsourcing particular functions to another company that specializes in those services can create performance improvement and cost savings if implemented correctly, but most importantly, it allows your employees to focus on your core competencies.

Here are some views about these restructuring changes that your employees may hold:

- **Possible (positive) point of view:** We'll have more robust and efficient support structures.

  Some employees will be thrilled to break free from the old way of things and gain better support in doing their day-to-day jobs. This emotion is often seen when the current support system is not proficient (or is nonexistent) and a dedicated group of individuals will be serving administrative functions (like benefits and help-desk calls), allowing employees to focus more on what they love to do.

  What can you do? You can leverage these positive perspectives by having employees talk about the benefits and how their work life will be improved after the change.

- **Possible (negative) point of view:** You are taking away my support structure!

  The downside of making support structures centralized or outsourced is that some employees feel they are losing the one-on-one relationship with their administrative support person. The employees' point of view is that the loss of administrative staff who knows them individually means the employees may have to do more work on their own.

What can you do? Validate the concern by acknowledging it in using both formal and informal communications. Administrative staff may have been able to identify a potential problem and rectify it before it happened, but as companies grow, this individual knowledge of the employee's preferences may not be realistic, and in some cases may be able to be solved with technology solutions. The employee's concerns in this case may be addressed by showing how the new system will be able to prevent many problems through more robust processes. Outlining the new communication process with the new centralized or outsourced support department may also ease anxiety over the loss of personalized connections.

Don't forget that one of the points of view may also come from the support group that is changing. When administrative staff is more centralized, those employees gain a greater chance for their own mobility for professional development and a larger opportunity to share resources and build a cohesive team. Check out Chapter 12 for more ideas on how to drive team change.

Moving smaller teams into larger ones or combining cross-functional teams

Business that are experiencing market consolidation or a decrease in demand may decide to combine teams in order to leverage fewer resources or to incorporate smaller teams into larger ones to increase management span of control (how many people and teams a leader manages), requiring fewer managers.

- ✔ **Possible (positive) point of view:** A larger team will allow me to learn more from my new teammates.

  Having new teammates always provides an opportunity for expanded relationships and learning.

  What can you do? To affirm this positive point of view, we recommend that you talk to people on the new team about what everyone will be able to bring to the table as part of the new larger team.

- ✔ **Possible (negative) point of view:** We have always done it our own way, now we have to follow someone else's rules.

  When restructuring includes moving a self-directed, smaller group into a larger team, fears are usually based on having to learn new work practices and losing flexibility and autonomy.

  What can you do? The best way to address this concern is to acknowledge the loss of the autonomy but reinforce the WIIFM (what's in it for me? — see Chapter 7). One WIIFM may be that restructuring with the new procedures and policies will help the company save money, which means the company will have more money to invest in their employees. Another way of stating this WIIFM: We'll have efficiency savings, which means we're less likely to have to make cutbacks in other areas of the company.

✔ **Possible (negative) point of view:** My title/location/office is changing to something worse!

If an employee doesn't like change, the possibility of relocation, office moves, changed roles, or new job descriptions/titles is not going to be met with open arms and a ticker-tape parade.

What can you do? Show genuine interest in them as people, not just names on a chart. Do your best to understand your employees' concerns, needs, and goals. Broadcasting organizational goals is easy, but it takes listening and patience to get to the heart of employees' goals and needs, which are what you need to understand in order to show how the change will benefit everyone. This information also may enable you to meet employee requests with little investment.

✔ **Possible (negative) point of view:** I am not sure if I have the skills needed in the new organization.

Restructuring the group may seem fairly straightforward, but don't forget to consider what expertise is needed to reach the new goals and priorities and their downstream impact. Even if departments are being combined for administrative positions, and you believe the work will remain fundamentally the same, employees may need to (or feel the need to) increase their skills.

What can you do? Providing training opportunities to help improve skill sets will go far in alleviating anxiety associated with job and department changes.

Taking away management layers (Making the organization flatter)

Eliminating layers of management can improve an organization's ability to more quickly make decisions by speeding up communication across the layers. Flatter organizations tend to be more nimble and less bureaucratic.

✔ **Possible (positive) point of view:** This change will put me one step closer to the executive team.

At times, middle-management layers create barriers to open and honest communication. By being closer to the actual decision makers, employees may feel empowered by having their voice more clearly heard by those that can make a difference.

What can you do? You don't need to do much here. Just make sure to continue to listen to employees and emphasize the positive.

✔ **Possible (negative) point of view:** Is my job next?

Changing management structures can be frightening for employees. If a manager is laid off or has her job role changed, employees may wonder if they are next in line to have their job cut.

What can you do? One of the best ways to work with this concern is to focus on the positive: Fewer management layers mean more opportunity to be more nimble and innovative. Build into the restructuring more effective leadership and equitable management processes. Management restructuring may be a great time to introduce a more-objective performance-review system and professional-development plan for employees. (We talk about this restructuring from a manager's point of view in the next section.)

Approaching restructuring from a manager's point of view

Even though managers have fancy titles, they still may have many concerns and views of restructuring that may or may not align to the goals of the organization. In this section we look at a few views managers may have when asked to lead or be part of a different organizational structure.

Combining departments

Although combining departments to address shrinking demand, increase span of control, or enhance collaboration are all good reasons for restructuring, the affected managers may not be so enthusiastic about the change.

✔ **Possible point of view:** I am losing control.

Relinquishing responsibility isn't easy. Loss of financial control and organizational power for managers and departments is seen as one of the greatest problems when departments combine. Although managers have to deal with this concern directly, it's not just a management concern. The rational for merging one department with another is most likely to drive better collaboration, but there may be more pain than synergy in the beginning because everyone loses some flexibility to do what used to seem easy (for example, upgrade equipment or provide on-the-spot incentives).

What can you do? A great way to address this negative point of view is to focus on the new opportunities for development: A larger department often means more diverse projects and a greater ability to try something new. This view is longer term, but if new opportunities can be developed and acted on quickly within the new department, the restructuring will gain valuable credibility.

Taking away management layers (Making the organization flatter)

Flatter organizations generally have better communication and faster decision making due to fewer handoffs between management layers. However, the affected managers have to deal with the loss of employment and stability.

- ✔ **Possible point of view:** I am losing my job.

  Many restructuring efforts focus on making organizations leaner and more streamlined. Unfortunately, this improvement really doesn't motivate someone who is being let go precisely so that the organization can get lean and make lots more money in the future.

  What can you do? If someone is losing his job, the best thing leadership can do is show respect and honor the past work. Even though the change in structure isn't personal, it will feel like it is to the person losing a paycheck. Now is not the time to focus on reasons like "making the organization agile and lean"; it is time to listen to the employee and ask if you can do anything to help with the transition. (We discuss how to work with the human resources department later in the chapter, which is a must when working with layoffs, job changes, and staffing moves.)

- ✔ **Possible point of view:** My job is changing.

  Whether managers are changing job roles or employees are being asked to do something new, switching from a well-understood set of tasks and responsibilities to something new can be frightening.

  What can you do? Having clear definitions and discussions on what is expected in the future will help avoid confusion and frustration at all levels. But outside of clear roles and responsibilities, the best thing leadership can do is to expect the best and not make excuses. This action may seem like tough love, but saying "I know you're ready for this new challenge" conveys a more positive meeting than "We'll try to make this work." Replace *kind of, sort of,* and *we'll try* with *I know, we can,* and *it is possible* and see how a few words can make significant changes in how people work.

Staffing Considerations during Restructuring

Boxes on a chart are easy to move, but people are not so two-dimensional. At the bottom of all reorganization efforts are, you guessed it, people. And because people, pay, and job positions are involved in every restructuring process (we have never seen an organizational change that didn't impact people), the process itself is anything but simple. Most leaders have the wherewithal to consider strategic plans and operational changes when shifting around the structure, but many executives may not realize the depth of the people side of the business. Staff-related concerns you may need to consider during reorganization include adjusting compensation; changing positions, titles, and jobs; creating new positions; and eliminating positions. In the following sections we discuss each issue. First, though, we briefly explore the difference between *staffing changes,* which are simpler changes in number and type of employees, and *restructuring staff changes,* which reflect a larger organizational change.

Staffing adjustments versus restructuring efforts

Before we continue to throw the big R word around, we want to differentiate between restructuring and plain old staffing changes. Restructuring is a big deal and often causes some significant changes in the organization. Teams move, job titles and responsibilities change, clients are often impacted, and the organization looks and feels different when the process is done.

Simple staffing changes, though, are just a regular part of business. Staffing changes may occur when someone is promoted and begins to manage a larger team or has a bigger span of control. Staffing changes may happen when a process is changed and new skills need to be infused throughout the organization.

Large restructuring changes often are out of date with what the market needs before they are even complete. The best way to avoid this problem is to be continually evaluating whether your team and staff need to upgrade skill sets, encouraging shared responsibility, and reviewing performance. A changing marketplace means that employees always need to acquire new skills and expand their job descriptions in order to remain competitive. By making simple staffing changes to meet the ongoing, changing needs of business, larger, more distributive changes may be unnecessary.

Many factors can drive changes in job and team roles and responsibilities that can make major restructuring staffing changes necessary. New market opportunities, changing economic conditions, improved technology, and new policies can all impact responsibilities and job roles and can prompt the decision of whether or not structural organization change is needed. Following are three big triggers that tend to initiate most restructuring efforts:

- ✔ **Acquisitions and mergers:** When two or more companies combine, it often causes job redundancies (a company only needs one CEO). We talk specifically about acquisitions and mergers in Chapter 14.

- ✔ **Significant economic or financial triggers:** Whether the economy has a downturn or an upturn, the change in business operations and the necessary alignment of staff to the new direction of the company often cause restructuring. Some examples may be the introduction of a new product line or a significant increase or decrease in company revenues.

✔ **New technology:** Changes in technology, such as the use of robotics in production and technology applications to do work formerly completed by humans, can dramatically change both the number of people working in an organization and the type of skills needed to run the organization. For example, if a software application is now going to take care of all customer complaints, the company may have a greater need for technology experts and less need for customer-service professionals.

Adjusting compensation (Up or down)

Compensation rewards employees for doing their work effectively. If the work an employee does changes, her compensation may need to change as well. In many restructurings, pay adjustments need to be made so that employees doing the same work don't have significantly different pay levels.

Few people will complain if they get more money, but most organizations run away from the thought of decreasing compensation because of employment agreements, collective-bargaining agreements, or employment law. If your company is considering lowering pay, these valid concerns need to be reviewed by a seasoned HR professional (see "Involving the Human Resources Department" later in this chapter).

Any compensation changes may impact government employment regulations and must be reviewed by the company's HR team. Leave terms like *FLSA* (Fair Labor Standards Act), *exempt/non-exempt,* and *collective-bargaining agreements* to the professionals!

Changing positions, titles, or job descriptions

During a restructuring, the makeup of departments and teams and what they do frequently changes. Therefore, you need to make sure that everyone understands who does what in the new structure. Make sure that job roles, titles, and descriptions are specific and clear. You may need to establish a realistic span of control for managers in the group (how many people and functions a leader manages), reallocate duties and accountabilities among positions or teams, or combine functions within a team. By redefining job responsibilities during a structural change, the change will be more than a reporting relationship change; it will be a change in how the business operates (and that should be the purpose of structural change!).

Even if job descriptions stay the same, now is a great time to review employee duties and goals to make sure they are aligned to the larger mission of the organization.

Adding new positions

Not all restructuring is doom and gloom. (We did say we'd tell you the good, the bad, and the ugly, and here comes the good!) Some restructuring efforts mean that a group needs to add new positions. Start by making sure your mission and vision for the restructuring are clear, just as you would for any organizational change you may undertake. Then, when you craft job descriptions, check back to make sure the position helps meet the goals the new structure is trying to achieve.

Hiring the right employees for the right jobs during a restructuring boosts morale on the team and fulfills your strategic priorities. Although adding positions can be time consuming, if done right it can often take the organization to a new level and infuse skills, talent, and fresh ideas throughout the team.

Shifting reporting relationships

Changing who is reporting to whom is the most common type of activity during restructuring. A company may be moving from a functional model for operations (in which people who do the same type of work all work on the same team) to a more cross-functional work arrangement (a group of people work together on a process or product rather than on a specific function). An example frequently seen during restructuring is separating or integrating support teams from operational teams. Another reason for changing reporting relationships may be to more clearly define accountability at a product, service, or regional level of operation.

As managers take on new employees in the new reporting structure, they should conduct a performance review and goal definition with each new team member. In essence, the managers should act like they are hiring a new employee, even if the employee has been with the company for years.

Eliminating positions (Layoffs)

A *layoff* is the elimination of a position from the organization due to lack of work or a restructuring of job responsibilities. Even just defining the word makes people cringe. No one likes to lose a job, and no one likes to be the one who tells people they are losing their job. Unfortunately, layoffs (which are now often called a *reduction in force* because it sounds nicer) are just a part of business. When team structures change, some work moves somewhere else in the organization or is no longer needed at all. Planning and communicating with the employees being laid off, the remaining staff, and clients who may be impacted have a significant impact on the outcome of the layoff process.

Layoffs are never fun, and few companies know exactly how to do them efficiently and empathetically. Taking the right actions through a structured approach helps alleviate some of the emotion and ensures that all legal requirements are met. If you have to conduct a layoff, here are the key steps you will take:

1. **Planning:** Planning starts with identifying the goals of the layoff (usually cost reduction) and then continues with creating a workforce plan that forecasts staffing needs over the next 12 to 24 months. By setting goals and forecasting needs, you get an exact number of the amount of financial savings the company needs to achieve. At this time you also want to look at alternatives to the layoffs, including executive pay cuts, hiring freezes, voluntary layoffs (when employees choose to leave the company, rather than being forced to leave the company), and transferring individuals to other departments in the company that may be growing.

2. **Assessing what worked in the past:** If the company has gone through layoffs in the past, evaluate what worked and what didn't work. Use this information to help make the layoff go as smoothly as possible.

3. **Verifying the layoff procedure, legal requirements, and budget:** If a layoff is necessary, you and your human resources department will have to set up procedures for who will be laid off. Additional areas that are unique to a layoff include legal notification requirements, establishing a support hotline for employees, and developing a process for which laid-off employees will physically leave the building, which supports the company confidentiality requirements and maintains the employees' dignity. A budget for layoffs is put in place during this step. The budget often includes severance pay, outsourcing assistance, and extended benefits.

4. **Creating the plan and layoff criteria:** The plan includes who is being laid off, how that individual or team was selected, who will be involved in the layoff process (who will tell the individual), and how and when managers will be informed of the process. Having managers deliver the message is often seen as a best practice because they are the ones closest to the individual. Additionally, the human resources department and a senior leader are often involved in the layoff discussion with an employee to answer any questions, handle any resistance, and provide support to the manager during this difficult time.

5. **Linking the goals of the layoffs to long-term metrics and performance:** Having a layoff is tough on the workforce, especially when productivity is expected to stay constant. Work with managers to put metrics in place

to track the effectiveness of the layoff. The goals and metrics should also identify the optimal staffing levels needed in order to not face another layoff in the near future.

6. **Conducting the layoff with dignity and respect:** When conducting the layoff, make sure employees are treated fairly. Give training to managers conducting the layoff so they feel comfortable with the process and can communicate why the layoff is happening quickly yet sensitively. There should be additional security and outplace counseling services during the layoff time as well as counseling set up for the survivors of the layoff.

Layoffs are not just about the bottom line. Peoples' lives are involved, so winging it is not a good option. *Managing For Dummies,* by Bob Nelson and Peter Economy (Wiley), can give you additional information on how to conduct a layoff and terminate employees.

Laying off staff can be one of the most difficult tasks you face as a manager. Work with your HR professional to help you understand your organization's layoff process and prepare you for the specific situation you may face.

Involving the Human Resources Department

The three Ps (people, pay, and position) have some fairly hefty consequences if not handled correctly, so during any large restructuring effort, you should consider working with the people who make people their business: human resources professionals. When you meet with HR during the restructuring process, you will most likely discuss why the restructuring is taking place (refer back to your mission and vision for change) and how you identified or would like to identify the impacted positions.

If you are unsure whether or not your HR department needs to be involved, we advise you to err on the side of involving it rather than worrying about what regulation or employment law may be impacted later.

What can your HR department do?

- ✔ During a layoff, HR makes sure that employees receive the proper information about outplacement services, termination of benefits, and other options and resources available to them.

- ✔ During a layoff, HR also makes sure that you correctly follow any specific company regulations, such as employee seniority or bargaining agreements. A *bargaining agreement* is a legal agreement between management and some labor groups that determines pay, work hours, and layoff terms, and it's definitely something the human resources team should handle!

✔ During any restructuring, even if it doesn't involve job eliminations, HR makes sure you stay in compliance with any employee agreements or employment regulations. Most states in the United States and many countries require a predetermined notification period if jobs are changing dramatically or are being completely eliminated. Leave these rules and regulations to the professionals so you can do your job and focus on the larger mission of the change, not the paperwork!

✔ Often, HR departments are able to provide you with a communication plan or at least an outline to help with restructuring and how to address any special needs caused by a potentially sensitive topic.

✔ When adding or changing job positions, HR can help write, rewrite, and evaluate job descriptions and review compensation structures to make sure the change is aligned with other potential plans or changes occurring within the company.

Mapping Out the Restructuring Process

Organizations come in many types of structures: flat or not-so-flat, centralized or decentralized, cross-functional or functional, or anything in between. We don't think there is one right way to structure an organization; many successful organizations operate in extremely different ways. As we explore how to map out the restructuring process in this section, our goal is to focus on the process of shifting to a new structure rather than determining the right structure.

Although no single way of structuring an organization is always best, we could point out plenty of examples of dysfunctional organizations that hinder innovation and change (you may be in one right now or have been in one in the past). If you find yourself in one, now is the time to leverage restructuring so that the new structure makes sustainable and significant change, not just changes to an organizational chart.

Guiding principles for structuring with purpose

Restructuring an organization immediately brings the three Ps to most leaders' minds (people, pay, and job position), but these details are really the last part of the change, the results of more significant changes. The restructuring process should follow four guiding principles:

✔ **Focusing on the customer:** Organizations are in business to deliver something to their customers — otherwise they wouldn't be in business, obviously. Restructuring changes should always start by addressing change that will improve the customer experience. Don't forget that the definition of *customers* can include stakeholders, the community in which the company operates, and employees as well as the people that buy your product.

✔ **Putting strategy before structure:** What strategy and goals are needed to deliver a better product or service to your customers? The company may need to revamp a product line or introduce a new one. Other strategies may include having a broader reach in new markets, reducing the cost of services for customers, making the organization a great place to work, decreasing its global environmental footprint, or increasing profits for shareholders. Strategy before structure simply means making sure leadership is clear about the goals of the organizational change before the change happens.

✔ **Changing processes to improve performance:** Restructuring should not be done just to mask poor performance issues or hand them off to another group in the company. Often, greater profits, lower costs, or higher quality can be achieved by making process changes and increasing skill sets within the organization. After you look at improving the processes that can impact your strategy and customers, then you can look at aligning resources to the new processes or strategy.

✔ **Building an enabling structure:** When restructuring does happen, make sure the structure is flexible enough to last in the long term. If restructuring is just a short-term fix, the company can get in the cycle of moving people around and never really getting work done. People need time to adjust to change, and the amount of time it takes is significant. And, as with all change, the work does not stop when change happens, so being strategic about how employees' jobs are impacted will help decrease any "Here we go again" change attitudes down the road.

Figure 13-1 outlines the restructuring process following these guiding principles.

Figure 13-1:
Guiding principles for structuring with purpose.

Developing your restructuring plan

If you decide that a new structure for the team is the best way to achieve your strategy and improve performance to deliver amazing results to your customers, you can get to work on a plan to make sure you identify and retain key employees and increase your competitive advantage after the change. Follow these steps:

1. **Define the goals and strategy the organization wants to achieve.** Refer to Chapter 4 for help developing your future state plan. Your goals and strategy will include starting to inspire a shared need, building a vision, creating a change road map, committing leadership to the change, and factoring in what will help or hinder change.

2. **Create the plan.** Your plan should include communication (see Chapter 7) and how the restructuring will take place. You will use the plan to guarantee that all members of the organization (at the suitable time) have the information they need to do their job in the future.

3. **Identify the critical functions necessary to support your core strategy.** By starting with the core positions, you're able to focus the organization around these critical elements. All the other positions support these critical functions during the change and long into the future. If you are having trouble identifying which roles are critical, look back at the vision for the change and ask, "What three things absolutely need to happen in the future to help us reach our goals? Who will (or should) do them?" If you find that you don't currently have an employee who can do this job, don't worry; adding positions can come later in the process. For now, write down what the role should do and then see if you have a person to fill it.

4. **Fill out the rest of the organizational chart to support these core functions.** This step prioritizes the focus of the organization. It's not the same as creating hierarchy in the organization; you simply define what roles are aligned with the core competencies needed in the future and what roles will support that core group as it works to achieve these goals. For example, if a company is betting all its marbles on building an application for smartphones that will change the entire world as we know it, then software engineers are probably a priority for the company. Human resources professionals, finance team members, and perhaps distribution channels would be logical support staff for the engineering group. If increasing the market for your product is the strategy, sales and marketing should probably be a top priority, supported by customer service, manufacturing, and so on.

5. **Identify any changes in reporting relationships, consolidation of job responsibilities, or increased spans of control.** These changes will become key talking points in your change communication plan.

6. **Create a high-level job description for the core positions.** Determining the core functions is the first step. Second, describe what the role will

be doing and what core competencies the person in the job should have, both now and in the future. A good job description should include the job title; purpose; responsibilities/duties; and the required knowledge, skills, and abilities. You can find excellent templates on the Internet along with sample job descriptions for many jobs.

7. **Fill in the names.** Finally! After you know the positions that will be needed to reach the strategic goals and what each position will do, fill in the names of people who can do the job. You may have some blanks, which means you will have to train or hire in individuals for the positions. You may also find you have some names left over, which means you may have to do job eliminations.

8. **If you haven't already done so, work with your HR department to review why new positions are needed or why a job is being eliminated.** HR conducts any appropriate review from a legal, compensation, and compliance perspective and can also help in posting positions as necessary.

We aren't lawyers or HR professionals, so for more on the HR function or legal requirements of restructuring, we highly recommend talking with your own HR team, picking up a copy of *Human Resources Kit For Dummies* by Max Messmer (Wiley), or contacting the Society for Human Resources Management.

9. **Finalize any new or changing job descriptions or compensation changes.** Again, we recommend working HR on this one. See Step 6.

10. **Finalize your communication plan.** Be sure to include in the plan what is changing, what work is moving, what work will be reassigned, and the new job descriptions.

11. **Go out there and change.** A new structure goes through the same change principles as any other large change. Some employees will be thrilled with the new opportunity; others will be upset by the change (see the earlier section "Looking at restructuring from an employee's point of view" and Chapter 9 for what reactions to expect during change).

Identifying the necessary process changes and their impacts

Although we generally recommend looking at process improvements before making structural changes (as noted in the earlier section "Guiding principles for structuring with purpose"), sometimes process changes come after structural changes in an organization. So whether you are doing the process review before a structural change or managing it afterward, you can use this section to help you identify process changes and their impact on the organization.

Process changes can be made in a number of ways, including Six Sigma, Lean, Lean Six Sigma, Kaizen, and many, many more (and yes, there is a *For Dummies* book for most of them!). These methods are great ways to make changes, but before a change can happen, you have to know it's needed in the first place. That fact seems straightforward, but you may be surprised by how many managers jump into "fixing" a process without clearly identifying the process first!

To identify what needs to change, first take a moment to review what is happening today. We call this *a process portfolio.* Just like a stock portfolio or a product portfolio, you need to occasionally review and adjust how work gets done. You would never just buy stock and then never look at it again, right? A company should never just invent a bunch of products and not look at how they are doing. The same principle is true for processes. Processes in many organizations have been created with years of toil, tears, and sweat, and taking a step back to make sure they are working and still make sense is the main goal of the process portfolio review.

Here are some questions you may want to ask during this review:

- ✔ **What is the most important goal for each process?** Many processes have multiple outputs, but when it comes down to it, a process should have an overarching goal; otherwise you may want to question why the process is happening in the first place. Is the goal of a report to provide information to executives? Is the goal of maintenance on a machine to ensure manufacturing doesn't come to a halt? If you can't think of a goal relatively easily, mark that process as one that potentially needs to change or be eliminated.

- ✔ **How can these goals be met more effectively?** Even in the most automated process, some person needs to do something along the way. Make sure that responsibilities are clear, the right training is provided, and that you have the right staff with the right competencies to make the process work. New technologies may be able to streamline a process to help improve quality and efficiency as well.

  Another way to meet the goals of the process more effectively is to look at areas of duplication; sometimes processes are created because another process was not operating effectively but the old process is still being done because it has always been done that way. Restructuring is a great opportunity to change any process that isn't meeting its goal or is delivering an output that no one uses.

- ✔ **Are there any changes in the organization that have affected or will affect the process in the foreseeable future?** You may look at processes that have been added, stopped, or significantly changed over the past few years to see if they've impacted the process you are reviewing. Processes are all connected! You may also identify new (or not-so-new) technology that may have changed the process. We talk more about technology change in Chapter 15. Finally, you may want to take a peek at customer demand. If customer demand has gone up or down recently, has the process adjusted to these needs?

Structuring performance metrics

In Chapter 11, we discuss how to redefine performance metrics during any change. Here we explore a few performance metrics specific to restructuring changes. As with all performance metrics, restructuring metrics should be built to inspire performance improvement, effectiveness, and efficiency, all focused on reaching the overall goal of the change.

A great place to start structuring your metrics is linking your process portfolio review and the guiding principles for successful restructuring. With these two activities complete, you will already have identified essential goals for the organization, customer requirements aligned to these goals, and your key processes (which by now all have clear goals attached to them too). The last step in the puzzle is to establish goals and measures to measure these vital processes.

Performance metrics are your key indicator of how well a change has been done and how well the change is being sustained in the future.

The key to making performance metrics tie back to the restructuring process is to align the strategy and goal of the change to the metric. We can't say this enough. If the goal of the restructuring is to improve customer satisfaction by adding more quality experts into key teams, you should measure product quality and customer service complaints (compliments, too). If the goal is to increase speed in delivery of products by restructuring the engineering and manufacturing teams into cross-functional pods, you should measure timely delivery of a product.

We walk you through this process with an example of a performance metric that can help judge the success of restructuring, in both the short and long term. In this case, the *vision of the restructuring* is to inspire innovation by removing extra approval layers in the organization. The vision to inspire innovation is being driven by the *customer requirements,* which are new software applications that are significantly updated and innovated at least once a month. This vision and requirements led to the following *restructuring goal* of improving the quality, frequency, and speed of application research, creation, and development.

Here are three possible metrics to measure the achievement of the restructuring goal:

- ✔ **Frequency:** Number of innovative ideas adopted across the company or number of best practices shared in the knowledge-management system (which now doesn't need as many approvals!)

- ✔ **Speed:** New product introduction timeline (time from when research has an idea to when it is ready to launch)

- ✔ **Quality:** Number of updates to fix "bugs" within 60 days of the new application launch

The measures help the organization determine if the vision, which is tied to a customer need for innovation, is being realized through the restructuring.

Is measuring the process of restructuring important? Maybe. But just doing something doesn't mean it's done well, so although teams should track the progress of the restructuring, that measurement shouldn't be the only one in place. Following are some metrics you may want to consider tracking during the restructuring process:

- ✔ **Were you able to retain key employees?** Retaining key employees helps to smooth the transition and retain knowledge within the organization. We talk more about retaining key employees and how to decide who is key in Chapter 14.

- ✔ **Do employees have their performance reviews in place in the new reporting structure?** When a large restructuring occurs, you can get a lot of benefit from kick-starting the new organization with a fresh view. Providing performance reviews for past performance and mapping out new goals for employees help facilitate this fresh start.

- ✔ **Did the restructuring follow all government regulations and company policies?** This concern is why you involve HR during restructuring. Many rules and regulations must or should be followed, and your HR professional can guide you through this process.

These metrics aren't long term, but they may be able to help future changes run even more smoothly.

Thinking about Communications Concerns

No chapter in this change book would be complete without us talking about communication! (We do love the topic.) Saying that restructuring needs communication is kind of like saying Mount Everest is a big mountain. Yes, you need communication. Yes, you need a lot of it. And yes, you will need to plan for it in substantial detail.

With all the amazing information in Chapter 7, you may already know that you and your organization have a wealth of communication options. Consider which method may be most appropriate by thinking about how the organization will react to change. For example, if you think employees are likely to have a lot of questions about why the restructuring is happening in one part of the organization and not another, you probably want to up your face-to-face communication rather than just sending out an e-mail, because face-to-face communication provides a more open exchange of information.

Explaining the need

The best way to inspire a shared need for structural change is to have a clear vision (what is happening), realistic yet aspirational benefits (why), and specific ways the new structure will help (the how).

One of the key issues that emerges during restructuring is employees questioning the need for reorganization. Often there is a lofty goal or aspiration, but when it comes down to hard data or specific examples, the communication falls short. Executives may circulate a document with the new organizational chart, but the chart itself may not be clear on how the new structure is going to facilitate change.

To have clear descriptions of how the structural change will impact employees, start with an accurate and realistic vision and goal statement, and then tie these to the benefits that will emerge directly from the change. Subsequently, talk about how things will be different.

Spreading the news of the decision

One question to consider is how early to inform employees that management is considering restructuring and staff changes. In general, we're in favor of providing as much information as legally possible as early as possible. However, some restructuring changes have legal implications and should be thoroughly planned out and approved by the human resources department before any communication takes place. In some cases, providing too much information too early can create unnecessary anxiety and confusion among staff without sufficient details of what is actually changing. In this situation, trusting your experience and instinct comes into play.

When you have fully developed your restructuring plan and are ready to communicate the change, we recommend you provide an overview to the entire organization outlining the nature of the changes and the affected departments and teams. At the same time, communicate to individual employees who will be affected how they will be personally impacted. If layoffs are involved, encourage all staff to be sensitive to those who are losing their jobs. Consult with HR on the legal and company policies around communicating the names of affected employees to other staff.

Even though it may seem uncomfortable, consulting key employees about the differences and opportunities that will emerge after the organizational change makes sure that the change has supporters from day one. No one likes to be told what to do without consultation, so whenever possible, involve employees in one-on-one meetings to discuss the changes before they happen. These conversations not only help create a shared vision for the change but also allow key employees time to adjust to the idea of a new role, position, or organization. Involving employees through communication is the best way to begin to build a clear and consistent picture of how the organization will operate.

Chapter 14

Organizing Change during Mergers and Acquisitions

Surprise, surprise: When two companies merge, change is going to happen! Mergers and acquisitions are increasingly commonplace today. Look in any business magazine and you'll read about some company buying some other company. But what you see in that article is just the tip of the iceberg, because a company negotiating a great deal is just one part of the M&A puzzle. Other pieces of the puzzle include getting employees on board with how the goals of the company and their responsibilities will change (or not change in the future), who will be part of the new company and who may not be, who is leading the new company, and what will be expected from employees in the short and long term. And that's just the beginning of the change list during M&A activities: Throw in new benefit structures, different organizational charts, and new ways of working with customers, and you start to realize how extensive change can be during a merger or acquisition.

If your company is facing an M&A situation, you have come to the right place. In this chapter we define the M&A change process, discuss some of the main reasons companies go through mergers or acquisitions, and take a look at what employees in both the acquiring and the acquired companies may be thinking. We provide you with an in-depth review of how to work with the common staffing considerations that mergers and acquisitions present and address what should happen to support the new company long after the deal is done.

Taking Change to a New Level: Combining Companies

Since the 1980s, a steady stream of mergers and acquisitions has taken place, launched by deregulation in the financial markets and by technology that empowers companies to operate in more markets and on a global level with greater ease. Most mergers and acquisitions occur for financial reasons: greater market share, lower operating costs, or a broader customer base. That being said, these financial goals would be almost impossible without a big effort on the "people" side.

The entire purpose of mergers and acquisitions is to change and grow stronger, bigger, or more efficient, all of which take a considerable amount of effort. As with all large scale changes, especially something as large as combining companies, in order to be successful, employees must accept the change and be willing and able to work in the new environment. In this section, we make sure you understand all your M&A jargon and break down all the possible reasons an organization may consider M&A.

Defining mergers and acquisitions

Mergers and acquisitions can be looked at like any other change opportunity, but in a much broader way because every department, team, product, and service is impacted. Add in possible regulatory and compliance issues, and you can see why M&A is a hot topic in organizational change circles. Before we move on, though, we need to first define what exactly we're talking about.

A *merger* is the creation of an entirely new firm through the combination of two or more equal partners. Neither company is being acquired or doing the acquiring. The new company may even take on a new name if an entirely new business entity is created. A recent example of a merger in the airline industry was the joining of Continental Airlines and United Airlines. The name of the final company is *United,* but the corporate logo was retained from Continental, and all the assets and liabilities were combined.

An *acquisition* is when one company buys another, either through a cash payment or the issuance of securities. One company is the buyer and another company is the purchased entity, and the bought company is usually combined into the company doing the buying. In some cases, companies are bought and sold multiple times. In 1999, Ford Motor Company bought Volvo for US$6.45 billion; just over a decade later, Ford sold Volvo to the Chinese car company Geely for US$1.5 billion.

Mergers and acquisitions are complicated and pricey undertakings. However, although each merger and acquisition has nuances, the change aspects are very similar because company culture and identity, reporting relationships, and business operations all change at some level regardless of who is buying whom. We focus most of this chapter on the change aspects of M&A, but first we walk you through the reasons why mergers and acquisitions happen in the first place.

Grasping the reasons for M&A

As you read through this chapter, you see that mergers and acquisitions are a big deal with a significant amount of work involved in order for the goals to be met. So why would any company want to put itself through such an ordeal? Why not just pour another cup of joe and rest on your laurels?

Mergers and acquisitions take place for many strategic business reasons, but the most common reasons for any business combination are economic at their core. Following are some of the various economic reasons:

✔ **Increasing capabilities:** Increased capabilities may come from expanded research and development opportunities or more robust manufacturing operations (or any range of core competencies a company wants to increase). Similarly, companies may want to combine to leverage costly manufacturing operations (as was the hoped for case in the acquisition of Volvo by Ford). Capability may not just be a particular department; the capability may come from acquiring a unique technology platform rather than trying to build it.

Biopharmaceutical companies are a hotbed for M&A activities due to the extreme investment necessary for successful R&D in the market. In 2011 alone, the four biggest mergers or acquisitions in the biopharmaceutical industry were valued at over US$75 billion.

✔ **Gaining a competitive advantage or larger market share:** Companies may decide to merge into order to gain a better distribution or marketing network. A company may want to expand into different markets where a similar company is already operating rather than start from ground zero, and so the company may just merge with the other company. This distribution or marketing network gives both companies a wider customer base practically overnight.

One such acquisition was Japan-based Takeda Pharmaceutical Company's purchase of Nycomed, a Switzerland-based pharmaceutical company, in order to speed market growth in Europe. (That deal was valued at about US$13.6 billion, if you're counting.)

✔ **Diversifying products or services:** Another reason for merging companies is to complement a current product or service. Two firms may be able to combine their products or services to gain a competitive edge over others in the marketplace. For example, in 2008, HP bought EDS to strengthen the services side of their technology offerings (this deal was valued at about US$13.9 billion).

Although combining products and services or distribution networks is a great way to strategically increase revenue, this type of merger or acquisition is highly scrutinized by federal regulatory agencies such as the Federal Trade Commission to make sure a monopoly is not created. A *monopoly* is when a company controls an overwhelming share of the supply of a service or product in any one industry.

✔ **Replacing leadership:** In a private company, the company may need to merge or be acquired if the current owners can't identify someone within the company to succeed them. The owners may also wish to cash out to invest their money in something else, such as retirement!

✔ **Cutting costs:** When two companies have similar products or services, combining can create a large opportunity to reduce costs. When companies merge, frequently they have an opportunity to combine locations or reduce operating costs by integrating and streamlining support functions. This economic strategy has to do with *economies of scale:* When the total cost of production of services or products is lowered as the volume increases, the company therefore maximizes total profits.

✔ **Surviving:** It's never easy for a company to willingly give up its identity to another company, but sometimes it is the only option in order for the company to survive. A number of companies used mergers and acquisitions to grow and survive during the global financial crisis from 2008 to 2012. During the financial crisis, many banks merged in order to deleverage failing balance sheets that otherwise may have put them out of business.

Mergers and acquisitions occur for other reasons, too, but these are some of the most common. Frequently, companies have multiple reasons for combining.

Even though management and financial stakeholders view mergers and acquisitions as a primarily financial endeavor, employees may see things a little differently (they're thinking WIIFM, or what's in it for me?). Combining companies has some potential downsides for employees, who have to deal with immediate fears about employment or business lines, but more positive sides of merging may include more opportunities for advancement, or having access to more resources to do one's job.

Considering the factors of success

What makes the M&A process successful? Although mergers and acquisitions have been happening for almost as long as organizations have been in business, companies still don't have a perfect formula for how to succeed with a business combination. However, two critical areas tend to lead to the companies meeting their strategic goals:

- ✔ **The process:** One of the most important areas successfully combined companies undertake is an organization-wide change process. This process starts with a clear strategy and specific goals, not only for the new company but for the integration process as well.

- ✔ **The fit:** The second area that helps to determine success is how complementary the products, services, *and* culture of the two organizations are before the change. The fit of companies often comes down to whether or not the other company's strengths complement your company's weaknesses (check out the SWOT analysis in Chapter 1) and how much risk the company willing to take (check out Chapter 6 for more on risk analysis).

Although each situation is different and each change and integration plan is different, these two areas are the make-or-break aspects of change during a merger or acquisition.

Following the M&A Process

The M&A process has three fundamental steps. (It is much more detailed than this, really, but we like to start with the basic steps and then dig into some of the details.) First, an executive (or executives) somewhere has some motivation to merge with or acquire another company and starts the entire process. The motives are important because they determine the strategic goals of the entire process. Second, the merger begins to happen (we did say this was a very fundamental view!). Companies perform their due diligence as they move from wanting to combine to getting ready to integrate as a new company. Third, the companies combine and the real change happens.

Because we love analogies, think of an M&A like two individuals dating and eventually getting married. First, there are just two individuals who decide they want something more (the first step: the motivation to merge), so they get engaged, start planning their wedding, and then tie the knot (the second step: the due diligence and integration process). After the wedding happens, their new life begins (the third step in the M&A process). The first two steps lay the groundwork for what is ahead, and the third step is when things really change.

Recognizing the need for enterprise-wide change and being realistic about how the two companies will work together in the long run, both operationally and culturally, should be continually addressed in the basic steps of mergers and acquisitions: during the decision to merge, during the due diligence and negotiation process, and as the new organization becomes one after the merger is official. In this section, we go a little deeper into these fundamental steps of the M&A process.

Making the decision to merge or acquire

Before any of the benefits of mergers or acquisitions can happen, a company's leaders need to know why they want to combine forces and what they hope to get out of the endeavor. Many organizations pinpoint their reasons by identifying their *core competencies,* the capabilities they have that create a competitive advantage for that company in the long run, are hard for another company to copy, are part of the company's culture, and are meaningful to their customers. These capabilities can be managerial, people driven, or technical. Some companies' greatest competencies are their people, especially for service-companies or for heavily R&D-focused companies where innovation and brainpower are at the core of the company's identity. The success of Apple has frequently been associated with its powerful innovation, research, and development, led by former CEO and chairman Steve Jobs.

Core competencies are by definition hard to develop any other way than through experience or by being purchased, and therefore, they are often at the center of M&A decisions. By understanding your company's core competencies, you can better evaluate what's missing and how other companies may be a good fit with your organization. For example, if you find that you lack the technical competence to respond to changes in the marketplace, you may want to seek out and acquire an organization that is innovative in the technical arena. You also may want to build on one of your existing core competencies to further strengthen your position.

It probably goes without saying, but the decision to merge with or acquire a company must be based on the strategic goals of the company. As you can tell by the volume and cost associated, these things don't just happen unintentionally or based on spur-of-the-moment reasons (at least not the most successful ones).

Performing due diligence and integration

Due diligence and integration make up an incredibly complex process that spans from the time the two organizations initially agree the companies should become one to closing the deal. The process is very analytical and methodical but at times can seem like chaos.

Due diligence and integration can be seen as an in-depth data-gathering and decision-making process before the deal closes. Organizations start by creating clear objectives and goals for the merger, and then they evaluate if the objectives can be met both strategically and financially. This part also includes negotiation and working through any regulatory or compliance issues that may arise. The goal of the due-diligence phase is to have a plan and agreement on how the companies will operate together after the combination is complete, which includes everything from which functions will combine and which will stay the same to what name the new company will have and how much the entire deal will cost.

This description is a very generalized, 20,000-foot view of the due diligence process. For more on the ins and outs of the merger and acquisition process, pick up a copy of *Mergers & Acquisitions For Dummies,* by Bill Snow (Wiley).

 During the integration and due-diligence phase, a number of steps are taken, departments are combined, and management decisions are made. Most problems in the post-integration phases come from lack of clarity about how decisions are made and who is making them. With so much happening in the integration and so much information being passed back and forth, M&A change leaders can help alleviate some of the pain by identifying differences and similarities in management style and facilitating decisions on how decisions will be made — both during and after the merger closes.

Supporting Employees during the M&A Process

During a merger or acquisition, you have to deal with the tangible aspects of change (better financial statements, new technology, and improved distribution networks) and the intangible aspects (organizational culture, employee morale). Although economic reasons drive the overwhelming majority of reasons to merge, employees bring significant value to the combined entity.

Even if the reason for merging is to combine manufacturing facilities, if employees aren't on board and supported during the process, the company won't obtain the full value of the integration because many employees will continue to do what they know — with a different company.

Combining two balance sheets is relatively easy; merging two cultures is not so easy. People are not like machines, and integrating teams of employees is much harder than changing the logo on their business cards. The goal of change leaders during the M&A process is to engage the people side of the business so the full financial value of the endeavor can be realized.

Why are employees so valuable in the M&A process? Outside of the change aspects discussed in this book, employees bring specific skills and capabilities to the table. Even if the merger or acquisition is intended to improve a process, gain market share, or cut costs, the functional skills of employees (including the routines, knowledge, and experiences) are the glue that holds all the processes together. Employees with leadership and management skills are also part of the overall M&A process, because they are the people who help set the corporate direction, financial controls, and overall management of the new company.

Assessing and assisting the employee transition

Following are the three benchmarks that successful M&A teams go through as they involve their employees in the process. By observing whether employees are acting in line with these goals, you can gauge your progress and increase assimilation efforts where needed.

✔ **Assimilating the new and old organizational culture:** Keeping employees in the dark about the future company is a surefire way to derail even the highest-value merger or acquisition. As soon as possible, employees in the acquired company should have the opportunity to work with leaders and employees on both ends to learn more about the history, culture, and company values of the new company. Employees need this opportunity to learn what has worked in the firm doing the buying, why the bought firm is attractive to the acquirer, and how they may be able to best contribute to the new organization.

Assimilation goes both ways: Acquiring companies also need to know more about the culture that their new peers operated in before being acquired because, after all, the acquired company must have been doing something right to make it an attractive acquisition candidate.

✔ **Being ready to work together:** Acquired employees may feel they're being forced into doing things another way. Just like a marriage, you can't just throw together two companies (or people) and expect them to coexist perfectly without some help. When one company is bought, they may feel like their company is losing out and the other company is winning. However, if leaders encourage employees to work with one another and reward them for doing so, old routines on both sides of the deal are likely to come together to create better ways of doing business in the new company.

✔ **Sharing capabilities and knowledge:** Value creation is the main reason for mergers and acquisitions, and sustainable value is only created when information is shared and capabilities are continually developed. Thus the merger or acquisition is not a once-and-done activity but a long-term focus that ensures the new firm has the resources (technical and human) to operate in the new way and also makes sure that employees are encouraged and rewarded for sharing knowledge.

We have seen some acquisitions that initially did a great job of cutting costs by buying another company and eliminating overlap, but the two firms continued to treat one another like evil stepsisters, with the employees never really wanting to share anything and always feeling a bit bitter that things had to change in the first place. Not surprisingly, the expected return on the acquisition was never fully realized. Sometimes, the M&A process can be a rather quick one, and after the deal is done it is a great idea to take a second look at what capabilities were expected to be shared and how this can really happen now that the deal is done.

Knowledge transfer (that is, learning) is a not just teaching another person how to do something. Long-term learning comes when a task or skill is taught in the context of why it happens. Buddy training, mentoring, and coaching can help facilitate this knowledge transfer and supplement any classroom or e-training as employees learn from one another.

Don't forget to get a dedicated change project team aligned to the integration. The project team should be a mix of both companies. Dedicated resources throughout the initial phases of the integration help speed the process, facilitate any questions from employees, and identify gaps and potential concerns early on in the process.

Considering what the "bought" company is thinking

One of the biggest conflicts "bought" employees try to come to terms with is that they were doing some things well but other things have to change. Their company was bought because of some value, which means they were doing something right. However, after the deal is done, these employees must integrate into the acquiring company's norms, culture, and way of doing things, leaving behind a good part of what they may feel they were doing right.

Take the case of two pharmaceutical companies. One was wildly success-ful immediately after the company was founded; the other had to pull itself up by the bootstraps and hammer away at research and development for two decades before it became very successful. The latter company felt it was successful because it had to do things efficiently and work together as a team. Employees had modest office spaces, reasonable benefits, and a can-do culture. When they were acquired by the "lucky" company, employees of the acquired company saw the acquiring company as a bunch of spoiled rich kids who never really had to work hard and who just threw money at problems because they had so much financial success almost from day one. This type of strife is common, because employees have genuine loyalty to the original organization and even anger or hostility toward the new organi-zation. Leaders in this particular pharmaceutical company were smart, and one of the ways they worked on integrating the best of the two cultures was to appoint "bought" employees to efficiency teams throughout the company with the goal of identify areas where innovation, rather than money, could better solve problems.

Change required by a merger or acquisition can be jarring for employees, who may have been thinking that everything was going along just fine. Even if their view isn't a realistic picture of what was really been happening, it could be the perspective of many employees in an acquired firm. How can leaders avoid this pitfall? While leaders "sell" the reasons for the merger or acquisi-tion, often on a strategic and financial level, leaders on both sides should take the time to get individuals and small teams to identify advantages that will impact the employees on a day-to-day basis. Value creation must take place for the employees as well as for the firm. Value for the employees may be more job security, greater benefits, or career advancement.

Although employees in both organizations need to understand the purpose of the acquisition and their role in the new organization, the needs in the acquired company are different from those in the acquiring company. Taking these needs into consideration and knowing when to allow employees the time to assimilate and when to push for results helps speed the change pro-cess in the long term.

Staffing Considerations during Merger or Acquisition

The goal of M&A activities is to create greater value for both companies through more financial power, increased market share, or streamlined operating effi-ciencies. Before any of these benefits can happen, however, productivity and employee engagement need to be taken into consideration.

Most organizational leaders recognize that M&A efforts are most successful when the people side of the deal is addressed. Like most changes, upfront and frequent communication partnered with proactive and sincere involvement in the process improves the business outcome. We like to call addressing staffing concerns as helping people deal with the deal. Mergers and acquisitions are a bit different than other organizational changes because of the rapid pace of change often associated with the process. Additionally, both companies experience quite a bit of uncertainty because even though plenty of planning, data collection, and strategic visioning for the future take place, until the deal is signed nothing is 100 percent accurate due to the limitations of what can and cannot be shared before the deal closes.

In Chapter 2, we discuss the productivity dip during change. During the M&A process, employees may become especially distracted by this uncertainty. The best thing leaders can do to decrease and shorten the productivity dip is to be upfront and honest about the changes ahead and clearly communicate what can and cannot be shared during the due diligence. Employees realize that before the deal is done there are regulatory, financial, and competitive reasons why everything cannot be disclosed. However, telling employees merely that much helps to create two-way communication that will benefit the company in the days to come. Besides communication, leaders want to focus on three staffing concerns common during the M&A process: minimizing employee attrition, retaining key staff, and maintaining employee morale. We discuss these three areas in the following sections.

We have seen successful companies try to keep acquisitions behind closed doors, leading to something of the white elephant in the room. Everyone knows something is happening, but rather than talk about it openly, employees take cues from water-cooler talk, become wary of company leaders and their messages, and may even hold back any extra effort because they have no real idea about what is down the road. All of these behaviors can destroy leadership credibility and have a negative impact on the overall acquisition. The best thing leaders can do is to be upfront and honest about the changes ahead and clearly communicate what can and cannot be shared during the due diligence.

Within the first 90 days of closing the deal, the change team should revisit the organizational and knowledge assumptions made during the due diligence and pre-close process and create a realistic plan regarding what needs to happen now that information between the two companies can flow openly.

Minimizing employee attrition

Employee attrition is when employees leave a company, either voluntarily (an employee may find a new job or retire) or involuntarily (they may be fired or laid-off). *Merger syndrome* (this is a scientific name, we swear) is when employees leave the company immediately before or after the deal closes. Lack of a clear future, stress from change, and uncertainty about leadership are all reasons employees choose to jump ship instead of seeing where the ship is going to sail, so to speak.

When a large group of employees depart during the M&A process, a significant amount of knowledge departs too. Employees who remain question whether they should be looking elsewhere, too. And we aren't talking about just minimizing the loss of your star players (we talk about them in the upcoming section "Retaining key staff") but also about losing institutional knowledge. Employees throughout the organization provide continuity that customers are craving during a merger. Customers are looking for cues from the new company about what is ahead and how their needs will be supported. If all the employees that customers know within the company say sayonara, customers may also soon leave for competitors.

Keep an eye out for stress in the organization and allow employees time to deal with the added stress of the change, learn about the new company, and do their jobs. If the number of sick days starts creeping up or if productivity is dipping significantly, do a gut check and ask employees what else can be done to help people work through the changes the merger has created. Remember that change does not happen overnight!

As you work on minimizing employee attrition, include these key incentives:

- **A bright and believable future:** Employees want to know that the company's best days are ahead of it, and they want to know how they will play a role in this future. Employees are smart and don't fall for an idyllic future with no substance, so be realistic and share as much detail as you possibly can. Leaders can paint the picture of the future, but employees must see and believe it is going to happen. To build credibility, keep 100 percent of the say-do ratio; that is, do 100 percent of what you say.

- **A positive work environment:** If employees are supported and feel they're making a difference, you have a higher chance of retaining them. A positive work environment includes trusting and rewarding employees for doing the right thing and thanking managers who retain employees. Have managers talk with each employee (if possible) to make sure they have the tools they need to do their job and manage stress. Listen to their concerns and treat employees as people. Respect and dignity in the face of change is one of the surefire ways to keep employees engaged and at work.

    Strong communication from leadership can greatly support a positive work environment. How management, notably direct supervisors, communicates during times of transition is a key ingredient to retaining staff.

When allowed by the laws and regulations that govern a merger, management can provide ongoing updates (meetings and e-mails), face-to-face communication, and recognition for behaviors that are consistent with the new or evolving post-merger culture.

✓ **Opportunities for involvement, feedback, and personal development:** No one likes being told what to do. By involving groups of employees throughout the process, the leadership team can gain valuable feedback, and individuals have a chance to voice ideas and concerns. Additionally, as part of the integration, be sure to identify the new ways employees will be able to grow with the company through expanded roles and responsibilities. A defined schedule for training and professional development sends a strong message to employees that they are valued.

✓ **Money:** We discuss financial retention strategies for key players later in this chapter, but keep in mind that each employee has financial needs and goals. Most likely, at least one of the companies in the deal will be changing its total compensation package (benefits, salary, bonuses), so as soon as you can, communicate the potential changes or additions. If employees don't hear anything about their pay, they may begin making career choices based on assumptions and fear rather than fact.

Employees will want to stay with a company if they feel they have room to grow, are encouraged to try new things, and feel valued for their work, both mentally and financially.

Although money is a great motivator, so are two words: thank you. If you can tell employees how their work effort is helping the team and the company, they will feel valued. And employees who feel valued rarely pack their bags and walk out the door.

Maintaining employee morale

Employee morale isn't just something that the perky new employee in HR is cheering about. It can make or break a company after a merger or acquisition. Why? When employee confidence is high, employees usually are more likely to work harder to make the change happen and maintain a positive view of the changes and challenges that lie ahead. You can imagine what may happen when morale is low: This negativity can filter through everything from lunchroom gossip to damaging discussions with customers.

The most important way to maintain and increase morale is quite simple: Ask employees what you can do. By engaging your employees, you can find out what the organization and its leaders can do better. Not only does this conversation create a dialogue between management and employees, but as long as leadership acts on the recommendations (or at least some of the recommendations), it also shows employees that their opinions matter. In Chapters 8 and 10 we provide ideas on how to motivate people to move forward, which helps maintain morale during change.

The view from the top and the view from employees can be quite different during a merger or acquisition. Leaders, especially senior executives, have access to information and have extensive decision-making responsibilities during the merger or acquisition, as well as (in most cases) significant personal financial benefits from a completed transaction. Often, when most employees learn about the change, leaders have been working on it for months (if not longer). Employees sometimes feel they may be coming to the party quite late, even if communication has been proactive, because the leadership has already processed the change and is ready to get moving. With new decisions and constant uncertainty, morale can easily drop. Here is what you can do to maintain morale during M&A:

- ✔ **Be honest with employees.** Really honest. During mergers and acquisitions, too many leaders say what their PR firm told them to say or what they think employees want to hear. Some leaders may talk about how the two companies will take the best of both worlds and make one perfect company, but in reality, even if this was the honest intention, identifying and creating the best of both worlds is quickly pushed aside to get operations up and running as quickly as possible. A high trust environment (which is one outcome of honest communication) creates productivity and innovation. It is great to be optimistic, but leaders also need to be realistic.

- ✔ **Focus on the future culture.** The culture of an organization includes a wide array of elements, ranging from what people wear to work to the way people address problem solving. When the deal is signed, the two separate and different cultures still exist and can exist for quite some time. Culture may not be tangible, but years down the road, employees may still refer to themselves as "from the old company." This perspective is a very vocal way of showing that the two cultures never really merged.

  The best way to address cultural issues is head on and with completely open and honest communication. Don't tiptoe around how the culture will look, feel, and breathe — tell employees what is expected of them, what is expected to go, and what is expected to stay, and involve employees in making it happen. Immediately re-vamp the onboarding process for new employees to focus on the new company. Redesign your performance-management system to align with the new values of the company. Make sure managers walk the talk so employees have a model of what they should do. For more on managing cultural change, see Chapter 16.

✔ **Talk about the process.** As soon as federal regulations allow it, clear communication helps keep at bay cynicism about the motives behind the merger or acquisition. Few employees have been through enough corporate combinations to understand the process, so explaining the process helps to build trust within the organization. Here are a few questions you can answer:

- *How will the new leadership team be created? When will employees know about the new executive team?* Everyone — customers, shareowners, and employees — will want to know who is running the show. For a number of reasons, most likely some senior leaders are not going to be part of the new organization or will be in different roles within the organization. This leadership change is often one of the first decisions made during the M&A process, and providing this information establishes the open and honest communication wanted by employees.

- *How will processes and technology be integrated? Who is leading the integration effort? How can employees provide feedback about the integration?* Most employees understand that every detail of the organization is not 100 percent set in stone before, during, or immediately after the merger. These things take time, so explaining what the process will be and who will be leading it helps to create certainty during uncertain times.

- *What can employees tell customers or other individuals who may ask about the merger?* Customers are smart and have lots of ears and eyes out in the marketplace. Sometimes they hear about mergers or acquisitions as quickly as employees (if not earlier). Work with employees who have direct and indirect customer-facing roles to let them know what they can tell them (and what they can't).

- *Where can employees go for more information?* Above all else, be sure to create a two-way resource for employees to ask questions during the process. Additionally, this forum provides a resource to collect any rumors that may surface. Rumors will start no matter how much information you put out there, but there is no better way to stop the rumors than by hearing what they are and addressing them head on.

Consider registering for social media–monitoring services so you can determine what is being said about your company during this critical transition. Make sure that employees understand your company's policy around posting to external social media websites to avoid leaking information or spreading rumors. For more on communicating during change, head over to Chapter 7.

Investment-only M&A

An increasing number of mergers and acquisitions are done just for investment purposes. In these cases, a private equity firm may buy a profitable company, and everything within the company is expected to the stay the same. But communication is important even if everything is staying the same. Leaders should tell employees early on that the status quo will continue and that their employment deal is not changing. Additionally, leaders need to address what employees should tell customers, whether any new resources are available to the organization (financial, technical, or management), and how the acquisition ties into the bigger picture.

More commonly, private equity firms buy struggling companies in the hopes that a combination of financial capital, industry expertise, and hard-nosed business decision making can turn around a weak company. When this type of acquisition occurs, you can expect virtually every aspect of the company to change. In these scenarios, constant communication, even if all you have to tell is bad news, is a must. Employee defections may be widespread. But bear in mind, without the acquisition, the struggling company may have failed. As much as you can, have your change leaders focus on the positive aspects of the "white knight" that has come to your rescue.

Retaining key staff

So you're doing your best to make sure there is not a mass exodus from the company post-merger, and you're engaging employees to ensure employee morale stays positive. You should keep your eye on one more thing as you consider staffing concerns during a merger or acquisition: retaining key staff. Your organization likely has some employees whom you really want to keep. We know, all employees are important, but about 10 percent of your team is in absolutely critical positions. People tend to get caught up in the word *key* staff, so in this section we define it and then tell you how to keep those people.

Knowing who they are

Key staff members are people in your organization whose sudden absence would create difficulty in delivering on customer requirements. They may possess a skill that is hard to replace or train, they may be your most amazing star performers, they have a strong relationship with important clients, or they may be the ones that hold considerable institutional knowledge. Some managers have a hard time admitting that some of their staff is key and that others are people that they just want to keep. We know this distinction is hard to make, but identifying key staff helps you target retention strategies above and beyond what you are doing for the entire organization.

Key staff retention strategies should target roughly about 10 percent of the organization. If you find you need to retain more than 10 percent of your organization through targeted packages, you may consider offering a general retention for all staff. General retention may come in forms of a modest bonus (about 5 to 10 percent of annual salary is a good rule of thumb) or restricted stock.

Your company may have individuals or teams who aren't necessarily key staff for long-term results but are needed to complete high-priority projects in the short-term. Offering these employees or teams some type of project-completion bonus helps make sure these employees wrap things up before they consider moving to another position or company.

Don't limit your key staff to the highest levels of leadership. Yes, having consistent and strong leadership will help dramatically in the days ahead, but so will your sales team and R&D team. Sales teams have relationships with customers that are often next to impossible to rebuild overnight. R&D teams have institutional knowledge that spreads much farther than any documented procedure or process could ever account for in the company, and they may hold the secret to your next dominant product.

Implementing strategies to keep them on board

After you have identified your key staff, you can work on how to keep them from jumping ship. A retention package is simply a way of formally (and usually financially) letting employees know that although they do have the option of leaving, it's worthwhile to stick around and see how wonderful the new company will be in the future.

Keeping key staff on board is all about timing. Retention bonuses often include some type of obligation or delayed payout, timed with how long you believe it may take to iron out any kinks in the new organization and timed with how long it will take to help the employee see the value of the merger. Other retention packages may be focused on the short term. You may have a group of employees who must stick around long enough to get the new organization launched. Often this group is in support functions like finance, technology, and human resources. Although you may be able to replace these positions if needed, knowing that the lights will stay on without much thought in the immediate months after the merger is a safety net worth creating.

Most retention comes in the form of a lump sum payment or additional performance bonus, but other parts of the stay bonus may be stock or stock options or additional benefits like vacation time, future paid sabbatical, or the option of flextime. You may not want to promise anything, but when you begin to communicate to key staff about how their retention is important for the success of the merger and the future of the company, you have a great opportunity to ask what they would consider an ideal retention package. Keep in mind that you'll have to perform some keen negotiation and boundary setting, because a few employees may ask for an unreasonable amount (and if they do, it may be an indicator that they are more focused on their own needs and don't have a vested interest in the future success of the company).

Retention of key employees (or any employees for that matter) is not just about keeping a warm body in a seat. Part of retaining employees may include offering options for tying company performance after the merger to financial rewards for employees. This deal, often called *gain sharing,* may be structured as profit sharing or stock. Along the same lines, adding performance objectives to retention plans is perfectly acceptable. The reason you are asking key staff to stay is that they need to keep doing what they have been doing!

As for the fine print: You need to work with your support team. Retention packages are not just a Christmas present coming out of the HR department, and you need to remember to work hand in hand with that group during the process. Additionally, you and the legal department will probably become quite good friends. Those employees are experts in covenants, contracts, clauses, non-competes, and other state or federal regulations that impact what you can and cannot offer as well as what employees can and cannot do.

One added detail you should not forget is that these 10 to 20 percent of employees are critical to your organization and could probably find another job relatively easily, even in the worst economic conditions. So don't delay communicating that they are valuable to the organization and you plan on creating a retention plan for them (even if you don't have all the details just yet). The last thing you want is for those hungry headhunters calling and planting seeds in your key staff's minds that the grass is so much greener somewhere else. Make sure you communicate any retention offers before the deal closes — even if everything isn't finalized.

Key employees have a way of seeing all, hearing all, and knowing all, which provides you with another retention strategy: The employees who are staying see how the organization treats employees who are leaving and may become more loyal if they see the company communicating truthfully, straightforwardly, and with empathy toward employees who are losing their jobs. Employees who are staying (or asked to stay) will believe the messages delivered to them about the future of the company too.

The Deal Is Done: How to Proceed Successfully

The deal is done, retention offers are signed, the communication plan is in full swing, and employees are beginning to explore the new environment with a positive attitude. Now your job as a change leader is to keep the momentum rolling so that all the value expected as part of the merger or acquisition can become a reality.

Here are a couple of things change leaders and executives can do to make sure the future is as bright as you expect it to be:

- ✔ **Keep your eyes and ears out there.** Change agents after the merger (see Chapter 3 for more on change agents) can help identify any unexpected obstacles that may come up. Conducting a 90-day post-merger assessment is a great checkpoint to ask what is going well, what still needs work, and what change lessons can be learned from the successes and challenges of the M&A process.

- ✔ **Retain, focus, and engage — in that order.** After employees feel secure in the new company (that is, they have a job and they may even have a retention package), you can then begin to refocus teams on the work at hand. Having objectives and projects to work on reminds employees that even though they probably still have a number of unanswered questions, work still needs to get done and should get done. Finally, when employees are back doing the work that needs to get done, then managers can work on reengaging employees around a common goal and mission. Trying to motivate employees and engage them in the new culture may seem artificial until employees have some experience working in it.

- ✔ **Give managers and supervisors the tools they need.** Give front-line managers the information and necessary training to address questions and concerns raised before, during, and after the integration. Executives are great at communicating the vision and direction of the company, but managers and supervisors are the ones who work on the details long after the deal is done.

- ✔ **Train staff to integrate them into the new organization.** The many changes that were identified during integration and due-diligence phase must now be implemented. Inform staff of all the decisions that have been made regarding changes in processes, organization structure, and organizational culture and provide training on how things will be done going forward in the combined company. Everyone needs to understand what is expected of them and gain the skills to be able to perform in the new organization.

- ✔ **Regularly check-in with employees about what is happening.** Often, communication efforts are quite significant during the early stages of the integration. However, stopping or dramatically decreasing communication a few months after the deal is done can make employees feel either that they're being left in the dark or that all the ideals about the value the merger would create never came true. Formally providing employees with the continued results of the merger every three to six months until all the expected value is attained helps to build a change-ready culture — one that knows leaders have the capability to set a vision for change and follow it through to completion. We also recommend that you conduct an employee-engagement survey before, during, and after the merger or acquisition to keep a pulse on what employees are thinking and feeling.

If the value of the M&A is not being seen, you may have a great opportunity to engage the bigger employee base on what else could be done. To promote two-way communication, you may want to provide an e-mail box or an internal social-media tool to encourage feedback and questions on the M&A. Employees recognize that all the goals set out at the beginning of the M&A process may not be met, and communication should address these changes as appropriate.

✔ **Recognize that the work is just beginning for some people.** Even though the job of the executives and M&A team is coming to an end after the integration winds down, lower-level employees will just be starting to pick up all the work that needs to happen to make the merger a success. Continue to provide support to these employees and managers, because some gaps in information or organizational assumptions may surface long after the deal closes.

Even after the merger or acquisition, people may still be afraid that they'll lose their jobs or that more things will change down the road. To help you address these concerns, check out Chapter 9 regarding how to work through resistance during change.

Chapter 15

Aligning Technology Change with Results

*I*n January 2012, Eastman Kodak, the maker of billions of Kodak moments for more than a century, declared bankruptcy. Why? One reason is that it didn't change with changing technology. Executives at Kodak may have never really imagined that digital photography and the growth of a little i-something would eventually replace the need for a camera. Not changing with the speed of technology or with the technical demands of customers eventually caught up to this photo giant.

Change and technology go hand in hand, and this chapter covers this type of change from beginning to end. We first explore the change solutions that organizations may want to consider when integrating technology and strategy, and we uncover what some change professionals consider the bread and butter of change: integrating technology, people, and processes. We then move into some of the specific changes companies face when they adopt new technology-support systems like e-Business, ERP (enterprise resource planning), CRM (customer-relationship management), and many more fancy acronyms. Next, we cover the somewhat newer social-media technologies that companies can integrate into their overall strategy, and finally we provide ideas to overcome common technology change pitfalls if you see them standing in the way to your next great technology solution.

Disclaimer! We are not technology engineers or programmers. We're change professionals who approach technology from a change perspective, but we do provide plenty of hot-off-the-shelves references for technology gurus throughout the chapter.

Tying Together Strategy and Technology

Technology is changing the nature of jobs, customer demands, product markets, and organizations. Organizations have technology coming at them from two sides. On one side, state-of-the-art technology enables companies to respond better and faster to customer needs. On the other, continuously changing technology can propel organizations to always be on the lookout for the next great thing to increase productivity and become more adaptable to change as new technologies emerge.

A decade ago, Amazon was more synonymous with a river in South America than the online powerhouse superstore. And these days, if a consumer-focused company isn't online, customers will pass them by for one that offers a one-click shopping experience.

This virtual shopping world has enabled another giant leap: Customers can be anywhere and buy anywhere. The global economy created with the help of the Internet means global competitors and global customers. Not only do companies need to beat out their traditional competitors, but they also have to fight for market share with a brilliant shop run from some basement seven time zones away. Just as the production line changed the face of manufacturing in the early 1900s, technology continues to change and challenge the face of business. It doesn't matter if you are from the Henry Ford or Steve Jobs generation — successful organizations change in response to new technology in a fast and focused manner. This response means tying strategy to technology and layering it all with a solid change-management effort.

In Chapter 4 we talk about creating a vision and strategy for change. You also need vision and strategy when dealing with technology, because you can't treat it as an afterthought; it should be integrated into the overall strategy and objectives. In the 1990s, more large companies were implementing an ERP (enterprise resource planning) system, which is technology that integrates management information across an entire organization. The goal of ERP systems is to make information flow seamlessly within the organization, resulting in higher productivity, but in reality, many people found fancy ways to upload spreadsheets but kept doing the same thing they had always done. The 2000s were focused on customer experience (customer-relationship management) and e-business. Although some companies did a wonderful job incorporating the related technologies into their operations, others just collected a bunch of data on customers that sat in a database somewhere. Today, smartphone apps and social media are the big areas to have a presence — but few organizations have successfully coupled investing all the time and energy into these endeavors with bottom-line results. This is where strategy comes in — and comes in strong.

When developing your technology-change strategy, make sure you answer the following questions:

- ✔ **What do we want to achieve?** Companies may create an online social presence to attract new customers or to help work through customer complaints. Implementing any technology should be tied to better results for the organization. Are you reaching more customers who then will buy more products and services? Is the technology going to help give real-time answers when a person is not available? As with most change, new technology should not be implemented just because someone else is doing it — there must be a goal in mind.

- ✔ **How will we measure success?** Here's the kicker. How do you *know* that reaching out to customers with 140 characters every hour is going to grow your customer base? Work with your fellow change leaders to determine how you will measure productivity after the plan and technology are in place.

If these questions sound familiar, they should. These questions (along with solid answers) are always at the core of any successful change.

There are two advantages to tying together strategy and technology with a change-management bow: Companies can deliver on customer demands and create a tech-savvy organization ready to change with whatever comes its way. We highly recommend checking out www.mystrategicplan.com and *Strategic Planning Kit For Dummies,* by Erica Olden (Wiley) to help guide your organization's strategic development.

Delivering on customer demands

We started this chapter highlighting what happens when a company doesn't change its technology to meet the demands of the market and tech-savvy customers. Technology is not just about meeting a productivity goal or making data more accessible to management — it can be the difference between giving customers what they want or going out of business. Eastman Kodak continued to focus on traditional cameras and films and declared bankruptcy; Fuji (a competitor) transitioned into flat-screen manufacturing when the smartphone camera was on the horizon.

Publishing houses and bookstores (something near and dear to our hearts) face similar challenges. E-books and e-readers have changed how people read books, news, and magazines, and an explosion in the self-publishing industry has opened the gates for any aspiring author and flooded the e-book market with millions of once-stashed-away-in-a-drawer-novels. Amazon sells books online but also created a whole line of e-readers and got into publishing their own books.

Changing with technology is not just about delivering on customer demands or selling a technology-based product. A large company may not sell what looks to be a technology product, but the backend that serves the customer, the lifeblood of the organization, may be the technology that supports the website or makes sure all the raw materials are ready for manufacturing. For example, Amazon sells everything from clothing to xylophones, but it is the technology for the website, vendors, and distribution centers that generates the overall customer experience.

Before the dot-com bubble burst, the "We need technology to attract customers at any cost" conversation like the one below was quite frequent in coffee shops around Silicon Valley:

> *Future Internet Millionaire (FIM): "Hi Mr. Venture Capital Partner. I have an amazing idea I want to sell on the Internet. I created an application that provides every person with a smartphone with an unlimited amount of oxygen."*
>
> *Mr. Venture-Capital Partner (MVCP): "Hmm. Sounds interesting. What is your business model?"*
>
> *FIM: "I figure I will have out-of-this-world traffic. Everyone wants oxygen, right? Millions of customers a day!"*
>
> *MVCP: "How much will you sell the oxygen for?"*
>
> *FIM: "My resources say not much. We may even lose money, but we'll make that up on volume and capturing market share."*
>
> MVCP: "Sold! Here is a check for one billion dollars!"

(Note: Mr. Venture-Capital Partner is currently working as a barista at the same coffee shop, and the Future Internet Millionaire moved back in with his parents.)

You can have the most wonderful idea or intention to integrate technology within your product or services, but if customers won't pay for it, you may need to revisit the business model.

Making the technology-innovation link

Setting a future-focused vision and strategy for the organization by embracing changing technology in its products, services, and operations brings a tremendous benefit: People want to explore and innovate. Although we can't tell you a scientific formula for innovation and being ahead of the technology curve, when the structure and culture allow an open flow of information and this flow is rewarded, innovation will likely follow. If the company is stuck in 1982 technology with bolted-on, home-grown systems, the level of innovation is probably in the same decade.

We are not saying that technology is the only enabler of change and innovation but that adaptability and open knowledge sharing are some common denominators when it comes to blending innovation and technology with strategy.

- ✔ **Adaptability:** Innovation means the organization can be flexible when things happen. An adaptable organization doesn't get set in its ways but looks for new ways to operate in a changing environment. Technology changes at the speed of light and requires organizations to move fast and think fast so they can be open to *what can we do?* versus *what is happening right now?* Being open minded to possible changes on the horizon is necessary to keep pace with developing technologies.

- ✔ **Open knowledge sharing:** How an organization distributes information to the right people at the right time can determine not only how collectively smart the organization is but also how quickly and reliably data is applied to problem solving. If information is hidden or hoarded, little knowledge is shared; when technology is used to its fullest, the technology can enable an organization to operate with more open processes and knowledge.

Just having the latest and greatest technology doesn't create an innovative organization; the technology must be used to improve processes across the company and to enhance customer value.

Most of this chapter focuses on how to rally the troops around changing technology. However, changing with technology is not just about adopting new technologies. From a product and service development perspective, it is about creating those technologies to be ahead of the curve — not just to keep up with the curve. This is where innovation comes in.

Matching Technology with People, Processes, and Strategy

As you can probably tell by now, technology encompasses much more than just flipping a switch and having a happy face pop up on everyone's computer. When preparing for a new technology, most executives and project managers thoroughly examine, plan, and plan again for all aspects of the technical integration; some of the better ones even include redesigning business processes. Many executives have also begun to slow down and make sure technology fits into an overall strategy and isn't just something to implement to keep up with the Joneses. To ensure success in adopting new technology throughout the organization, a fourth piece of the change needs to be addressed — the one we have been talking about all along — the people. The people factor is what makes the technology last.

Your people determine if the technology gets used in a way that supports your strategy. A few ways to help people adopt new technology are to include key users in designing the process and technology solution and communicate how the technology change will enable them to better do their jobs and how the technology will help reach new levels of productivity and service:

- ✔ Create a change ambassador group or front-line council to help reduce negative reactions to the change and eliminate uncertainty or concerns in the organizations. These individuals can help in a number of ways, including

  - Working with the project leaders to identify site or department-specific needs for communication, training, or functionality related to the technology

  - Working with the change team to communicate and gather feedback on the progress of the change (change agents are a vital communication link between employees, the project team, and the executive sponsor)

  - Working with the change leader to make sure solutions meet the functional needs of the site or department

- ✔ During communicating and training opportunities, remember to focus on the opportunity and what's in it for employees. Many times people like the idea for change but they just don't want to have to pay the personal cost of learning how to do things differently. If employees see the value in learning a new technology, they are more likely to do it. Show employees how learning new skills and doing things differently will benefit them in the long run.

As you begin to implement your change, pay careful attention to your training plan to ensure that the users will feel confident in their ability to successfully maneuver the new system.

In a well-functioning business, people, processes, and technology are in balance and aligned with the overall strategy and vision of the organization. Changing one aspect of the business means that the other areas should adjust to reestablish balance. Figure 15-1 illustrates how to create this balance.

No matter which technology you implement, the model stays the same. As we walk through all the various options for technology change, you'll be able to develop a clear picture of how working with the four elements shown in Figure 15-1 will make you and your organization achieve results.

Not all audiences will adopt the new technology in the same way, because one size does not fit all. Remember to let employees know what they can expect from the system, what is expected from them, and how the big picture relates to their work.

Figure 15-1:
Strategy and vision of the organization at the center or people, process, and technology.

Making Room for New Technology

A great deal of money, time, money, effort, money, and resources are invested in technology. Some leaders may assume that the technology changes will be greeted with open arms because they paid so much for them or have been told by the salesperson that this technology is going to solve all their problems. Other leaders (who obviously did not read this book) may approach change from a "need-to-know" basis, holding information and communication about changes close to the vest. By not preparing people sufficiently or by withholding information, leaders are likely to encounter significant resistance to new technology adoption.

Making room for technology is all about creating a change-ready environment by reaching out to stakeholders, users, and teams who are impacted by technology through facilitated involvement, two-way communication, and practical training. To integrate the technology successfully, employees need to be trained on how to use it, processes need to make the technology easy to use, and employees must trust that the technology is going to do what it should do. You also need to involve the business users and people who will support the technology in creating or modifying what will be used. In other words, talk with the users about how the technology can best serve the stakeholders' needs. No texting, no e-mailing, no online survey — just sit and talk with them (we know, a very novel concept!). A system can have all the bells and whistles, but if employees don't use it or if employees still need to upload-download-reload data manually, you'll have few efficiency gains, no matter what the system is capable of doing.

Ask stakeholders for their experience and insight into how the technology can support better business operations, and then make the technology fit the needs of the user, not the other way around. Although sleek technology demos can show businesses how wonderfully a process can flow, remember that the business need and the business process should be supported by technology and that the technology should not (in most cases) run the business.

Joining the online e-business revolution

At this point, if your organization isn't online with an e-business strategy, you're missing out on loads of customers! For traditional brick-and-mortar companies, e-business change has often meant a complete overhaul of how the business connects with customers, or at least a reengineering of the sales processes. Start-ups sometimes find they have to slow down the dot-com speed and make sure a product is sellable by fully integrating e-business.

What makes a company an *e-business* company? If you're doing part of your business on the web, you are using e-business. This includes advertising, providing customer support, selling products and services, and anything in between. Because e-business spans a pretty wide domain, achieving clarity around why, how, and when the organization will use online technology helps eliminate confusion and bring focus to the e-strategy.

Before picking a change strategy, identify how your organization may want to use (or is already using) e-business:

✔ **Traditional online presence:** Since the 1990s, lots of companies have offered a listing of products, services, and company information online. No bells and whistles, just sharing basic information with customers. Let's say you're running a local flower shop, Blooming Blossoms. You put pictures of beautiful blossoms online, testimonials from clients who just loved your designs, and a phone number to call to order flowers for Mother's Day.

✔ **E-commerce:** The next level is e-commerce, or selling products or services directly over the Internet. For example, Blooming Blossoms may put an Order button by your flower photos online, so anyone with an Internet connection can order flowers the day before Mother's Day and have the flowers delivered right to Mom's door that next morning.

✔ **Web 2.0:** At this level, an organization implements online customer service, does business with other businesses online (called *business to business,* or B2B), provides services directly online, and cultivates and maintains an online, often user-driven community using social media for marketing purposes. Your flower shop orders flowers just in time from the flower supplier. Your customers create arrangements themselves by choosing and dragging flowers around the screen and can enter their card message directly into a text box. Your website has a blog where you share helpful hints and updates about your company. You have a Twitter feed and maintain a Facebook page, engage directly with your customers there, promote special offers, and monitor both accounts to handle customer service questions and keep your reputation spotless. You may even be thinking of creating a smartphone app to make things even easier and more fun for your customers to order flowers.

You can see how e-business has dramatically changed how business is done. Therefore, if an organization is moving from one e-strategy to the next, a change plan is a good idea. Your change plan should include training on how new technologies integrate with all the systems your employees may already be using and a clear vision of what the technology will achieve for the employees (remember the WIIFM) and the company.

E-business is not just about putting a checkout cart on the home page. In order to make e-business change successful, the organization must be ready to do business differently, and processes should be revamped to support how e-business will be used.

Just because everyone seems to be doing e-business doesn't mean everyone in your organization is going to be happy when you start doing it too, and it definitely doesn't mean the endeavor will be easy. In our flower shop example, the person who used to take the orders on the phone now needs to fulfill orders processed online. It could be as complex as aligning the forecast for how many flowers are needed every day with the supplier's order system.

You can imagine how much more complicated things get when your organization does business around the globe. The same change principles presented in this book apply to e-business, but you need to pay close attention to a few special considerations: integrating old technologies with new and aligning processes to the new technology.

Integrating old, new, and emerging technologies

Most likely, by the time an organization gets to the e-commerce level, it probably has some type of these technologies:

- CRM (customer-relationship management)
- SCM (supply-chain management)
- ERP (enterprise resource planning)

We touch on those technologies later in the chapter. E-commerce is not as simple as just layering on a website that does a bunch of stuff. Not only do the systems need to talk to one another to make it work, but the people who work with the multiple systems also need to talk with one another.

Let's go back to our little flower shop, Blooming Blossoms, which has really taken off. You have thousands of happy customers and have hired an entire staff of customer-service agents and florists. The CRM system and the online order form need to talk with one another, but your advertising team may want to know how to pull data on customers to better market your services. Customer-service reps need to know how to point clients to the site to do future booking or make personal reminders for anniversaries and birthdays. Your florists may need to know how to order more flowers from suppliers using the SCM. E-business practices build on most software applications already being used in the company (or may need to be implemented). This integrated view of the business is the art and science of balancing people, process, and technology, and e-business is speeding up the need for this balance faster than you can say Blooming Blossoms three times quickly.

Technology can have all the capabilities in the world, but if the people who use it don't support and know the value of it, it is useless.

Adjusting or redesigning business processes

When e-business is in full swing, how customers and businesses interact will be dramatically different than it was before the new strategy was created. Changing how the work gets done behind the scenes is commonly called *business-process reengineering.* Most of it happens in the *back office systems,* the systems that support business operations like finance, HR, inventory management, and so on. We cover how to make these process changes later in the chapter, so for now we just look at the potential scope of process redesign during an e-business transformation.

These processes will, at a minimum, include almost anything employees do before, during, and after working with the customer:

✔ How customers can provide feedback on products

✔ How feedback is reviewed and responded to

✔ How customers can receive updates on orders, returns, and shipping

✔ How customers pay for their service

In a true e-commerce company, SCM processes change as well; gone are the days of the purchasing department sitting in a cube in the back of the building; now SCM is in real time and online, feeding just-in-time information to suppliers on an organization's raw-material needs. This change dramatically impacts how people do their jobs (especially everyone in the purchasing department).

With new processes come new reporting relationships, new training, new job descriptions, and probably new career paths. We have not even begun to talk about how e-business can open global markets for companies (like it did for Blooming Blossoms), and these new markets will impact financial reporting (finance), building new business (sales and marketing and business development), and hiring new employees and training the ones you have (human resources).

Whether you are a one-person shop or a Fortune 500 company, e-business really does touch and change every aspect of the business.

Including ERP and integrated systems

ERP (enterprise resource planning) was made popular in the 1990s when companies quickly realized that the spreadsheets and home-grown information systems weren't sufficient to compete within the emerging global Internet economy. ERPs and integrated information systems were set up to create a powerful tool for knowledge (data) to be shared quickly among lots of employees. For anyone who hasn't had the chance to work with such a massive technology system, here is the basic premise: Finance people link to the human resources system so they can better understand the costs in specific organizational cost centers. Manufacturing professionals link to the supply chain system so they know when and where to expect raw materials and can plan their production schedule accordingly.

Although ERPs and integrated systems have the power to truly transform a company, they are basically just big and very expensive databases sitting alone in a cold, dark room if they aren't integrated with the culture, policies, goals, communication channels, and infrastructure of the organizations using them. In other words, technology can't just be thrown at users; it must be part of how business is done, and this means . . . drumroll please . . . change.

In addition to an amazing communication plan (Chapter 7), expert change agents (Chapter 3), and a solid vision for why technology is changing from leadership, you need to take care of some tactical concerns that need to happen during these system changes, including training on the new system, redesigning processes to maximize efficiency, and redesigning job roles to reflect the new technology strategy (these cornerstones of technology change should be starting to sound a little familiar).

Training right

Two types of training go on during ERP implementations: how to use the new system and how the system relates to how employees will do their job. Adults learn best when they have context around the training, so you probably shouldn't bother just putting a bunch of people in a room to teach them which button to press. Instead, ask them to integrate tools into an overall process; they will learn even more when they can apply the training to their day-to-day jobs and get hands-on practice with the new tools.

Just like all other parts of change, the training has a strategic component as well; training with no strategic goals is just a bunch of manuals soon to be collecting dust. Here are a few common goals when it comes to training:

- ✔ **Employees are ready to perform at launch.** Users of a new system usually are not big fans of waking up in the morning and having a new system they must learn while also doing their existing jobs. On the other hand, few people like to learn about a system way in advance and then be asked to recall everything they learned five months later. You should design training to give users the information they need to do their jobs as close to the time they will be making the transition as possible.

- ✔ **Everyone impacted achieves the required competency levels in their areas of their responsibility.** The training will develop a set of skills and competencies that employees need to do their jobs. If you can tie these skills and competencies to predefined performance objectives, the training will be well aligned to the strategy of the organization.

- ✔ **End-users own the technology.** Having technology pushed down employees' throats is not the way to win over their hearts and minds. Give users the opportunity to play with the technology, use it in real world scenarios, and then give feedback.

- ✔ **You establish a foundation for continuous skill development.** The worst thing an organization can do is force employees to go to a mandatory training on a new system and then say, "Hasta la vista, good luck, bye-bye." Periodic training and a method to incorporate improvements and changes to the system (as well as provide the structure for ongoing training of new employees) is always the best approach.

✔ **The training supports rather than stalls the effort.** Hands-on training that is applicable to how employees will use the system when they do their jobs should be balanced with not trying to train in everything at once. Training can be done systematically: The first training wave trains on the day-to-day activities, the second training wave may train on monthly activities, and so on.

Being smart about process redesign

During an ERP implementation, you can easily get caught up in how wonderful the technology looked during the sales demo. But the technology can only go so far to enhance productivity without substantial process change. You need to do more than provide a fancy user interface — ERP implementations should help facilitate changes in how work is done. If the process is not changed, you may risk just automating an inefficient process.

Process redesign can be broken down into five steps:

1. **Define what the future process should accomplish.** This step is where you benchmark other organizations and processes as well as use strategic tools like a *SWOT analysis,* an acronym that stands for identifying the strengths, weaknesses, opportunities, and threats to the organization. Here's an opportunity to set customer-focused goals and critical success factors for the process as well as create service-level agreements between departments and with suppliers. When the future goal is defined, check back to make sure customer, cultural, financial, business, and technical considerations are all accounted for and voiced.

2. **Define the as-is state.** The as-is state should include what is happening today: the good, the bad, and the ugly. Process mapping is a powerful tool frequently used in improvement initiatives, but keep it to one or two pages and tackle the big steps each function does in the department.

3. **Create the future state process.** Have the team decide how it wants the process to work.

4. **Tie technology to the new process.** Remember that technology should support a process and make it easier; processes should not be built to make technology work the way it should.

5. **Identify the differences in the current- and future-state maps.** This step is often called a *gap analysis.* Focus your energy and resources on the areas with the biggest gaps.

We love process tools so much we can't contain ourselves to one chapter. For templates and info on how to use the tools mentioned in this chapter, head to www.leadingchangeguide.com.

Analyzing job roles

When new systems replace old ones and automation and knowledge transfer are better leveraged, job roles will change. A job-description analysis is basically a "who-does-what" chart and can be used to help retrain employees on new processes. It follows these steps:

1. **Identify who is impacted.** It may be a team, a person, or a function within a department. Let's return to Blooming Blossoms, your flower shop, because you're now implementing a finance system to better report the skyrocketing profits from the e-business implementation. One of the roles that will change is the financial analyst.

2. **List out what major tasks are changing or may be new for the role.** Now think of how work will be different for the people impacted. For the financial analyst over at Blooming Blossoms, the changes may include how reports are run, how quarterly information is reported back to executives, and how forecasting models are created.

3. **Identify what skill is required to do the new task.** Using the information above, start thinking of what skills may be needed. If someone has been running spreadsheets or manually entering data for years, he may need to be trained on how to check the accuracy of data feeds in the new system or how to make the data flow from one area to another using the new technology.

4. **Identify how to close the gaps between skills needed and the current state.** Find out which skills can be taught and which need to come from other resources. Remember that technical training is not a good fit for theory and lecture! Just-in-time training or practical examples are often the best way to make sure employees know how and why they need to do something different.

You can find a job-role-analysis template at `www.leadingchangeguide.com`.

The new trend in technology is to move away from the massive hosting servers and hardware at a client site to cloud ERPs. *Cloud ERP* basically means all the information and applications are hosted on the Internet (up in the invisible cloud, hence the name), taking away the hassle of handling data storage locally, often resulting in a faster implementation. But the general concept of change associated with ERP implementations is still the same: Companies that transfer organizational knowledge from one part of the company to another will be able to serve customers more efficiently.

ERP implementations are notorious for causing turf battles in organizations and facing tremendous resistance. Yes, to most people, doing away with physically entering in data eight times throughout a process may seem like a brilliant solution. Yes, eliminating the need to photocopy everything and then walk some type of data over to another person who is sitting on the other side of the building may seem like a really good idea. However, when the person who enters in the data or walks it over hears that he isn't needed anymore, well, he may fear for his job and resist change.

Change, especially when it relates to gaining efficiencies and changing job roles, is a very real threat to individual status, position, and power. A great way to avoid this turf battle is to bring the people who are going to be impacted into the decision-making and design process. It may take more time, but the solution will be more widely used, and involvement and partici-pation is one of the best ways to create lasting change.

Actually using CRM

Customer-relationship management (CRM) is about building ongoing connec-tions with your clients. CRM systems provide a place to collect information about who is buying products or services so a company can market, up-sell, cross-sell, and provide a more in-depth customer experience. The big kicker with CRM systems is making sure the data is used, not just stored on a big server or cloud somewhere. Imagine how happy Blooming Blossoms custom-ers would be if they picked up the phone or went online to order birthday flowers for Mom and were able to hear or see exactly what they bought in the past and look at recommendations for flowers she might like.

The big organizational change piece of CRM is identifying how the data is used (process), who is going to use it (people and job roles), and how the information can be accessed (training).

Effectively using social media and the next "it" thing

An organization's success (or failure) is often based on what employees do or don't do. Change is all about giving employees, customers, and other stake-holders the ability, flexibility, and power to adapt and share knowledge. Social media is often an easy tool to promote this behavior.

Some organizations treat social media as a random, over-caffeinated typing fest that is haphazardly thrown together because all the cool businesses are doing it. We don't recommend this approach, as you may have guessed. Social media — Facebook, YouTube, Twitter, LinkedIn, or whatever the next great social channel may be — is best used when your organization has an intentional, goal-oriented plan and, you guessed it, a change plan to go with it!

You can utilize the major social networks in a number of ways. Companies use these opportunities for everything from customer service and product training to customer research, marketing, and PR. For example, Google uses YouTube training videos to attract and inform millions of potential viewers using or potentially using Google applications. These simple and short videos are geared to ordinary people, not just programming-savvy web developers.

Large companies, such as GEICO and Comcast, use Twitter to communicate in real time with customers. Rather than wait in the online phone queue, users can Tweet their issue and see a resolution in 140 characters or less. This system can also help companies create an online repository of issues and solutions to proactively manage. Internally, Yammer can make companies more productive by allowing employees to privately exchange short answers to simple questions with one another. Tools like Basecamp help employees on projects organize to-dos, manage calendars, and keep every piece of project information in one central repository. All these social-enterprise tools are part of the bigger communication picture when it comes to using technology to build awareness of what is happening in the organization, create understanding within the organization, and gain commitment and action from employees.

Companies are using social media not just to mass market their products and services but also to help support customers and encourage problem-solving employee behavior. These are perfect examples of how innovative behavior and social-media technology can go hand in hand.

For more on social media, check out *Social Media Marketing All-in-One For Dummies,* by Jan Zimmerman and Doug Sahlin (Wiley). For more on communicating effectively using social media tools, pick up a copy of *Communicating Effectively For Dummies,* by Marty Brounstein (also published by Wiley).

Avoiding the Common Pitfalls of Technology Change

Often, organizational change is guided by reactive initiatives or wishful visions rather than by a plan based on sound principles. Because the impact of technological change is so far-reaching, it frequently becomes the trigger for transformational change in an organization. Technological changes present a unique set of challenges, and stories of disasters are multitude.

Following are the most common causes of these failures and how to avoid them:

✔ **Competing priorities and perspectives:** Sometimes the decision to use a new technology is not understood among key players on the project. Other users may have used a different technology to do the same thing in another company and don't understand why they need to learn yet another technology tool.

If you are faced with a number of other initiatives and options, communicate to the stakeholders why this technology is being used and how it differs from the alternatives or other products.

✔ **Inconsistent procedures:** Often, technology is used to streamline a process or processes, but if a thorough process-improvement effort from beginning to end doesn't have enough stakeholder involvement and resources, a big pitfall can be the notion of "garbage in, garbage out." If a new system is put in and users are still receiving poor information to do their jobs, the system will just get the bad information out sooner but not change the way business is done.

Spend extra time creating solid (and mutually agreed on) definitions, processes, and procedures across all the users who work on the system, have input into the technology, or are customers of the data or service the new technology delivers.

✔ **Skepticism:** Skepticism on the functionality kills buy-in. Although employees (at any level) may have many ideas about the benefits of the data warehouse, they may also have a wait-and-see mentality to find out if the technology can really do everything the vision, strategy, and sales guy promised. This is particularly true if the company has tried implementing technology in the past and those change initiatives failed. People will be jaded and feel like past efforts were a waste of money and ask, *why support this one?*

The best way to avoid this problem is to have clear expectations and measurements of the project, to communicate them throughout the stakeholder group, and then to start measuring performance on day one to show how the system is delivering on promises.

✔ **Lack of clarity around the scope of the technology:** After you announce that a new technology is going to be implemented, you can be pretty darn sure some groups in the company are out searching the web for what this new technology can do. The other half may be out rewriting their resumes. All this distraction halts productivity during the transition from the as-is to the future state.

As soon as possible, provide an outline of what processes will be impacted and which will not. Also, begin to filter functionality even when the system may be in test mode. Individuals can hear and read about what the technology can do, but when they see it live they start believing it.

✔ **Poor project support and poor communication:** Support, whether it is leadership, communication structures, or an unrealistic project plan, can bring technology to a stop.

Avoid this problem by making sure the project support doesn't end with leadership saying the technology is important. Create a support structure that includes a well-trained project team, a robust communication process, involvement from end users in creating the solution, and solid measurements for the project and the technology results.

Many people are surprised that the problems cluster around people and cultural issues and not around the reliability or effectiveness of the technology (not you, of course — you read this book!). Generally, the technology works well, but the soft issues will be the ones that can set implementation and project plans into a tailspin. Devoting effort to getting the technology *and* people working will launch your technology change to great heights.

Chapter 16

Shifting a Culture: Managing Cultural Change

*O*rganizational culture tends to have a life of its own. Even though you may have spent a great deal of time focusing on communicating and implementing a new strategy or carefully maneuvering through a merger or acquisition, you may still find that old beliefs and assumptions about "how things are done around here" remain. These beliefs and behaviors can be like an anchor to a previous time that no longer works for the organization. It may well be time to take a serious look at shifting the culture. No, we're not talking about cultural change like moving to a different country. We're talking about changing the underlying assumptions that employees hold about the company, shared values, and ultimately the behaviors that drive success in the organization.

Although it's an undeniably large undertaking, culture change can happen. It just takes careful planning and patience. Rome and old culture weren't built in a day; nor will they change overnight. In this chapter we help you get the process moving and make culture change achievable.

First we walk through all the major elements of culture to help you grasp the extent of what will (and will not) be changing. Next we move into a real-world plan that helps you create successful change by aligning executive support and work systems (a fancy word for processes and reward systems). Because culture is such a big change deal, we also provide some tips to safeguard against failure. Finally, you'll want to know what to do after the culture change is a crazy success, so we point out some good techniques for how to hire in employees that fit the new culture and how to work with those that don't.

Understanding What Organizational Culture Is All About

Changing an organization's culture is one of the most complex leadership challenges anyone can undertake. Although all change requires you to create new goals for the organization, improve how processes are done, use multiple communication channels, and handle the usual suspects who resist change, a culture of an organization runs deep and is personal.

Culture is ambiguous but can be seen, felt, and heard around the building. Culture is whether or not employees show up on time to meetings. An organizational culture writes the unwritten rule as to whether someone picks up the phone to ask a question or shoots an e-mail off to someone sitting 50 feet away rather than getting up and talking face-to-face. An organizational culture is also visible, involving what people wear to work and whether leaders keep their doors open and invite employees in or sit in a mega office somewhere out of reach to the common employee (maybe even with a private bathroom as well as a remote control that opens and closes the door on command; but we digress).

Employees and executives can often take culture for granted. Because people see and work with it every day, it is just "there." Organizational culture is no different than a national culture. If you're American, imagine if turkey was no long the signature dish of Thanksgiving. What if cricket was no longer played in India? Or the red double-decker buses in London were replaced with silver one-level buses? You can begin to imagine how hard it is for employees to change their cultural mindset if they have worked for the same organization for a long time or perhaps for their entire careers.

Many people are creatures of habit and get used to doing things a certain way over time. Employees may believe there is only one right way to do things. Until these individuals are exposed to a different corporate culture, they may have no idea that other people have different approaches that can actually work.

Breaking culture into three components

MIT professor and management consultant Edgar H. Schein points out that culture has the following three components:

- **Artifacts:** Artifacts are simply anything that can be seen, felt, or heard in the company. This category includes how offices are set up (cubicles, virtual, or formal offices with big heavy doors), the work hours (does everyone come early or late — or come late and leave early?), and the dress code (formal, informal, pajamas, tuxedo). But it may also include how family and work are balanced among employees, level of formality in the organization, and how meetings are run.

Other artifacts may be jargon, how disagreements are handled, what social events the company has for its employees, how people hear about things that are happening (through the grapevine or formal communications), and how formal the language is between peers and managers.

A very formal, hierarchical culture probably has some form of formal dress (button-down shirt with the occasional casual Fridays), meetings that begin and end on time, no decision made without the approval of your manager's manager, and offices resembling something like an ancient fortress. On the other extreme, a casual culture that values freedom probably has people coming into the office with their pets, a casual dress code allowing shorts and sandals, decisions made by consensus, and virtual offices or cubes with very low walls so everyone can interact with one another. You can begin to see how these physical aspects drive the organizational culture and how work is done.

✔ **Espoused values:** The espoused values are the mission statements and mottos you see up on the wall, on business cards, and on the website. Some executive team came up with them a while back for the company, and they are the values they tell customers, new employees, and almost anyone else.

Enacted values are the norms that are exhibited by employees and can be inferred by the actual behavior in the organization. If the company really stands behind its espoused values, its enacted values are the same as the espoused values. However, sometimes they aren't, because the company doesn't practice what it preaches (we told you culture is a difficult thing to tackle!). For example, innovation, advancement, or some other form of that idea is often an espoused company value. However, if employees are never rewarded for risk taking, the enacted value is that innovation is okay as long as you don't fail. If a company values quality but shuns any formal quality program and only rewards people for fixing things instead of investing in getting it right the first time, then firefighting, not quality, is really the enacted value.

✔ **Basic underlying assumptions:** Assumptions are all those unwritten, unspoken things that happen in the company. They are what people really pay attention to in the organization. Assumptions are the hardest to tackle because they are usually somewhat unconscious. Did everyone's eyes follow a senior leader walking down the hall for a meeting with the reclusive CEO (who only comes out for board meetings and Groundhog Day) and assume it meant the senior leader was fired? This assumption is cultural. When people saw an unknown silver-haired man in a conference room with that same CEO, did everyone assume the company was being bought, or did they assume some exciting new client had been signed? These assumptions are hard to pinpoint, but the conclusions people jump to in a culture and theories (good or bad) about what something someone does means are basic underlying assumptions in an organizational culture.

Digging into the layers of culture

To double-check your understanding of these three levels of culture, consider the metaphor of peeling an onion. Each layer of the onion and component of culture reveals a deeper understanding of what is driving individual and group behavior. Here we take a closer look at these three levels and peel back the proverbial onion.

Imagine you are walking into the headquarters of a company. What do you first see? Most likely you observe the layout of the offices and posters and art hanging on the wall. You also notice what people are wearing. These visual cues are all artifacts. They're the physical characteristics that you can directly observe about an organization.

For example, you may notice a great number of awards hanging on the wall from customers acknowledging the organization's commitment to quality and customer satisfaction. These displayed awards give you a clue that the organization has a culture of quality and customer service. In another organization you may observe photos of the founders and CEO hanging in the lobby. These pictures may give you some indication that history and the founding principles laid out by the company's founders are deemed important to preserve.

Looking a bit deeper in the organization, you start to come across formal written statements such as strategies, goals, philosophies, and organizational values. These are the statements that you may see also hanging on the wall for all to read as reminders of what is important. You also find these statements commonly on corporate websites and in strategic plans. These espoused values, which we talk more about later in this chapter, are important building blocks of culture.

If you spend enough time in the company observing office activity and talking to employees, you can begin to see the core of the culture onion: the basic underlying assumptions held by members of the organization. These assumptions include deeply held beliefs (including beliefs about customers, how employees should be treated, what is required for success, and so on), perceptions, and feelings. Often they're taken for granted and unquestioned and may even be unconscious. In very strong cultures, these beliefs can be quite dogmatic and strongly held by organizational members. This level of culture is quickly communicated and passed down to new employees. It doesn't take long for someone to figure out "how things really work around here."

Although a strong company culture can be an asset to an organization by providing stable, shared beliefs and values, culture can also be very hard to change. Simply announcing a new set of company values isn't enough. Change leaders must demonstrate what these values look like in action and reward people for the desired behaviors. Then employees will know that you are serious about cultural change.

The Starting Line: Defining the Current Culture

Whether the old company culture was something that evolved naturally or was purposefully put into place years ago, changing culture is something that must be handled proactively. Clearly defining mission, vision, and values is the first place to begin to define the organizational culture. We talk in Chapter 4 about how to develop a mission and vision, so here we go into a little more detail about the importance of organizational values. Then we discuss how to assess what values and culture are currently in place so that you can begin the transition from the appropriate starting point.

Taking a deeper look at company values

We introduce the key middle layer of organizational culture earlier as consisting of espoused values (see "Breaking culture into three components"), and here we go a little deeper in explaining how company values play an important role in defining and maintaining your overall culture. Values serve as an ethical foundation on which to build an organization's culture. They are driven by the core shared beliefs regarding what is important as you go about conducting business. Values set the tone for acceptable and desirable interactions between co-workers, customers, and suppliers.

Here are some examples of common values for organizations:

- ✔ Trusting people and having the highest ethical standards
- ✔ Respecting decisions and choices of other employees
- ✔ Innovating to propel the company forward
- ✔ Using teamwork to drive results
- ✔ Putting the customer first

We just gave you 80 percent of the values for 80 percent of organizations in the world. Not that we are cynical, but as we note in the discussion about espoused values and enacted values in the preceding section, anyone can put values up on a wall. Not everyone can live them and reward them day in and day out.

No company is perfect, but one organization that we feel lives and breathes their values is the United Stated–based health-food giant, Whole Foods. Yes, we like their food. And, yes, U.S. President Barack Obama got in trouble during the 2008 campaign for talking about buying arugula there. But customers see, feel, and come back to buy highly priced food at Whole Foods because of the quality and service. Here are Whole Food's values they hang on their wall and what they are doing to make them real:

- ✔ **Supporting team member happiness and excellence:** Call us crazy, but we really think Whole Foods has some happy juice in the break room. Employees are always polite to one another and the fish guy is so happy cutting salmon, you'd think he just got back from a year-long vacation (but we know he didn't, because he was there last week).

- ✔ **Creating wealth through profits and growth:** Obviously, Whole Foods doesn't operate just to make the world a better place. The company wants to make money. But instead of just using profits to line the pockets of a few wealthy executives, Whole Foods invests in the company to grow and prosper, opening new stores and hiring more employees.

- ✔ **Caring about our communities and our environment:** The compost bin in Whole Foods stores is about four times the size of the trash can. But caring about the environment doesn't stop there; Whole Foods actively promotes local products and asks customers to help give back to the community to support healthy lunches in schools and raise money for microloans to businesses in developing countries.

- ✔ **Creating ongoing win-win partnerships with our suppliers:** The footprint of Whole Foods gives tremendous opportunities to their suppliers. Fresh burrito soon-to-be giant EVOL got its start at Whole Foods in Boulder, Colorado. A back-of-the-truck burrito guy was able to partner with Whole Foods to put his wraps into hungry hands across the country.

- ✔ **Promoting the health of our stakeholders through healthy eating education:** Whole Foods frequently sponsors educational seminars on how to eat healthy, gluten-free, low-fat, vegan, vegetarian, and any other dietary need out there.

- ✔ **Selling the highest-quality natural and organic products available:** This one goes without saying — after all, you can't charge $3 a pound for apples if they aren't the best apples around.

- ✔ **Satisfying and delighting our customers:** Many Whole Foods locations have put in automatic feedback systems that allow any customer to walk up to give feedback. The store leadership wants to hear from customers. From offering easy returns to giving kids free, healthy snacks while their parents shop, customer delight is an obvious value that is espoused throughout the organization.

To us, it looks like Whole Food walks the talk!

Many organizations tie their standards of business conduct to their core values. Training on core values supports employees to make ethical decisions in their daily work routines.

One problem we frequently see with organizational values is that a small leadership team at the top goes off on a two-day retreat to articulate the values and then puts up posters announcing the values and claiming that they're what the company believes in. This approach is not enough to make the company values real for the average employee in the trenches. Line managers need to have practical conversations with employees on what it means to live the company values.

One best practice is to have dialogue sessions that discuss examples of what the values look like in real life. Examine ways to live these values as well as examples of what missing the mark looks like. For example, trust and respect may look like talking to a co-worker directly when you have a conflict. Lack of respect in this case would be to talk about that co-worker behind his back to his boss without first talking to him about the conflict. Even worse would be spreading rumors about him.

Another best practice is to tie your performance-management process and rewards system to your company values. Some organizations have specific sections on employee annual performance reviews that address each of their company-wide values. Pay for results for executives can also be tied to goals that support the company values. For example, valuing diversity may be one of the corporate values, which can be measured by the percent of minorities and women hired and promoted in a given year.

Examining your current organizational culture

As a change leader, one of the first things you need to do to understand organizational culture is to get a clear picture of what your employees believe. To gather this information, you need to do a variety of cultural assessments to dig at the third level of culture, the hidden assumptions (see the earlier section "Breaking culture into three components").

You can choose from a number of methods to examine a company's culture, including the following approaches:

- **Interviews and focus groups:** Interviews and focus groups are powerful tools to get firsthand information regarding how employees view your organizational culture. You may also want to include customers, suppliers, and vendors in your evaluation to get an external perspective of your organization's culture as well.

  Because the act of simply asking a question can itself change the culture, we recommend that you carefully craft your questionnaires and interview protocols in such a way that you drive a positive change in the organization. For example, a good question to ask would be, "What do you like the best about working at this company"? Another best practice question could be, "What changes would result in you being able to provide higher customer satisfaction?" Avoid negative questions such as "What bothers you the most about working here?" which can open the floodgates to faultfinding and finger-pointing. This purposely positive approach is commonly known as *appreciative inquiry* in academic circles.

You may be saying, "But I want to hear about the bad stuff, too!" Of course you want to understand what is not working. A best practice to get at this information is to ask employees what changes going forward would make the organization even better. By using this approach, employees tell you what is not working *and* share their ideas about what better would look like. Our experience has shown that focusing on what you want is much better than focusing on what you don't want.

✔ **Quantitative assessments:** A number of commercially available instruments can be used to quickly capture a snapshot of an organization's shared assumptions and behaviors. These instruments go by a number of different names, such as employee-satisfaction surveys, employee-engagement surveys, and organizational-culture indicators. Most of them are administered by third-party companies that provide online access to employees to complete the typical questionnaire in less than 30 minutes. One of the advantages of using an independent third party is ensuring confidentiality and the anonymity of the employees providing feedback on the survey. Another advantage is that most of these instruments are well researched and verified to measure key indicators of organizational health.

Assessing the leadership culture

Leadership is one of the important aspects of organizational culture and deserves a closer look. The leadership styles and behaviors that dominate in your organization can impact organizational performance and employee morale. One of our favorite cultural-assessment tools is the Leadership Culture Survey, published by The Leadership Circle. Decades of research went into the tool and its 31 dimensions of culture. The Leadership Culture Survey provides a powerful examination of your leadership culture. Used for your entire organization or for just a leadership team, the survey tells you how your people view their current leadership culture and compares that reality to the optimal culture they desire. The gap between the current culture and desired culture reveals key opportunities for leadership development. The Leadership Culture Survey also measures how your leadership culture compares to that of other organizations.

A Leadership Culture Survey does the following things:

✔ Establishes a compelling rational for change in leadership behavior

✔ Focuses leadership-development efforts

✔ Delineates leadership cultural challenges associated with acquisitions, mergers, and restructuring plans

✔ Correlates leadership to productivity, profits, turnover, and other bottom-line metrics

Although the entire survey is far too extensive to cover here in detail and probably contains more information on culture than you may want to ever know or learn, in this section we briefly walk through the elements to give you an idea of what a formal assessment may look like for your organization. To access the Leadership Culture Survey, you can obtain certification training through The Leadership Circle or hire a consultant who is certified to administer and interpret the survey.

The leadership cultural model, shown in Figure 16-1, consists of four major interrelated dimensions: relationships, tasks, creativity, and reactive behavior.

✔ **Relationship dimension:** Are relationships based on interpersonal skills or compliance with direction and directives? Complying cultures maintain a sense of self-worth and security by complying with the expectations of others rather than acting on what they intend and want. On the other hand, relating cultures work with one another to bring out the best in people, groups, and organizations.

✔ **Task focus:** Do people want to achieve great things or great control? Positive cultures offer visionary and authentic leadership. Cultures with a controlling task focus often have leaders who exert too much control, push themselves and others excessively hard, and pursue results at the expense of people.

✔ **Creative leadership competencies:** Creative competencies are well-researched competencies measuring how you achieve results, bring out the best in others, lead with vision, enhance your own development, act with integrity and courage, and improve organizational systems. Is leadership authentic or is it masked by organizational politics, looking good, and winning approval? Courage to try the unknown (that is, creativity) in the workplace involves authentically and directly dealing with risky issues in one-to-one and group situations.

✔ **Reactive leadership styles:** Opposite of creative cultures, leaders in a reactive culture protect themselves and establish a sense of worth and job security by remaining distant, cynical, and superior. Reactive tendencies are leadership styles emphasizing caution over creating results, self-protection over productive engagement, and aggression over building alignment. These self-limiting styles overemphasize the focus on gaining the approval of others, protecting yourself, and getting results through high control tactics.

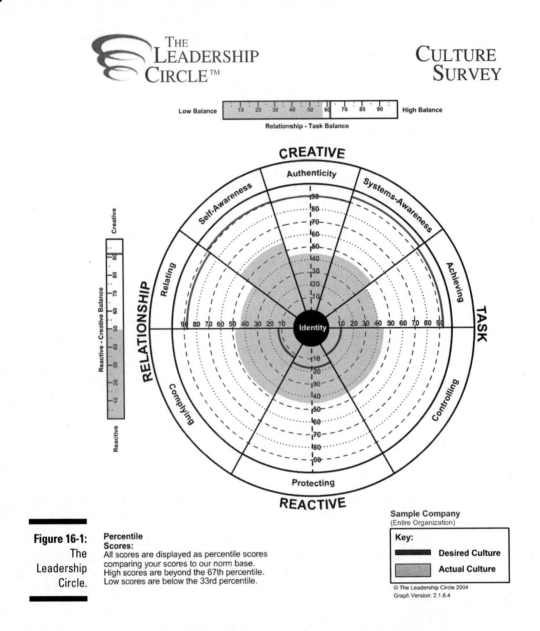

Figure 16-1:
The Leadership Circle.

Percentile Scores:
All scores are displayed as percentile scores comparing your scores to our norm base. High scores are beyond the 67th percentile. Low scores are below the 33rd percentile.

Sample Company
(Entire Organization)

Key:
- Desired Culture
- Actual Culture

© The Leadership Circle 2004
Graph Version: 2.1.6.4

The Leadership Culture Survey assessment is administered via a confidential online questionnaire completed by employees and management. Respondents are asked to rate not only the current state of the organizational culture but also what they want as the desired future state. This tool can be a quick and cost-effective method to understand some of the deeper underlying assumptions driving an organization's behavior.

Commercially available cultural assessment instruments and tools can save you both time and money in the long run by leveraging best practices based on years of industry research by these survey companies.

The Next Step: Creating Successful Cultural Change

Now that you have done the hard work of gathering an accurate picture of what your current culture looks like by engaging employees and management in formal or informal assessments, you're ready to design the culture that you want. Although some best practices are established for creating a positive culture, as we discuss in the preceding section, you still need to define a specific culture that works for your strategy and your particular organization.

This process of defining the desired future state is best done by engaging thought leadership from all levels, including executives, middle management, and individual contributors. Culture doesn't simply rest in the formal statements issued by managers; it's in the hearts and minds of all employees. You need to engage everyone in the organization to create the new culture.

Uniting executive support

One of the most common reasons for cultural change is new leadership at the top. New CEOs, especially when hired from the outside, come into organizations with strong beliefs and assumptions about how an organization needs to operate to be successful. Savvy change leaders quickly recognize instances where the new leadership's beliefs clash with the long-standing culture of the organization and take steps to bring everyone together.

As an example, we use Barry and We Make Airlines Fly, a manufacturing company with a number of locations in California. One of the founders, John, decides to retire and sells the company to a larger firm, Worldwide Airlines That Really Fly, with multiple divisions that also serve the airline industry. To serve as CEO, Worldwide brings in Barry, who has a long history of using a very competitive bidding process to lower the materials cost from vendors. The founders of We Make Airlines Fly, on the other hand, believed that its suppliers should share in the success of We Make Airlines Fly and built long-standing relationships of trust with these vendors to increase quality and maintain low costs. Barry immediately announces to the procurement department that all supplier contracts going forward will go out to bid to the most competitive supplier every three years. The head of procurement can't believe what he's hearing. He finds himself dumbfounded on how Barry could expect this approach to work.

What you have just witnessed here is a culture clash. Barry now needs to learn how to successfully lead a cultural change effort if he is to change the procurement department's deeply held beliefs about vendor management.

The executive team plays a critical role in setting the right cultural tone for the entire organization. The role includes leading the effort to develop changes to any of the core values, vision, and mission statements. It also includes developing new artifacts that represent the underlying changes in key assumptions and beliefs about the way the organization should work.

One of the most powerful ways to create a new culture is to create new stories and images that symbolize the new way of doing things. For millennia, people have maintained their cultural heritage through storytelling. This technique also works in the business setting. We recommend you spend significant time with your executive team to create a new story of what it means to work at your organization. Leaders need to develop and emphasize stories that demonstrate in vivid detail the desired future behaviors and beliefs in the organization, which may include specific stories about employees who have gone the extra mile to exemplify the desired behaviors. You can also have these stories tie back to the vision of where the company is going and its core mission.

Stories can be captured in writing and used by people throughout the organization to retell in speeches, small group meetings, and more. It should also be woven into your new-hire orientation or onboarding. You can develop ways to continue to elicit new stories. One idea is to request submissions through the company intranet, if you have one.

Frequently, the changing culture is associated with a change in brand strategy and external communications. We view this as a best practice that enables you to align your internal culture with how customers and others see you in the world.

Another technique for reigniting employees' commitments to core values is to dust off some of the older stories from company founders that exemplify the desired culture. Storytelling is a powerful way to communicate culture, because stories connect with employees at an emotional level.

Develop and tell stories that exemplify the behaviors and values that you wish to promote as part of the desired future state.

Successful executives do everything they can to walk the talk of espoused values. Employees can be naturally skeptical of any changes to the company's core values. They watch vigilantly to see whether management is serious about these changes or just giving lip service to them. Communications as well as actions, including the reward system, need to reinforce the desired behaviors.

Burritos and other food for thought

Simple stories that remind people of the roots of the company do so much to drive culture. We love the story of EVOL burritos. Phil Anson, founder of Phil's Fresh Foods, loved mountain climbing in Colorado. But climbing made him hungry, and he and his climbing buddies were tired of eating horrible frozen food from the local gas station. Phil began making burritos and selling them out of his van to fellow climbers.

Everyone who ate them loved them. He worked nights and weekends in his kitchen. He woke up at 3 a.m. thinking about burrito flavors. And even when his burrito shop moved from camper van to legitimate business, the extra tasty burritos came from his heart. He loved fresh, healthy, easy food (you may notice that EVOL is love spelled backward).

Aligning all work systems

You have done the hard work of rewriting the core documents, including vision and mission (see Chapter 4) and company values that set the tone for your organization's culture. You've created new images and stories to communicate the desired culture. The next step is turning to the rest of your work systems to ensure they align with and reward the desired behaviors. In Chapter 15 we talk a lot about aligning technology and processes during change. Here we emphasize changing your reward and recognition systems to fit the changes you're making.

Think about how you can recognize and reward employees' behavior that supports the new culture and at the same time eliminate old reward systems that emphasize the old culture. Out with the old and in with the new! Too often we find that organizations leave in place outdated systems that result in a mixed message to employees.

For example, imagine you have announced to your company that you want everyone to spend more effort on quality. However, your primary measures for calculating the annual employee bonus only consist of on-time delivery and cost-reduction goals. Given this situation, can you realistically expect employees to now focus on quality given that their pay is tied only to cost and delivery? Of course not! You need to add in a new quality measure as part of the bonus calculation to drive new behaviors toward quality products and services. This change will no doubt create dialogue among employees on the relative importance of quality versus on-time delivery and cost. How you address these questions around priorities determines the fate of the new culture you wish to create.

Public recognition for employees who exemplify the desired future culture is another powerful technique to encourage the new culture to take root. You may want to create new monthly or quarterly rewards that symbolize each of the core values you wish to emphasize. For example, if sustainability is a value you wish to incorporate, you could consider an annual competition among employees to think of ways to reuse, reduce, and recycle consumables used in your business. Recognizing the winner as well as other teams with significant achievements at company events and in company communications emphasizes the value that both executives and employees place on sustainability.

Corporate citizenship may be another value you wish to promote in your company culture. Giving employees the opportunity to volunteer their time at local nonprofit organizations one day a year is a way to show your company's commitment to local communities. Many companies also support corporate giving by allowing employees to deduct a percentage of their paycheck every month to go to a charity of their choosing. We have witnessed annual giving campaigns at corporations where local nonprofits get a chance to share with employees onsite what they do and how they support the local community. These events not only show management's commitment to corporate citizenship but also create a sense of pride among employees that they are making a difference in the world.

Old habits die hard. Employees may want to hold on to old ways of doing things. One best practice to ensure the old ways are actually "dead" is to hold a wake for them. Yes, we really mean a wake or a funeral that celebrates the successes of the old ways but symbolizes that they've passed on and the time has come to embrace the new. Some CEOs have physically cut the wires of old servers that ran old-generation systems to physically show a move from the old to the new.

Safeguarding against failure

Culture change can be uncertain. But with the right tools, methods, and vision for the future, it can be done. A few things help leaders safeguard against failure, and if used correctly, they serve as a safety net that catches you and the organization if you veer off course.

- ✔ **360-degree assessments:** A 360-degree assessment allows peers, managers, and employees to rate leaders on a number of areas. A cultural 360-assessment can give leaders in-depth information regarding how employees view the leaders' embodiment of the values of the new culture. These assessments are most effective when done at the three-month mark of the initial launch of the new culture programs so that executives have enough time to change behaviors and catch potential pitfalls early in the process.

> ✔ **Employee-engagement reviews:** Many companies use employee-engagement surveys to determine the pulse of the organization. A one-time survey provides valuable insights into how content employees are with a wide range of people issues (compensation, management, ease of getting work done); annual surveys can show employers trends in the overall workforce attitude and satisfaction. These surveys can also give individual departments relevant data on how they compare to other areas in the company. The surveys are based on past experiences, but if they're done at the 3-, 6-, and 12-month marks of the cultural-change process, the trends can help alert leaders to potential concerns as well as positive improvements.

Working with the New Culture

Why do some hires come in and hit the ground running and others just seem to stall out at every turn? Knowledge and skills have something to do with it, but usually the make or break for an employee is whether or not he or she fits in with the organizational culture. Whether you are changing a culture or just tweaking the current one, a bad fit with a hire is a big waste of money and time. And the problem is probably not that the hire doesn't have the skill set to do a job or overstated past experience significantly; the misfit usually involves personality clashes with the culture.

Hiring new employees into the new culture

Ask any recruiting expert, and you'll find that the best way to find the perfect employee is to look beyond the job description and the skills required. You have to look at the personality and make sure that the role you are filling fits this person's personality. When you hire someone purely for their skill, you miss out on an opportunity to enhance your team and your company's culture. Sometimes you can't uncover this fit with typical interview questions, so you need to plan out the interview to get what you want and what that new employee wants.

A perfect match between an employer and an employee is about so much more than mutual prosperity. The best employee takes a basic job description and broadens the role. Within weeks, she becomes a vital contributor and part of an effective team motivated to bring success. Too often, recruiters provide a stack of resumes to hiring managers and simply check off whether or not key words match the resume. On the other hand, when hiring to fit candidates to the organization, magic happens. Employees and employers go through a rigorous process to understand not only the strengths and capabilities they both offer but also what each potential employee wants to do next.

Trying to put a candidate into a company that doesn't fit his work style is like trying to put a square peg into a round whole — it just doesn't fit! But when the fit is good, your new employee is going to bounce out of bed every day ready to go to work.

When a job opens up, you have to get a warm body into that seat. But slow down one bit. Keep a pulse on the short-term need but look three years out: Could this individual grow with the strategy in the organization? Do you see the individual fitting into the culture (work style, work hours, decision-making process) for the long term? You want to hire in the best person for the job, but make sure to pick the best person for the job and for the company's growth as well.

Many hiring managers look at bright, eager recruits and just think, "Wow, they could really change things around here!" This goal is lofty and worthwhile, but try not to put all the success or failure on the new person's shoulders. One person can come in and ask questions and stir things up in the company, but he can't single-handedly change the culture. Many of these great prospective employees leave within two to three years because they don't feel that they can make dramatic changes alone.

What to do when the new culture doesn't fit employees

Cultural fit is not just for new employees. Every employee at the company is impacted by a new culture. If you have not been working too much on the culture of an organization but after reading this chapter you find yourself fired up to start making your culture more creative and collaborative, go for it! But don't forget that just like with other changes, some employees won't be 100 percent on board with changing things. Many people will come around, but not all. These employees in the "not" column will eventually be the Achilles' heel of the company. Culture, job fit, employee engagement, and employee satisfaction all go hand-in-hand. If an employee is way off the reservation (in a bad way) with the culture, forming relationships and getting work done may be very hard for her.

Although it's tough, the best thing for an educated change leader like you to do when an employee doesn't fit in with company culture is to look at performance. You need to look at both what employees do and how they do it. Many top-talent organizations use the *how-and-what* type of model for performance management, and looking at a simple example can give you an idea of how a manager would evaluate performance using the how-and-what model to judge what to do next when an employee does not really fit in.

- ✔ *How* refers to how the work gets done, often referred to as the softer skills like collaboration, respect, communication.

- ✔ *What* accounts for the hard results from an individual's performance.

Putting the two concepts together, for example: Does the individual respect others' opinions and make a fair judgment about what to do next (the how) and then go out and gets the work done in a collaborative style (the what)? Or does the individual ignore everyone's opinions, yell at co-workers, and run over anyone in her way (the how) in order to meet their monthly sales targets (the what)? In both situations, the individual may be meeting her numbers, but most people would prefer to work with the former example.

Table 16-1 summarizes the performance reviews for a group of leaders and notes what the boss may consider doing next using the how-and-what model for performance. For this exercise, keep in mind that the company wants to create a collaborative and creative environment for all employees.

Table 16-1   The How-and-What Performance Review

Employee	How the Work Gets Done	What Gets Done	What to Do Next?
Albert	He doesn't build relationships, and he follows a command-and-control model that leaves employees in tears.	Meets numbers 100% of the time	Coach Albert on how aligning with a collaborative culture at times will make everyone work better. If coaching doesn't work, Albert may need to be let go.
Tobin	He spends most of the day gathering opinions from others; people go to Tobin when they have concerns or ideas.	Has not met a single target in six months.	Train Tobin on time management and balancing discussion with action.
Sally	She makes great relationships and treats employees with respect.	Always makes her numbers and gets things done on time.	Make Sally CEO!

The lessons learned through culture assessments and leadership discussions can be used to determine what type of "how" the organization should hire for in the future. These results should also be a primary feed into the development of all the current employees and should be the basis for who gets promoted, who is given the sought-after training opportunities, and who gets the best assignments.

In this chapter we only begin to start peeling the onion of organizational culture and organizational-culture fit. For more information on organizational culture and fit, check out www.leadingchangeguide.com, our website filled with information, templates, and examples for how to lead organizational culture change.

Chapter 17

When Everything Changes: Working with Complex Change

Sometimes it hits you unexpectedly; other times it seems like a good idea at first but then you begin to have second thoughts. What are we talking about? Complex change. Chaos. We mean when everything, absolutely everything, is changing at once. Customers, technology, company culture, economic conditions, leadership teams; you name it, it is changing. This amount of change is not impossible to handle, it just takes a fine balance among assertive leadership, aggressive goals, realistic project timelines, near-perfect communication, fully staffed change teams, and a little luck. Not much, right?

Although we can't give you luck, we can prepare you to deal with complex change, whether it is planned or unexpectedly winds up on your to-do list one Monday morning. In this chapter we provide real-world examples of complex changes to use as reference for your own situation. We give you the tools you need to create simple, immediate changes during complex change and show you the fine art of balancing cooperation and creativity with necessary bureaucracy and structure. We also introduce the idea of a program-management office and knowledge management and tell you how to create these change structures within your organization.

If you want complex change to stick, you need to avoid the dreaded "flavor of the month" club, which can happen when everything is changing at once. In this chapter we tell you how to set your change apart. And finally, we tie everything together with how to make change easier in the future by integrating a change mentality into the organizational culture. We cover a lot of ground in this chapter, and if you're in the midst of complex change, you've got no time to lose.

Getting a Handle on Chaos: When Everything Is Changing at Once

What does managing multiple changes look like? In 2010, the merger of United Airlines and Continental Airlines was seen by some as a matter of survival for the U.S.-based airlines. In the post-9/11 world, with the economy slowly coming out of the worst recession in decades, economic factors required companies to go big or go home. We'll call those economic factors Change #1.

The merger meant a new name and logo. Former United employees said that it would be odd not to see the big United "U" on the back of planes. Continental employees would adopt a new name. These changes just touch the surface of all the changes that go into creating a new company from two different cultures, which is Change #2: forming a new company.

The former CEO of Continental, Jeffery A. Smisek, took over as the new CEO of the new United. (There's Change #3: new leadership.) Updating planes, upgrading services, and changing routes meant the company was creating a new product for its customers (Change #4: new product offering). When you factor in dealing with two customer bases, multiple labor unions, and other airlines declaring bankruptcy, you have multifaceted change.

Changing everything at once can work out well for all the stakeholders involved. It can also be a complete failure that takes years, if not decades, to recover from. Even if everything really is *not* changing at once, when there are multiple initiatives, priorities, messages, and leaders talking about change, employees, customers, and shareowners may feel like they are in the middle of complete chaos, and this perspective doesn't easily go away. But you can manage the chaos to make the change more palatable to customers, less disruptive to employees, and more profitable to shareowners.

Managing what seems like chaos comes down to executing change variables perfectly from the perspective of shareholders, customers, and employees. Here are the key elements to keep in mind:

- ✔ **Structure:** Make the change effort cohesive. Even though a number of changes may be occurring, try to show external and internal stakeholders how they all relate to one another. (Chapter 5 gives you the tools to build a plan using common change goals.)

- ✔ **Communication:** Create two-way communication methods for customers and employees being impacted by the changes. (See Chapter 7 on getting the message out through communication.)

✔ **Leadership:** Get leadership out there talking and walking the change. For more on leadership, check out the roles leaders play in Chapter 3.

✔ **Shareholders**: Make sure the change makes sense to external parties, like shareholders who want the company to make a profit. Learn more about measuring the change from many angles in Chapter 6.

Whenever large-scale change takes place, you can safely assume there are going to be a few opinions (an understatement) about how well the change went. Some customers, employees, and shareholders will love the change; others will hate it. But if you keep those points as your main focus, the likelihood of successful change will rise exponentially.

Creating a Snowball Effect with Small Wins

Creating simple and immediate changes, or "wins," helps reduce the uncertainty of an environment in which everything feels like it is changing. This snowball-effect strategy — making one simple change, followed by a slightly bigger change, and so on — reduces resistance by making discussions tangible and results-oriented early on during the change.

Creating a list of early wins, no matter how small, gets that snowball moving. As you plan the changes, rather than waiting to celebrate and communicate when everything is done, take a phased approach with clearly stated milestones for quick wins. Quick wins are low-hanging fruit because they are relatively simple to tackle, raise team confidence, and provide a sense of accomplishment along the long journey toward change. You may be able to measure these early wins with quantifiable returns on investment or through increased employee morale and productivity.

Quick wins are out there — you just need to make sure people know about them! Here are three questions that can help you find some quick wins with all the changes going on:

✔ **Can people see progress?** Getting executives together in a room to create a vision is not a quick win. You need to make real progress at the employee or customer level. The program may also be seen from a structure point of view. Did you train a core team of front-line employees and were they immediately able to go back and apply the training? That is a quick win. Employees can see it for themselves.

✔ **Are things getting easier, faster, or better?** Olympic athletes don't only gauge their performance once every four years, and the same is true for organization-wide change. Find ways to test success and progress. Ask a client to pilot a few of the changes being made in the organization. Test these changes out and see if jobs are getting easier and processes are becoming more productive. Offer employees the opportunity to trade jobs with each other or with another department for a day to get another perspective on if the changes have made things easy to do. Having an "outsider" point of view will also give valuable feedback on other opportunities to make the changes even better.

✔ **Is the early win influential?** Early wins don't have to be enormous, but they do need to be meaningful. Just checking an item off a project plan will hardly get doubters to jump on board the change train. Find something significant that makes you take a step back and say, "Wow, we're doing it." If a company is going through a merger in a challenging industry, this first wow may be a sales team that landed the first client for the newly created company or a production team that shipped the first product for the merged organization out the door.

Communicate early wins to gain momentum for change. Treat early wins as a winning sports-team's fans do. People like success, and when they see it they want to be part of it.

Structuring and Organizing Complex Change

The word *bureaucracy* may conjure images of an outdated workplace with workers getting approvals for even the most repetitive, meaningless task, but a certain amount of bureaucracy is a fact of life in organizations. We don't promote a highly controlled culture where only a few people make decisions and everyone else must get 20 signatures before anything happens, but you do need to balance the bureaucracy of management with the creativity needed for successful change. The structure, as you probably can guess, taps into a few of the chaos-management factors we discuss a bit earlier in this chapter.

In this section we introduce the concept of program management to assist leaders in keeping projects on track when they feel like they are trying to juggle multiple changes at once. We also take a look at how to manage the unexpected chaos that may surface during massive changes.

Using program management to establish structure

Program management establishes a structure to make sure project milestones are met on time and on budget. The goal of program management is to mobilize and align employees and provide them with the tools they need to quickly function as a team and get things done. It is not to hold a microscope up to every little thing that is happening during large-scale changes. Program management is like being the conductor of an orchestra: Although she doesn't create the music, she helps to make sure all the music is aligned.

A good program-management office does three things: Creates a road map of critical phases, coordinates project planning and schedules, and manages change acceptance.

Creating a road map of critical phases

First, the program manager creates a road map that's aligned to the bigger vision of the change project that helps people work together on common problems. A road map is bigger than a timeline or project plan. It walks teams through critical phases of major change and then links these common activities together over the course of the initiative.

Coordinating project planning and schedules

Second, the program manager facilitates agreement on key activities and due dates. Aligning the road map to various project plans helps make sure things get done. But program management works best when the focus is not on just getting things done but also making sure critical milestones and activities are coordinated with each other and contribute to the large-scale change as best they can. Imagine how chaotic it would seem to employees to have multiple communication messages and training invitations bombarding their e-mail inboxes. A program manager acts as a shelter from being overwhelmed, aligning dates for key training, messages, and activities so employees aren't confused about what's expected from them.

Managing change acceptance

Finally, program management works best when the manager goes out there and monitors the overall organizational acceptance of the multiple changes. When multiple changes are underway, change leaders are most likely focused on one or two key initiatives that impact their department or team. A program manager looks across the board to see how one initiative may be impacting another or how one success may help propel success in other areas.

Being a good program manager

Now that you have a good understanding of how and when program management works, you'll want to find a fabulous change leader to lead the program management effort. Here's the job description:

✔ Working with the team to create processes and templates for the overall change. A program manager can take the best of all change worlds and help facilitate knowledge sharing from one team to the next.

✔ Giving input to teams and frequently checking in with senior leadership to make sure all the changes are on track.

✔ Keeping track of resources and frequently reviewing the outcomes of change along the way.

✔ Working with change teams to develop repeatable processes and templates for future and ongoing changes.

✔ Gathering information and feedback from employees and providing this information to senior leadership. Program managers tend to take the pulse of the organization from an objective point of view.

A program-management office does not take the place of change leaders or project managers. Nor should it try to dictate what employees do. Rather, it should support functions during large-scale change. When introducing company-wide information systems or significant changes to how work is done, the program office can help the local leadership take ownership of the changes by giving them tools, templates, and plans to make the change happen. Local and team leaders already have a full-time job, so the program office must be seen as a way to make the change easier, not as an extra layer of bureaucracy.

Program management can also work effectively by capturing lessons learned from the changes and then developing a change process that works for the company. A program manager can facilitate the lessons learned workshops, compile all the information, and distribute it throughout the organization to increase the collective knowledge of the company on what does and doesn't work.

By making sure overall timelines are established and milestones are tracked, leadership time is freed up to concentrate on the overall performance and results of the project, not the nitty-gritty details.

Organizing manageable but complex change

One of the big things we hear from leaders when they are going through complex change is that they want to make sure work continues to get done, even though the change needs to be fast and efficient. Many leaders want to make the change happen quickly and efficiently, a bit like ripping off a bandage: It is painful when happening but soon over. The alternative is to feel like the company is suffering death by a thousand fish bites, or many small changes that may not be that painful but just keep on coming and coming until the organization can take no more. Quickly ripping off a bandage helps teams move to the future state of change and minimizes disruption from multiple initiatives.

Organizing change management is a balancing act. Change leaders need to work within the constraints of business realities but also make sure that projects don't go so slowly that they lose steam. *Manageable complex change* means looking at the changes your organization is going through as a system that needs to keep flowing.

Seeing chaos as mere complexity

What may look like chaos is more likely just complexity. Your role is to manage the complexity so you and your organization can adjust to changes rationally.

Think of the New York subway system: With more than 420 operating stations, more than 200 miles of track (over 300 kilometers), and an average of 5 million riders on weekdays, you don't need a book to tell you that it looks like chaos at times (especially rush hour). People are running this way and that, but for the most part everyone gets to where they need to go, when they need to get there. The system seems chaotic, but it has order.

Although you may not want your change to have any chaos, there will always be something you can't control (financial markets tumbling down, an irrational customer, internal turnover). These things are part of everyday business, but when paired with multiple changes they can feel a bit like chaos. Your job as a change leader is to manage as much of the change as you can through a controlled, and systematic approach. Your goal when managing multiple projects, multiple changes, and the perception of chaos: Be sure order is underneath it all.

Figure 17-1 shows how you can bring chaos into control and even alignment by managing patterns and creating acceptable and unacceptable rules for operating. We don't get too "PhD-talk" on you, we promise.

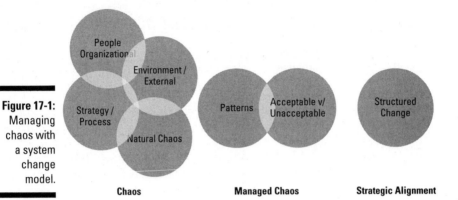

Figure 17-1:
Managing
chaos with
a system
change
model.

The more complex change is, the more it may *seem* like chaos. In Figure 17-1, chaos can come in four main forms:

- **People and organization:** People may be changing jobs, not sure of what their job is, not really sure who they report to or who they will report to in the future.

- **Strategy/process:** When a strategy is seen as unclear or when processes seem to continually change, no amount of change management is going to make the organization operate better. Without a clear vision or plan, the organization will be running around chasing whatever is thrown its way.

- **Environmental/external:** This type of chaos comes from customers, shareholders, or other people outside of the organization. Is everyone in a panic, selling shares of the company because the stock market plunged? This situation can be seen as chaos. Did a giant snow storm in an unusual area cause everyone to run for cover, thinking the world is coming to an end? Another external source of chaos.

- **Natural chaos:** Well, you really just have to deal with this type of chaos, because it doesn't go away. Some things just don't work out, and people or organizations panic. This is just the natural level of chaos out in the world; the important thing is to manage as much of the change and chaos as you can so the organization can deal with them rationally.

Building scenarios and setting standards

Your job as a change leader is to identify all the major complexities in your organization and build possible scenarios. Start by using the four major categories just mentioned. You don't need to list everything, just the big ones. After you list them, start managing these elements of the organization (that is, the system) by first identifying patterns in the complexities. You do this by collecting data and observing what is really going on from employees', customers', and external stakeholders' points of view. Then, with this data, you start doing something to set standards for what is acceptable and what is not during the change. Standards come in all forms, ranging from developing new answers for the sales process to new metrics to determine how a process is working to new performance management expectations of employees.

As a change leader, if you can find themes, the chaos begins to feel more organized, which means you can put the appropriate structure around it — which leads to the final step of managing chaos systematically: structuring it. After you're able to identify patterns in complexity (through observations, metrics, and review) and then use them to redefine how the business will operate in the future with new acceptable and unacceptable norms and processes, you can move the organization into a more structured change approach. Things calm down and people no longer feel like their world is being turned upside down, so you can take a deep breath and align all the changes, whatever their sources, to the strategy of the organization.

Example of managing complexity: A call center and its merger

To see what can happen when managing complex change, we look at an example of a call center that's undergoing significant change. Delightful Benefits helps companies manage their benefits, like retirement, healthcare, and bonuses. Delightful was bought by Hue Healthcare, and together they're combining various centers to save costs, opening new operations across the globe, and changing how they sell products and services to customers. Here are a few of the complexities the acquisition change team identified:

- ✔ **People and organization:** Combining two different company cultures is creating tension, and some superstar performers are leaving the organization unexpectedly. Because the acquisition just closed, many people out in the field are still unsure of what centers are combining and what it means for their jobs.

- ✔ **Strategy/process:** People at Hue Healthcare are a little upset about the lack of process Delightful brought over to the new company. Delightful is a bit put off by the stringent processes for everything from getting a badge to posting information on the internal website. The future way of doing business is still unknown, because teams are still working to create those processes.

- ✔ **Environmental/external:** Although Hue-Delight has been in a great space with few competitors, the market is quickly growing, which means more price competition and a demanding customer base. This change adds complexity to the sales cycle and a bit of chaos based on the base of change in the market.

✔ **Natural chaos:** With the opening of locations around the globe, the company must deal with an expected bit of complexity with new government regulations and local cultures.

What did the call center do? Step one was to set up a program office, headed up by a senior leader in the organization. Step two was to re-communicate the vision and shared need of the acquisition (see setting the vision in Chapter 4). Employees from the two companies had vastly different perspectives on the change, and executive leaders went back to talk with their employees about WIIFM ("what's in it for me?"). With visible leadership at the sites, the program manager continued to work on creating a change road map that addressed the risks of each of the two areas as well as how success would be measured in each area.

Next, senior leaders in the two companies were partnered with one another and signed up to own one of the four areas in addition to their regular jobs. One team of senior leaders went to each of the major call centers and talked about the people and cultural issues to find out what could potentially help or hurt the merger. Another team took on strategy and spoke with managers and executives across the company to make sure strategies and goals were tied together from the top to the bottom of the organization. Another team of senior leaders took on working with customers and gauging the external market to understand what additional external or environmental complexity may be on the horizon. The last team addressed the natural chaos expected from multiple regions, governments, and cultures.

These four teams, working together with executive leaders and reporting their ideas, concerns, and recommendations to the program manager office, put significant structure around a potentially chaotic merger. Within one year of the merger, productivity was 20 percent higher than before the merger, and 90 percent of employees said the merger was a change for the better. But managing complexities didn't stop there: The senior leadership team continued to find patterns in complexity and how to manage this complexity in the future. The following sections detail how.

Step one: Identifying patterns in complexity

The acquisition team quickly got to work by identifying patterns in an increasingly complex environment. One of the first patterns they saw was in the customer feedback on sales calls. Customers continued to demand more technical capabilities, one-stop-shops for their employees to call when they had questions, and the metrics to prove everything was working as the sales team promised. These unmet needs gave a sense of chaos because none of the old client contracts mentioned Internet or web access to serve clients.

Customers calling in were no longer happy waiting for something to come in the mail or being told to go find something on an outdated website. They wanted to have all the answers without having to call multiple times.

When leaders at Hue Healthcare started talking about these complexities, Hue's employees began voicing similar concerns of not really knowing what they were supposed to be doing when they did not know the answer to customer questions.

Step two: Defining acceptable and unacceptable complexity and chaos

With these patterns of complexity coming at the organization from every angle, the sales group and customer service team invited a few key clients to discuss what the best approach would be to refine what was satisfactory (acceptable) service and what was not. The joint team came up with a comprehensive list of when it was okay to send customers to the website and when customer service team members should give personalized care. They also made the website more user-friendly so clients didn't even need to call if they prefer to have self-service from the website. The sales team was then able to translate all these items into a new standard offering for potential clients.

Changing businesses that strategically place competent change leaders throughout the organization are the ones that change fast and remain competitive. However, business change can't just be a bunch of high-potential people running around changing whatever they feel needs changing — that would just be chaos.

Developing organizational knowledge during complex change

Knowledge management is not a separate part of change — it is one of the key ingredients of creating a sustainable structure. Managing knowledge across an organization means putting knowledge out there, building agreements to share knowledge, and equipping employees with tools to make it happen. These three steps put a structure in place for capturing all the information out there and make sure the information is available long after the changes happen.

1. **Put knowledge out there.** With so many changes flying around at once, you'll have plenty of questions and concerns to address. This first step in harnessing knowledge is about getting knowledge out there. Whether you're talking about change, encouraging discussions on how work is done, or trying to figure out what to do after an unexpected change falls in your lap, keeping it all in someone's head benefits no one (and probably

gives that person a big headache). Reward employees for discussing and documenting old and new work processes to help make changes transparent.

2. **Build agreements to share knowledge.** It never fails to amaze us when leaders just assume that employees know exactly what they're supposed to do during change or assume that knowledge is being shared perfectly. Get people in a room and let employees help define what knowledge needs to be shared and how it can be shared more effectively. As a change leader, one of your greatest feats will be facilitating these initial agreements.

   Sharing information is not just going to happen overnight if the company has never had a structure to share knowledge in place. Helping employees build relationships with one another is the first step to making sure they are talking with one another — and talking leads to sharing.

3. **Prepare and equip employees to leverage and harness knowledge.** Even the best-laid structure of knowledge management can go by the wayside if it isn't supported by the right tools. If none of the systems "talk" with one another, getting teams to actually converse will be an uphill battle. If you currently have a knowledge-sharing database with hundreds of naming conventions and even more ways of storing information, you may need a better approach. A company wiki site, searchable blogs, or weekly informational webinars or podcasts are all tools that can help spread knowledge in the organization.

Knowledge is best shared when it is easy to do so. If an employee has to request software, learn how to use it, and then go off and search for the information in an unending maze of drop-down menus, it probably is an indicator that the system needs to be more user-friendly. Here you have a perfect chance to include employees once again. Do any of your employees have a skill for creating interesting videos? Ask them to help create informational videos on lessons learned during the change. Do you have employees who love social media? Make it part of their job to socialize the knowledge internally. Involve employees who can affect the success of the initiative so they can take action to support knowledge sharing.

When processes aren't documented, some employees may feel they have job security because they're the only ones who know the entire process. This situation is obviously not good for the company, and it puts those employees on their guard because they always feel like they need to hoard information to protect it. When you involve these employees from the beginning and give them some control or leadership opportunity, they do come around.

Keeping the Interest High

So far in this chapter we have given you ways to break free from the chaos cycle by finding patterns in the complexity and starting to approach change from a more systematic, structured level. But sometimes the structure can have an unwanted result: the *flavor-of-the-month syndrome,* the employee belief that the company initiates a new change practically every month and none of them matter after a while. This evil step-sister of chaos brings the perception of multiple changes coming at employees from some program office in the sky, and some employees will just think, "Well, if I wait around long enough, another change will come flying at me and this one, which I'm not too fond of, may just go away."

To avoid or get over the flavor-of-the-month syndrome, start by answering these two questions (honestly, please):

✔ How have most change projects or new programs ended up in your organization? Were the outcomes sustained and are they still living, or did they fizzle out when the project teams disbanded?

✔ Is anything different about the change you are working on or are about to embark on? If so, what makes it different from the past projects?

The answers to these questions tell you a lot about where your current path toward change may end up if you keep going about change in the same way. You have to do something different to expect different results. After you have implemented the change toolkit (Chapter 4), crafted a reasonable project plan with a trained change team (Chapters 3 and 5), created a stellar communication plan (Chapter 7), identified any risks that may jump out at you along the way (Chapter 6), and put a structure in place to make change last (Part III), you will be 90 percent of the way to accomplishing the change goals. Now it is time to fine-tune your change skills.

To make changes memorable, some organizations like to brand change with clever acronyms or inspirational thoughts. Take the branding path with caution. Branding or fun names are fine, but every changes does not need to be branded for memorability, and branding can lead to a bad taste in employees' mouths (especially if too much money is being spent on "marketing" to employees if jobs or other benefits may eventually be cut out of the budget). Communication is important, but a sincere discussion from leadership can mean more to employees than a creative slogan.

Solving problems, not generating them

Some change programs start with an in-depth review of what is wrong with the company, which can lead to a negative start. What is the alternative? Why not start solving problems on day one? Going out and collecting a bunch of data takes time, money, and energy. You probably could have gotten the same result days or weeks sooner with a problem-solving approach, not a problem-generating approach.

A problem-*generating* approach to change goes out there and tries to uncover as many problems as possible, takes people out of their day-to-day jobs to do it, and then delivers results in 6 to 12 months. A problem-*solving* approach to change finds out what the biggest pain point is quickly, begins working on problems to generate momentum, and gathers more information along the way. The problem-solving approach gets you away from the flavor-of-the-month feeling because within a month, things are getting done. Things are different, which builds momentum to continue on with the changes.

To get you started on solving problems on day one, here is what the first six-weeks will look like for your change when you focus on solving problems from day one:

Week 1: Change leaders coach teams on what the change toolkit is (see Chapter 4) and then create their own change plan using these tools.

Week 2: Change leader holds a process-mapping session on the biggest pain-point. Real live changes that need to happen are identified (check out www.leadingchangeguide.com for process-mapping templates).

Week 3: Project teams work on the quick hits, identifying the real cause of problems.

Week 4: Teams present their findings back to one another, learn from one another, and start brainstorming solutions.

Week 5: In-depth solutions begin to be developed, quick wins are implemented, and additional problems are captured in real-time from leaders and employees.

Week 6: Visible results banish most fears of the flavor-of-the-month syndrome.

Breaking out of the annual cycle

The problem-solving approach gets momentum going and helps employees feel that the change is real and that something is different this time. Change leaders should continually tie this approach to the strategy and vision. A good model is to start with a vision and initial change toolkit, earn credibility through real improvement, and then revise the vision and toolkit as needed to get ready for future changes. This approach means teams will need to break from a traditional annual planning cycle and adjust change plans in real time (more on that in a second).

Most companies are really good at reviewing their business models, employee performance, and finances every year. An annual cycle is needed for financial reasons, but not for change. During change, the review cycle needs to happen more quickly in order to keep momentum going for the long haul while insuring the change plan reflects and anticipates reality.

A good tool to use during change is the *Plan, Do, Check, Act* method (PDCA):

1. **Plan the change (your change toolkit).**
2. **Do some of the changes.**
3. **Check how the changes are accepted by employees, customers, and external stakeholders.**
4. **Act on those results.**

This method is simple, but it works. The cycle may happen on a six-week basis or quarterly basis, but let the change dictate the timeline, not the calendar.

Climbing out of chaos: Using a belay system

Thomas Edison had it right when he said, "Good fortune is what happens when opportunity meets with planning," and everyone knows that he who fails to plan, plans to fail. Yes, it pays to plan ahead. So now we're ready to talk about how to combine this notion of continuous change with smart planning.

Ideal change links goals, roles, processes, and people skills, something that takes a significant amount of planning and coordination. Successful change also takes into account all the moving pieces that can create a domino effect down the road. Combining real-time change and planning is a lot like climbing a mountain. You have to plan your course in order to get from the base to the summit, but you may not be able to see some obstacles or opportunities from where you are starting. Similarly, you will start out on your change with a solid road map, great vision, and a capable team. But things will happen and you'll have to adjust course (see Chapter 10 for more on revising the change plan after the original plan has been put into action).

The way you stop adjustments from seeming like changes to the core vision or plan (and therefore causing confusion, chaos, or that horrible flavor-of-the-month taste) is to do what mountaineers do: Use a belaying system. The *belay* is a spike or other device securely anchored to the rock every few vertical feet that prevents the climber from falling too far if he happens to fall. During large-scale change, you create a change road map with "belays" built into it that prevent the change from falling back to square one (or falling off the map completely) if and when changes need to occur.

The pattern to support the balance of real-time change and planning is: Plan and make decisions (belay), take action (climb), adjust plans as necessary and make new decisions (belay), take more action (climb). You get the idea. You and your change team continue this pattern throughout all the changes your organization is undertaking.

Here is what your organizational change belay system may look like in a bit more detail:

- ✔ **First belay:** Vision is set for the change.

- ✔ **Climb:** Create some quick wins aligned with the vision and start uncovering patterns in the complexity and chaos (people/organizational, strategy/process, external, natural).

- ✔ **Second belay:** Adjust the plan and decide (and agree) on what to do with the information the teams have gathered based on quick wins and initial reactions to the vision.

- ✔ **Climb:** Communicate what's happening (again), gather feedback on how initial changes are going, and begin to create solutions to problems.

- ✔ **Third belay:** Use the feedback to revisit the communication plan and identify any gaps in how leaders or employees may be supporting the change.

- ✔ **Climb:** Go out and implement the next round of changes, all aligned to the initial vision the team created. Don't forget to communicate (we're sure you didn't need the reminder, but we just needed to say it).

These planning and decision points can be incredibly useful in keeping change teams on track, engaging the wider employee population, and adjusting plans to fit with the current realities of the business while staying aligned to the vision for the change. Teams can come together to make decisions and plan, but they don't need to solve everything on their own. After the planning, teams go back out among the people who are affected by the change and draw them into the change process.

The belay method of securing a place on the change road map and then moving forward has an added benefit: You don't often need to bring everyone together to make decisions along the way because the change team is going out into the world frequently to coordinate action and facilitate results in real time. It is much easier to continue making forward progress and keep moving up to the next level when you don't fall back to the starting point whenever a decision is questioned or a concern is raised. The process has no closed doors or ivory towers, because information is flowing in and out of the core change team on a frequent (not just annual or quarterly) basis.

Embedding Complex Change within the Culture

The more complex an organization, the more likely it is to feel chaotic during change. We have talked about some highly visible, massive changes out there, but change doesn't only come with a high-profile name or event. Think about some of the changes that may be impacting all businesses, big and small, over the next decade:

- **Technology:** Even if your company isn't implementing a large technology product, technology is changing. Fans, friends, tweets, and professional networks are changing business at a near-constant pace.

- **Global businesses:** Customers, partners, and maybe even employees can be in different time zones, countries, and continents.

- **Regulations:** From Sarbanes-Oxley in 2002 to the Dodd-Frank Act of 2010, from Medicare changes to uncertainty of international markets, a number of regulations and political decisions mean real change for companies.

- **Employee base:** Some markets, like the United States, are facing an aging workforce. Other markets, like India, are helping to create the new middle class.

More likely than not, your company has faced or is facing a few, if not all, of these changes. You can embed the ability, will, and energy to work through change in your culture by creating a structure that controls what you can control, plans for what you can't control, and resolves conflict productively to reduce the stress associated with change.

Controlling what you can

One thing that's always in your control is your own behavior. And through your actions, you can influence the behavior of others. When employees see leaders doing their job differently and making the changes they're talking about, employees are more likely to believe the changes are real and will start acting differently as well. In the midst of complex change, you can define and clarify the vision, scope, ownership, organizational structure, and leadership. Yes, that leadership word again — specifically, visible leadership. During large-scale, multiple-focus changes, you can take action and control how some aspects of the project turn out by doing the following things:

- ✔ **Get leaders talking.** The best way to do this is to create agreements with the leadership team regarding the vision for the changes, how decisions will be made, and who will make them.

- ✔ **Understand ownership and scope.** If you can make sure the financial, people, and time requirements that will be necessary for the change are clearly understood and agreed on by leadership in the company, as well as making sure everyone is on board with the role they will play in the change, you will be controlling a large aspect of change.

- ✔ **Agree on key messages.** Although you can't control how communication will be received, you can control the messages you and the rest of the leadership team will send. Before the changes start happening, agree on key messages that need to go out to all the stakeholder groups. Put a communication structure in place for the duration of the change.

Planning for what you can't control

During times of change, some things are out of your control. For example, the economy, though predictable for some analysts, is not controllable for the most part. Few people can predict, let alone control, what country's currency will be the next to put pressure on international markets. Closer to home, you can't always control employee satisfaction and acceptance, customer buying behavior, or how the communities in which the business operates will respond when faced with a tragedy or emergency. Planning for what you and the organization cannot control means assessing your risks accordingly and adjusting course as needed. We cover these topics in Chapters 6 and 10 in detail, so we will just touch on some of the most important areas for complex change here.

When dealing with complex change, you absolutely must plan for risks. When you realize or are planning to go through substantial change, stop and do a change assessment to identify where your highest risks are. You can use the risk assessment in Chapter 6 to start focusing on the specific risks associated with your project, but the change assessment is a bigger, broader view. Conduct your assessment with quantitative answers (ranking how you are doing), and then dig deeper with more discussion.

Table 17-1 shows an example of a change assessment. Score yourself by answering the questions on a scale of 1 to 5:

1 = We are very vulnerable in this area (high risk).

2 = We are doing some things right, but the area still has many concerns (high/medium risk).

3 = We are doing okay in this area. Not great, but no major shortfalls (medium risk).

4 = We are proficient, and if nothing else is done, we would be just fine (low risk).

5 = We are experts in this area. We read *Leading Business Change For Dummies* 27 times, implemented everything, and are awesome (no risk, in fact a great place to leverage other risks).

Table 17-1	Change Assessment
Question	*Score*
Building a sustainable structure	
Are rewards set up to help change happen quickly and productively?	_____
Do we have a plan to adjust processes in order to make changes sustainable?	_____
Is training in place to support both short- and long-term needs?	_____
Do we have resources to implement all the changes?	_____
Creating two-way communication	
Are people satisfied with the amount of information about the change?	_____
Are conflicts dealt with proactively?	_____
Are solutions to problems communicated?	_____
Is feedback encouraged and happening?	_____
Working from your customer's point of view	
Do customers see a convincing need for the change?	_____
Are customers aware of any changes directly impacting them?	_____

(continued)

Table 17-1 (continued)

Question	Score
Making change (and life) easier for your employees	
Do employees expect and want the change to flourish and last?	_____
Do employees have ample opportunities to participate in the changes?	_____
Does everyone who will be impacted by the changes know about them?	_____
Visible leadership: Getting leadership to talk and walk the change	
Do we have a clear vision tying all the changes together?	_____
Can leaders state the purpose of the change?	_____
Do leaders know the benefits and expectations of the change?	_____
Do all changes have one clear sponsor?	_____
Shareholders: Ensuring the change makes sense to external parties	
Will the change benefit external stakeholders and shareholders?	_____
Are measurements in place to track expected outcome of changes?	_____

After the results are in, you'll be able to add up all the scores and then discuss the details. Using the 1 (We are very vulnerable in this area) to 5 (We are experts in this area), here is how you can interpret the results:

✔ **Fewer than 36 points:** Although your organization may have a few people who really want change to happen, the structures, communication channels, and leadership are not ready to make the commitment necessary to make change last. Does this change really need to happen? Is the change part of the strategic goal? Work with senior leaders to prioritize if the change is necessary and if the organization is willing to commit the resources to make it happen. If so, go back and start creating the structure for change so the change will be meaningful and last long after the change is complete.

✔ **36–72 points:** Change doesn't need to be perfectly planned out in the advance, but not having a plan and not having senior leaders visibly supporting the change can make the entire process an uphill battle. Find ways to communicate with employees, identify the best way to train people on the change, and ask leaders to define the benefits of change for employees (the WIIFM). Even though the change may be urgent, sometimes it is in the best interest of the organization to slow down, put the change structure in place, and then move full speed ahead.

✔ **73-99 points:** You have some of the change tools ready; others may just be starting. Go back and make sure your leadership is all in agreement with the change and what the change will mean to your company. Next, make sure employees have ways to give real-time feedback to senior leaders about how the change is going. With open channels for communication and a committed group of leaders, your change will have the basic structure it needs to get the change going.

✔ **100+ points:** You are off to a great start for change. With the majority of change tools in process or already complete, your employees, customers, and other stakeholders have a good understanding of why the change needs to happen, what change is happening, and how they can make the change happen. Keep tracking progress, and you are on your way to change success.

Remember, the lower the number, the more risk there is in making change happen.

Take some time with your change team to review some of the risks associated with change, especially complex change. This step can't be done in an e-mail. But don't sweat the time it will take to sit down with the change team or one on one with senior leaders — reviewing the change-assessment questions will deliver exponential time savings in the long run.

The second part of planning for what you can't control is setting a vision and then adjusting accordingly. Your business change will work out in the end, not because you controlled everything and stayed the course no matter what's thrown your way but because you will be able to change plans and goals often, if not continuously. However, the one constant of these plans and goals must always be that they are aligned to your vision and continuously communicated. Staying the course is admirable, but so is changing it when it makes sense. An organization can't plan for everything, but the vision for the future should not be changing constantly.

The perfect plan means setting a crazy-wonderful vision of the future and going after it, changing course as is needed to get there.

The rule of three

Change leaders often try to overschedule things when chaos is flying right past them, but not even the President and his staff could actually pull that off. There are only 24 hours in a day, and at some point in time you need to sleep.

The point is that you cannot be all things to all people or do all things for all people. Set aside time in the evening to write down what you want to accomplish the next day. Then identify the three most critical things to get done (this selection is easier said than done). These three things are your top priorities, and all the other to-do's will have to wait until the critical list is done. You can still write them down on the list, but a list is only as good as what gets done. By focusing on the top three items, you'll move from planning to doing.

Resolving conflict productively: Revisiting the four As

In Chapter 8 we discuss how to resolve conflict during change with the four As: awareness, agreement, acceptance, and action. We take the four As of conflict resolution up a notch here, because when everything is changing, you have plenty of opportunities to resolve conflicts (because many of them occur).

Keep in mind that not all resistance or conflict is bad. In fact, it can lead to new and better ideas than you had planned.

Here are a few tricks to leveraging resistance and resolving it proactively before it turns into a political battle within the organization:

- **Awareness:** Awareness during complex change and complex conflict starts by saying the conflict exists. Acknowledge that differences exist as soon as you know they do. This awareness is not about blame or finger pointing; it is simply observing that differences exist.

- **Agreement:** Agree to the bigger goals of the project and what you are trying to achieve (outcomes, objectives), and recognize that you can reach desired outcomes in multiple ways. Take the time to develop multiple options to achieve the desired outcome, identify the pros and cons of each, and then decide how to get to the acceptance of the solution.

- **Acceptance:** Acceptance during change is not just about nodding yes or no. It gets down to having everyone state personal preferences, even if they are different than the way the group wants to go, and then identifying what everyone can and can't support. The proactive resolution to conflict (or even just differences of opinion) doesn't need to be a unanimous decision, but everyone must be willing to visibly support the outcome and be willing to communicate it to employees and other stakeholders where necessary (that is, to be a change leader).

- **Action:** When everyone is in agreement, put a plan in place and move on, but remember that this is not a one-time-solves-everything deal. Conflict will come up again, and as a change leader your goal is to handle it proactively so you can grow and maintain relationships. Maybe the solution isn't exactly what you think it should be, but if all the people involved can support it and take action, you have created a sustainable structure for change and conflict resolution.

When resolving conflict, make sure all parties involved visibly take ownership of the accepted and agreed-on solution, use two-way communication to solve the problem, and make solving conflict part of the way business is done. In addition, if the action plan takes into account the viewpoints of employees, shareholders, and customers, success will surely come your way.

Part V
The Part of Tens

The 5th Wave — By Rich Tennant

"I'm demonstrating my commitment to change."

In this part . . .

Expert *For Dummies* readers are familiar with how the books end: with a few top ten lists grouped in one convenient location. In this book, you find the ten essential principles of leading successful change, ten creative ways to lead change when someone else is running the show, and ten ways to energize your MVPs.

Chapter 18

Ten Essential Principles of Leading Successful Change

*L*eading business change is not easy. The difficulty arises in trying to keep the business going while the change is happening — some equate leading business change to changing the oil in your car while driving. But with the right team and right method, your change can be sustainable and impactful and maintain productivity while it's happening. The ten tips in this section give you the overview.

Creating a Consensus of the Change

When you know your business is changing, begin creating a concise vision of the future state and the reason why the organization needs to make this change. This common understanding of why the change needs to happen links the vision of the future, the core values of the company, and the mission of the organization. The vision is generally provided by the senior leaders, but it should include the perspectives of everyone impacted by the change. It is much easier to generate a shared understanding if most of the people who will need to change how they do business already agree with where the organization wants to grow and change.

The case for change needs to grab the attention of employees. Some reasons for change include achieving higher customer and employee satisfaction, creating long-term sustainability in a volatile market, increasing revenues and profits, or creating an innovative and open company culture.

To build a powerful case for the change (check out the tools in the change toolbox in Chapter 4 for how to do this), you need to work relentlessly to generate understanding and consensus. You will know if the vision and need are shared when everyone in the organization knows what needs to change and why they need to change in the first place. Storytelling and visioning a brighter future illustrate how the company will make positive change for their employees, customers, and external stakeholders.

Developing a Clear Plan and Strategy for the Change

Creating a strategy for change moves the organization from simply having a vision of the future to having a plan for how the organization will get there. Making a change strategy includes creating objectives and goals that are long-term focused on financial performance, people management and employee retention, customer satisfaction, and robust operations. Change requires people to act differently, so the strategy should also include designing new measures that are consistent with the new goals of the business.

A documented and detailed action plan eliminates confusion and false starts associated with the change. A project plan for change includes definable phases of the change, measurable steps to track progress, and assigned responsibilities for these steps. Aligning the change plan to strategic objectives helps set short-term goals, creates clear action items, and quantifies milestones along the way to turn change slogans into change substance.

Engaging Executive Sponsorship

Strong leadership is required if the change is to be momentous and sustainable. Good leaders inspire the employees to rally behind the change and make it happen.

Grassroots change (change that begins at the employee level) can happen. It just takes much longer. Leadership from the top puts the seal of approval on the change and can help align change initiatives to the broader mission of the company. When executives actively participate in change from beginning to end, they automatically build a coalition of other leaders in the organization for employees to rally behind.

The number-one rule for engaging leaders during change is to make sure executives do what they say they will do. It's hard to admit, but most leaders are really bad at follow-though. Projects get started and then stop because of lack of funding, lack of interest, or another idea that came along. Executives (like you, perhaps?) should be honest with employees about why past projects stopped and what they're going to personally do to make sure that this one doesn't. And then they should get things done as promised.

Executive sponsors can help create a continuous conversation about the creation of value for all parties involved. Leaders often have a broader view of how the changes may impact other departments and teams and will therefore be able to make the tough calls when it comes to sharing resources or resolving dissent.

Outside of building a vision and creating a shared understanding of why change needs to happen, executives are also connected to both internal and external customers of the change. From this position, they're able to rigorously examine the customer needs and help the change team prioritize the needs of the customers.

Building a Powerful Change Team

If leading business change is like an oil change while driving, you need a stellar pit crew to make sure you don't skid off the change road. Building a powerful change team isn't just about getting a bunch of superstars in the room and giving them the authority to change the organization. It's recruiting people who work well together, who have extraordinary communication and conflict-resolution skills, and who will actively engage other people.

Involve team members from the different departments that will be impacted by the change on the change team. Bringing in people from around the company builds commitment and significantly increases the likelihood of a successful transformation.

Powerful change teams don't just follow a project plan; they facilitate ideas. Encourage teams to come up with new and better ways of doing things instead of just doing what they're told. Team members who develop a new process or solution are likely to be advocates to other employees.

Ideal change team members should have the desire to challenge the status quo, be optimistically persistent, cultivate relationships within the organization, and balance short-term goals with long-term objectives. The team should have a good mix of individuals who foster ideas and creativity and those who get things done.

Defining Change-Management Roles Clearly

A powerful change team works together to make things happen because the members have clear roles and responsibilities on the project. Just like a pit crew on the race track, change-team members all have their own responsibilities and trust that other team members are doing their job.

Common change-management roles include a *change agent* (the project leader), a *change sponsor* (the executive ultimately responsible for making the change happen), and four to eight *core members* who represent the departments and job roles going through the change. Most teams also have team members who support the core team; these team members may have specific talents or information that is used at various points during the change but do not have a full-time role. Many of these team members will be your change advocates or change ambassadors (check on change-leader roles in Chapter 3).

Using the RACI (responsible, accountable, consulted, informed) model for change-management roles helps eliminate confusion around who is doing what and who is responsible. Each change project should have the following roles:

- ✔ **Responsible:** The individual or individuals (limit this role to one or two people) in charge of getting the job done. These people are your change agents.

- ✔ **Accountable:** Change sponsors are often the ones who have the ultimate decision-making and approval authority.

- ✔ **Consulted:** Change advocates are often part of a group that can provide input into a decision or action before it occurs.

- ✔ **Informed:** This group is the individuals or teams who must be informed that a decision or action has taken place. Be sure to include people who will be most impacted by the change.

A change network can help foster organizational acceptance in real time. Individuals in positions of influence in the organization can help communicate messages out to employees, solicit feedback from individuals in the field, and provide input to the change team throughout the project. These agents are the eyes, ears, and heart of the organization; they also are brutally honest and optimistically realistic on how the changes are being viewed and accepted in the larger employee population.

Removing Critical Barriers to Implementing Change

Identifying barriers to change is the first step to being able to knock every barrier or obstacle down. Executive leaders can help change teams align agendas and balance interests to reduce concern and conflict. Some of the common barriers to implementing change include

- Lack of experience or knowledge on how to change
- Undefined goals and objectives
- Fear that employees lack the skills to do the job needed in the future
- Lack of planning, structure, support, and resources to make the change real
- Poor communication
- Insufficient leadership support

The following suggestions can help you overcome these common barriers to change:

1. **Be sure to create, communicate, and stick to a strategic plan.**

2. **Don't jump into change without explaining the process to employees.**
   Even though the change team and leadership team may be on board with the amount of work that needs to happen to make the change work, give employees ample time to learn about the new process.

3. **Use productivity measures throughout the change process.**
   Measurements don't just come at the end of the change project; check to make sure the team is on track during the entire process of transition.

4. **Communicate, collaborate, and communicate again.**

It's hard for employees to be against a new idea or way of doing business if they helped create the new way.

Managing the barriers to change is a fine balancing act between purely moving ahead and moving ahead while cultivating relationships to make the change last. Just blowing past barriers because a leader has the power in the organization to do so may get the change to the finish line faster, but this approach is rarely sustainable. As you work through barriers, treat each barrier and its owner with respect and ask others for help in removing the barrier, even if the person's ideas of how to get rid of it (or whether it even needs to move) are different from your own. Building agreements on how to remove obstacles takes time, but the investment will pay off with a change everyone can agree with and support in the long term.

Managing Employee Resistance

Business changes can result in people resisting new ways because they fear losing status, power, or even their jobs. Employees may also become so used to a certain culture or way of doing things that they greet a new approach as they would a three-headed alien. Employee resistance can take many forms, everything from absenteeism to outright disagreement with the change.

To counter this resistance, keep everyone informed about what is happening, how they will be involved, and where employees should go if they need more information. This communication may be easier said than done for traditional, hierarchical organizations with a poor history of encouraging open discussion of issues, problems, and ideas. Managing resistance in these organizations or departments should start at the top with heads of departments talking with one another and visibly changing their behaviors to break down the walls that exist in the organization.

Whether your method for encouraging new ideas and communication is social media or employee meetings, you should give visibility and ownership to the event and recognition to people who contribute. Give people the power to make appropriate changes to the way things are done in their organization. Put a plan in place to act on good ideas and suggestions and let people know why you may not implement ones that don't fit with the organizational strategy.

Sometimes the best way to eliminate resistance is to show success to the employees who are hesitant about the change. Although most change leaders want to make a significant impact with the change, be sure to balance out long-term goals with short-term wins. You can generate much-needed momentum by creating short-term milestones that employees can use to visibly demonstrate the positive influence the changes will have in the long term.

Creating and Using Communication Plans

For many employees, change may seem like an overwhelming task. Beyond the work involved and the emotional impact of changing the way business is done, many questions may pop up: What do I need to change? What do I need to do? When do I start? As a change leader, your job is to tell the truth and listen for feedback.

For your change to succeed, you must communicate continuously. Organizations with a high degree of trust and communication between decision makers and other workers minimize productivity loss during the transition from old to new. Keep employees informed about changes that will be happening before they happen. Clear, succinct messages will be understood. Honest messages will be believed.

You need to consider two main communication audiences during change:

✔ Internal audiences usually require dialogues between employees and leadership.

✔ External audiences, such as customers, suppliers, and other stakeholders, need communication from the organization. Often it is the CEO or public relations team communicating with large external audiences, but sales-team members and customer-service employees also speak with these audiences on a daily basis.

Keeping both sets of audiences informed about the process of change, the expected outcomes, and the results helps reduce resistance and increase buy-in and excitement for the future.

A communication plan should encompass the type of communication being used (company website, podcasts, e-mail, social media, meeting, webinar), the key message (what are the two or three things that people should learn), the channel for communication (how people will know about it), the owner (who is delivering the message), and the audience (who is receiving the message). The communication plan should appeal to your target audience and focus on accomplishments and success stories throughout the change cycle.

Building Competencies through Training and Educational Programs

A natural productivity loss is associated with all complex changes because of the learning curve required to move from the old to the new. Building competencies from the beginning of the project helps to lessen the significance of the productivity loss. You can build competencies in the organization in a number of ways, ranging from formal in-class training and virtual webinars to less-formal mentoring and networking opportunities.

Adults learn best when the training is relevant and can quickly apply to how they do their job after they leave the training. Role-based training is most effective when it is based on defined needs that address gaps in competences and when employees see the connection between the training and how they do their jobs.

Creating informal networks within the organization is a great way to encourage ongoing training and learning. Training should not be a "one and done" activity; make sure you have a plan to continually educate individuals on new best practices, refresh what was learned in the original training, and provide the same training opportunities to new employees.

Anchoring the Change

Anchoring the change involves celebrating successes, whether they be milestones or the completion of the change. But it's not just about holding a party and shaking hands, although these aspects of change are important. Throughout the change process, to maintain focus and check your direction, take time to talk and document what is going well and why. And then properly acknowledge the completed change in various ways, from public celebrations to individual verbal acknowledgment to cash rewards for performance.

Paying for performance makes change sustainable because you're rewarding the behavior the change set out to accomplish. Giving outstanding performers rewards for their contributions helps to motivate continued high performance. Remember to link the accomplishment to the reward and keep in mind that rewards do not need to be monetary. Non-momentary rewards include recognition from senior leadership, leadership-development opportunities, or creating an award of excellence. These forms of recognition can cost little but mean much more than a $10 gift card for coffee.

To celebrate the individuals with verbal acknowledgement, take the opportunity at the beginning of regular team meetings to highlight the successes and praise extraordinary accomplishments by team members. Giving credit where credit is due builds support and relationships. Be authentic with your praise and thanks.

Larger milestones and the overall completion of the change project need celebration, too. Taking a break during the long change journey is a great way to re-energize teams to keep moving forward and to take a much-needed look at how much progress has been made during the project. Outside of recognizing all the efforts and formally closing a project, celebrating success is a great opportunity to review expectations of the future and how the team can leverage lessons learned during the change in the future.

Chapter 19

Ten Creative Ways to Lead Change When Someone Else Is Running the Show

Surefire elements of significant, sustainable change are a clear vision for the future co-developed by leaders and employees, visible executive support, and two-way communication throughout the organization. Employee-led grassroots change, although possible, often lacks the long-term resource commitment to make transformation worth the necessary time and energy commitment. However, if you see a change that needs to happen and you don't yet hold the keys to the corner office, don't just sit back and wait to be told what to do. This chapter offers ten ways to be proactive. Being an advocate for change, regardless of where you fall in the organizational chart, can put you in the position of being a team leader — and someone who has great career potential.

When someone else is responsible for the change journey, jump on board and show your commitment in creative ways, and next time a change to lead comes around, don't be surprised if you're asked to be the one running the show.

Aligning Individual Priorities with Organizational Goals

Experienced change leaders create change objectives and goals to move a company from its current state to the future state of doing business. Although many leaders take the next step in creating team-specific goals to support the change, you shouldn't wait around twiddling your thumbs. Look at the change goals and create your own SMART goals that support the overall company objective. (See Chapter 4 to read about goals that are SMART: specific, measurable, action oriented and agreed on, realistic, and time bound.)

For example, say your company just announced that it's acquiring another company to strengthen its product lines and services. One of your individual priorities may be to learn more about the other company, its customers, and what it does. Ask your manager if you can research these areas and present ideas on how they may impact your team. Most likely, your manager is already thinking about this and would be thrilled to have help. Or your manager may offer other ways you can help with the change.

You can also look at your current list of responsibilities and identify which of your own priorities can strategically help the overall change initiative. Make the link between what you do on a day-to-day basis and how that can support the overall change initiative. This understanding works well when your company is going through any type of process or technological change because you can begin to recommend better ways of doing what you already do.

Learning to Live with Ambiguity

Change is not certain. In fact, it's often anything but. Even the most change-capable executives may not be able to answer every question the second it pops up. If you are not running the show, the best thing to do is just accept the unanswerable. Ambiguity goes hand-in-hand with large-scale change, and it may be in your best interest to roll with the uncertainty.

Many executives would be relieved if they could just tell everyone in the company everything about the change from day one, but they usually have a reason why they don't. First, as you probably guessed, although there's a change road map early in the project, not all the details are worked out yet. Second, although you may be more than willing to jump at the chance to change the way work is done, others may not be as comfortable with significant and immediate change, and therefore the communication plan may focus on a more cooperative approach than on a let's-just-do-it approach.

Executives also may have other legal reasons for not releasing information, including involvement with labor unions, competitive information, or regulatory requirements. When it comes to mergers and acquisitions, executives are often required by law to keep some information about change limited to a small number of people.

This explanation all boils down to just accepting that some questions don't have answers right away. Raise your concerns and ideas, but then keep focused on your task at hand.

However, if you feel that the ambiguity is disturbing the workplace, speak up. We have seen executives who have brought potential buyers for their company into glass-walled conference rooms and then blatantly ignored questions from employees and analysts who ask, "What is going on?" This type of closed-door communication resulted in bad press and distrustful employees; there is a not-so-thick line between ambiguity and ignoring. If you see executives ignoring real concerns, let your manager know the downstream impact in a polite yet firm manner.

Understanding Your Leadership Style First

Even if your business card doesn't have a powerful title, you are still a leader. If you know what type of a leader you are, you can work on your personal strengths to help guide change more effectively. You can use a number of different leadership assessments to narrow down how your leadership style is seen by others, but most assessments come down to four different types of leaders. (For our recommendations on which ones are most appropriate for your situation, check out www.leadingchangecoach.com.) Knowing your own change leadership style and then applying it to maximize your strengths shows that you're a team player who's ready to support any transformation the organization undertakes in the future. Here are a few common styles:

- **Loud and proud:** Some leaders are powerful and vocal, chasing after goals like they're in the World Cup. If you're this type, ask to be part of the change team or take on responsibility for the change goals on your team.

- **Cheerful and optimistic:** Other leaders rally team members and can be seen as the company cheerleader and eternal optimist. If you think of yourself as someone who always see the glass as half-full and getting fuller by the second, you may be a perfect fit for being a change or communication agent for your individual department.

- **The strong, silent type:** Senior leaders value the honesty and sensitivity of these individuals because these employees often know the pulse of the organization and people's reaction to change before senior leadership does.

> If you are more likely to listen and be a sounding board for other employees, you are in the perfect position to communicate general thoughts, fears, and concerns up the chain of management.
>
> ✔ **Data driven:** Some employees lead through their ability to synthesize and look objectively at data. During change, emotions can run high, and if you lead by knowing and analyzing data, offer this strength to senior leadership as a way to measure and track how the change is going from an objective, data-driven point of view.

You may also be a combination of any of these leadership styles. In any case, knowing your own leadership strengths and style can help you effectively manage up the organization, coach employees and peers, and lead future change projects. By understanding your style, you also start to realize how other people may have a different leadership preference from your own. Use this awareness to start framing feedback and communication to meet the needs and preferences of others.

Changing What You Can Change: Yourself

There is an old saying that too many cooks spoil the soup. Similarly, too many leaders during change can make everything confusing and fragmented. If you are not in a position to formally influence the change, instead of trying to create a leadership role, take the opportunity to change your own attitude, beliefs, and behaviors. Have you been around the company for a while and kind of like the way things are done? Strong change leaders (even if you don't have the formal title) recognize this feeling in themselves and reflect on what they need to do to help drive the change forward.

Although you may be daunted by the idea of making sizable change in attitudes and behaviors, start small by setting realistic goals for yourself and then elicit feedback on these goals from peers, managers, and perhaps even customers. Tackle changing your own behavior the same way you would change the organization if you were running the show. Organizational change and personal change have strong similarities: Clearly identify what you want to change (your change objective), what the change looks like (your vision for the future), and the specific next steps and milestones for meeting them (your change road map).

Influencing What You Can't Change: Others

Just because you aren't the one running the show doesn't mean you can't influence the direction of the change. Not having the change leader title on your ID badge may benefit you in the long term, because employees are usually more receptive (to change) when they trust the people involved, and being "one of them" can give you a boost. One of the best ways to build this kind of relationship with employees is to give meaningful and timely feedback with the sole intent of helping employees increase effectiveness and job satisfaction. The feedback is more likely to be received as objective and sincere coming from a peer rather than coming from a formal leader who may be seen as having ulterior motives of getting the change project complete.

If you are wondering how to influence without a formal leadership title, start by building an atmosphere of openness with your peers by asking for and listening to other's concerns. After you know people's motivations and interests of others, you can help them see how the change project will meet their needs. Remember to keep your own motivations in mind — authentic feedback and recommendations build trust. Feedback with ulterior motives destroys relationships.

Another way to influence is to model the behavior you want to see in others by providing constructive feedback and opinions, especially to project-team and change leaders. Often, leaders would love to have someone give them critical feedback, and they'll welcome the opportunity. If something is going well, speak up and state the specific situation when the change worked. If a change event did not go well, provide examples of what did not work, ask for ideas on why the process did not work as well as it could have, and then offer to help in the future.

Here are a few ways to help you craft your first feedback messages to leadership:

- **Provide examples.** Don't just say it was bad — provide context, facts, and examples, like: "In the staff meeting today, it seemed like you were not interested in how the change would really work because on three or four occasions you didn't let John complete his thoughts and kept cutting him off and redirecting everyone back to the slideshow."

- **Ask why something happened the way it did.** Most people have good reasons why they do things, so find out why a certain behavior happened. You may say something like, "I guess you are so excited about this project and passionate about your work that you wanted to share that excitement. Is that right?"

- **Be supportive and offer ideas for improvement.** For example, tell your change leader: "You say that unless you keep John on point you will not be able to get through your presentation, but actually, people were only paying attention to the fact you that you were interrupting John, not your presentation. I think many people in our department would love the opportunity to discuss the change, not just hear about it. Can I help you set up a feedback session to get opinions on what may and may not work?" This type of feedback is positive and can help build your reputation as a straight-forward change supporter who comes to the table with data and ideas, not problems and complaints. Whether you are communicating feedback up the chain of management or to employees, critical feedback looks the same and can have positive results for everyone involved.

Although you may not have the formal power to influence or direct change, influence can come in many forms: having information or data on a topic, being an expert in an area, or having relationships within an organization. Keep in mind that influence is not the same thing as name-dropping. Name-droppers usually get nowhere; people with influence have insight into how someone may react or know the best way to present something to a larger audience. For example, you may help influence the change team leader by helping him understand how your boss may react to certain information or how your team likes to be trained on new processes.

Becoming an Early Adopter and Ally for Change

Adapting early to change and being an ally for it is one of the simplest and most visible ways of leading change when you are not running the show. During change, people usually fall into one of four types: *Champions* want to get the change going now, *allies and early adopters* want to make the change happen as soon as they have a sufficiently logical explanation to show them that the change is worthwhile, *followers* get on board after the change is proven with hard data and a physical demonstration, and the *stucks,* who, no matter what, will never, ever, change. Be an early adopter and ally for the change. Explore the rationale for change, and then volunteer to be one of the first to make the change happen. An added benefit of being an ally and early adopter is that you will be seen as a pioneer for many of the followers in the organization, and they will jump on board the change after you've proven it works. This is a chance to lead by example.

The nice thing about being an ally and early adopter is that you aren't seen as someone who is just giving face time to the change; you are actually doing it. Being an ambassador for change by adopting the change early demonstrates genuine excitement for the future ahead.

Creating a Community of Peers

Many change projects have front-line staff or employee councils that serve as the eyes and ears of change; relaying information, ideas, and concerns back to senior leaders to help adjust the change plan as necessary. If your organization has a change council, ask to be part of it. If your company does not have a change council, offer to help organize it.

Employee councils are communities of peers that all have a vested interest in the success of the change. To make the change happen, these employee councils advocate for local or departmental issues facing the business that may be impacted by the change project. This community also helps facilitate decision making by assessing and commenting on ideas, changes, and approaches related to the project. The council may not be making the decisions, but they do make recommendations. Another key purpose of this community is to provide regular feedback on the effectiveness and acceptance of program activities and changes. There is no replacement for direct feedback to change leaders on how the communication and change are really being perceived out in the field. Finally, the community of peers is often the best resource to help communicate plans, goals, and messages to employees.

The community doesn't take the place of a strong leader building the vision for change, but it does help to make the change real for the people doing the work. A good way to look at the community of peers is to focus on creating alignment throughout the project. The group is the eyes and ears of the project on the front line. Leaders need this help to align the site and department perspective back to corporate needs.

Helping Other Employees Cope with Change

Executives and team leaders are often focused on getting the work done and may be seen as too busy to have the time to slow down and help others cope with tough transitions. Without the formal title as change leader, you can help employees cope with change by being an objective participant in the change. Step back and observe what is happening; sometimes employees give substantial signals that they need help in coping with the change, like absenteeism, depressed or despondent behavior, or attacks on team members. Observe and make the judgment of when to intervene. Intervention may be one-on-one or in a group meeting that quickly becomes a bickering session rather than a change session.

Another way to help others cope is through active listening. Active listening is much more than just parroting back what an individual says. It can be used in many situations, including helping someone with an emotional issue, leading a problem-solving meeting or group discussion, or working through anger or resistance directed at you. All these approaches are ways of helping employees cope with the change.

The first goal of active listening is to reduce emotionality and increase rational discussion. When people are upset about a layoff or other significant job change, feelings are involved and often the other person needs to have a sounding board to express his opinions before he can begin to think logically about what to do next. Chapter 9 provides step-by-step advice on how to work through the negative reactions to change from employees.

Encouraging Communication Among Your Peers

Remember, the sum of the parts equals more than the individual contribution levels added together. How can you help build a better organization without giving a single presentation? Encouraging communication helps diffuse confusing or conflicting information and provides a conduit back to the core change team and change leader about what needs to be clarified or recommunicated. Encouraging communication also means reaching out to other employees. Each department or site is unique, but some similarities come to the surface when people start talking. When the change gets underway, other employees tend to be a useful source of information for one another.

Communication between peers and up through management does a number of things to make your job a lot easier in the future. By encouraging peers to talk about the change, you help to uncover what is valuable to the business and what is not. This communication helps to minimize the amount of time required to achieve the goals of the change by spending time on things that are beneficial to the business. This communication also helps minimize the loss of time during the productivity gap by quickly voicing issues rather than letting them fester. Productivity will drop regardless of how well the change goes, but the goal of a well-led change is to lessen the dip and quickly get team members back on their way to high levels of performance.

Often, communication takes on a negative tone during change, listing everything that teams need to give up rather than the things teams and individuals get. Use the phrase *appreciation for the change,* rather than *adjusting to the change,* to create an encouraging communication environment among peers. Take a look at how different the organization can become by simply changing communication to a positive tone rather than a pessimistic tone:

- ✔ Rather than developing corrective action plans to problems, design the future you want.

- ✔ Instead of looking for the root cause of the problem, ask what the root cause of success will be.

- ✔ Focus conversations on what people want as opposed to what people do not want. Some examples of what people may want are the opportunity to learn and grow or feel they are making a meaningful impact with their customers.

- ✔ Look at the change as an opportunity to uncover a treasure chest of potential, rather than a chance to solve all the problems that are wrong within the organization. Although being empathetic is important, staff and managers alike should begin to create a healthy attitude with positive messages such as, "As we move forward with this change, our customers will start seeing us as their partner, not just a product."

A purposefully positive approach to change, formally called *appreciative inquiry,* identifies the best of what is already happening, considers the possibilities of what might be, and helps to create what will be. Not to mention, being negative all the time is such a drag!

Believing in the Change and Speaking Up

Believing in the change is not about self-help; it is about making change a reality. Start imagining what the change will do to help you do your job better or make customers happier. If you've been unhappy in your job, you can probably easily identify ways that change can improve the situation. After all, surviving in a job that has inefficient processes or a subpar product is not sustainable.

Regardless of whether you are a change leader or not, when change starts happening, start talking about how great the change can be. If the change is not happening just yet, think back to a significant team accomplishment. Talking about these accomplishments captures the emotions, excitement, and energy the team had in the past and is often enough to push the team into making the current dream a reality. Just talking positively about the change does wonders for making it happen. Whether you are the most junior employee in the company or the CEO, show your enthusiasm for the project. Change comes from the heart, not from corporate messaging. Believing in the change makes others want to believe in it too. Remember that a sense of possibility for the future of the company is contagious.

Chapter 20

Ten Ways to Energize Your MVPs

In This Chapter

▶ Communicating goals and expectations

▶ Providing ownership and rewarding desired results

▶ Setting up leadership opportunities

▶ Becoming flexible, authentic, and honest

▶ Getting and using feedback and making a positive work environment

*T*here is nothing like a great employee — one you can depend on to deliver anything you throw her way, one who picks up the slack when others fail to perform at their best, and one who never backs down from a challenging assignment.

Leaders are always looking for ways to continue to energize, support, and motivate these superstars, because even though they may be able to leap tall cubicles in a single bound to get project deadlines complete, they are only human.

These employees are often the "go-to" people, but it's easy for them to take on too much and get burned out. Although these employees are your top players, don't forget that they also may be *other* people's top players: Even in a recession, good employees always have career opportunities.

This chapter suggests some ways to motivate your most valuable players and keep them playing strong on your team for the long term.

Setting Clear Goals and Expectations

Many people make the mistake of thinking that their MVPs need little direction and will just accomplish everything they are assigned. Needing little direction may be accurate, but *little* doesn't mean *none*. Setting clear goals and expectations for your best team players not only makes sure that both of you are working towards a common vision but also provides an opening for MVPs to talk about their career needs. Most MVPs have high professional goals, and linking how the work they do today will get them to where they want to go tomorrow is one of your best tools to keep them engaged and working on your team.

Some managers feel apprehensive when setting goals and expectations for MVPs; these managers may think goals could stifle an employee's creativity or make the employee feel micromanaged. The opposite is true. These clear goals and expectations also give MVPs the flexibility to go out and accomplish everything asked of them without worrying whether or not they are on the right track. If they agree with the goals you set, high-performing, high-potential employees will be empowered to make decisions and act fast. Just make sure they are aligned to organizational goals.

Performance plans aligned to the larger vision of the company and the business change are often called *lines of sight.* Create a visible link between change project objectives, company goals, and personal responsibilities to make sure your employees can see how what they do flows all the way up to the bigger picture.

1. **Identify the employees' career goals.** Do they want to move up in management or become subject-matter gurus for the entire company?

2. **Write down the career goals and create performance goals that will help your employees get there.** (This step is part of the second element to performance planning: goals and expectations.) Working with your MVPs, who should be involved in the process from beginning to end, come up with four or five key goals to accomplish in the next year.

3. **After you agree to the goals, discuss with your MVPs what big steps they need to take to accomplish these goals.**

4. **Talk about how to measure the success of the goals and when that measurement will be done.**

 Don't forget to keep all the goals in a SMART framework: specific, measurable, action oriented and agreed on, realistic, and time bound. For an example on performance planning for MVPs, go to www.leadingchangeguide.com.

Giving Ownership: Going Beyond Delegation

Ownership is a highly underutilized tool in business change. Typically, a number of activities or collaborative initiatives are delegated to individuals, and your MVPs probably have a few of these activities on their to-do lists. But although ownership and delegation are related concepts, they're different things.

Delegation often means identifying a task, putting together timelines, and letting someone else get the work done. You may find yourself delegating the creation of a project plan for a change or having someone else review or edit your communication messages.

Ownership means handing over a part of the change from beginning to end and allowing your MVP to be the one who makes the big decisions. You could delegate the creation of training materials to any employee, but imagine the difference in accountability and development if you asked your MVP to take ownership of the training during the change, including everything from who needs training, when it happens, and how it is delivered.

 Your MVPs are often innovative people who have great ideas on how to streamline processes and develop new ways of addressing problems and concerns that arise during change. If you give them ownership, they will make things happen.

Because ownership and delegating can be a bit confusing at times, start off by defining ownership roles using the RACI ownership method:

- ✔ Who is *responsible* for the project getting done?
- ✔ Who is *accountable* for measurable results?
- ✔ Who will be *consulted* as a member of the project team?
- ✔ Who will be *informed* regarding how the project will impact the organization?

Ownership falls into the first two areas: responsibility and accountability. An executive sponsor or senior leader in the company is often accountable at the end of the project to make sure it meets the organization's goal and is there to support employees and break down larger organizational barriers. This person (often the change sponsor) is not doing the day-to-day work, but he is the one who signs the check or gives final approval at the end of the day. On the other hand, the individual who is responsible makes decisions on a day-to-day basis, makes sure project milestones are met, and has ownership to getting the job done.

Recognizing and Rewarding Desired Results

With a robust performance plan focused on the future (created during the goals and expectations session in Chapter 11 and linked to the goals of the change created in Chapter 5), your most valuable player is probably off and running to get these items accomplished. Some rewards are intrinsic — just seeing goals accomplished can be satisfying enough. But you want to be sure to physically and externally reward some of the goals, especially the big ones on the employee's performance plan. When an employee accomplishes one of the big goals on her performance plan, don't wait until her annual performance review — recognize it in real-time.

Rewards may range from a simple thank-you note to a small, on-the-spot cash bonus. Your MVPs are probably always accomplishing something, so keep rewards fresh and inspiring, as the same $100 spot bonus or thank-you card can get old. Other ideas for unique rewards include

✔ Extra vacation time

✔ Flexible work schedule

✔ The opportunity to work from home

✔ Tickets to a local game or show

Not all corporations allow you to give these specific rewards, but that should not stop you from making a genuine gesture. Bleacher seats mean much more to an employee if the employee knows they are from the manager personally, not the manager's expense account. Check out Chapter 10 on more ideas on how to reward high performers.

Providing Leadership Opportunities

For newer employees who continually step up and make things happen as individuals, providing leadership opportunities is a wonderful reward for performance and an exceptional way for employees to practice for their next career move.

Don't just think of leadership opportunities as running a team or managing a part of a project. These outlets are great for showing and practicing leadership talent, but they are just the beginning. MVPs may thrive when offered a chance to teach the rest of the team about an accomplishment or facilitate a training session on an element of business change.

High-performing individual contributors may appreciate the chance to coach other employees in a formal mentoring program or on an informal one-on-one basis. They are often great at helping to jump start more efficient group processes. Ask your MVPs to help with meeting facilitation, leading group

problem-solving activities, and helping others develop expertise in group communication skills.

MVPs are often great change agents during a large-scale business change. In this role they can provide subject-matter expertise as well as change-readiness information back to the larger change team. Some MVPs jump at the chance to resolve issues and be the single point of contact for your team as the change progresses.

Another leadership opportunity is having your star player act as a liaison to other related projects and functions. Doing so provides him with visibility throughout the organization and expands his own scope of knowledge by interacting more frequently with other leaders and MVPs in the business.

Change can be an opportunity to grow and develop your MVPs as leaders. Look for opportunities to give these individuals stretch assignments and provide mentoring and coaching to individual contributors jumping into the management ranks. This jump is often seen as a reward for highly performing individuals, but managing and doing take two different skill sets; help these new managers flourish.

During change, it's important that your MVPs have good access to their bosses. Supervisors and bosses must be transparent with MVPs about their role before, during, and after the change so they don't walk out the door.

Being Flexible

Ask any high-performing employee what is in her top-ten list for the perfect career and job, and flexibility is likely to be on it. Maybe an MVP employee wants to work virtually one day a week to eliminate a long commute but your company doesn't support a virtual workforce. Many policies have some room for exceptions when it comes to working with the cream of the crop in the workforce. If you are unsure about what you can and cannot be flexible about, work with your human resources team.

Flexibility may also come in the form of how a project gets done. Even though you may have the perfect picture of change in your mind, your top performers may have ideas that can help make the vision and case for change even stronger. Flexibility demonstrates that you're willing to make things happen for your MVPs and you are eager to take their opinions, ideas, and needs into consideration throughout the change project.

Being a Coach

A number of coaching models are used in workplaces; some are good, some are great, and some are even better. Whatever model of coaching you choose, or if you choose to have an external coach help in the process, incorporate coaching as a discussion, not as training. Coaches create a conversation on leadership, and both the coach and the coachee come up with the right solution to issues. In contrast, training merely teaches the specific elements needed to get a job done.

Coaching isn't something you can just throw people into and hope for the best; it involves starting a dialogue on big-picture visioning, tactical goals and expectations, and discussions on personal and professional ambition. Coaching can help build skills in specific group processes and teamwork management (like how to meet committed milestones or better facilitate discussions), but the solution is crafted together, not just handed over from the wise coach to the eager employee. Coaching is less about advising and more about asking powerful questions to enable your MVPs to develop solutions on their own.

A great model to coach employees from is what we like to call the EDGE coaching model: explore, decide, go, evaluate:

- ✔ **Explore:** Explore options and opinions on what your MVP wants to accomplish or be in the next three to five years.

- ✔ **Decide:** Decide on specific goals for coaching: Does the employee want a sounding board, does she want to test new methods for tackling problems, or does she want to have the opportunity to learn about new ways to address issues or challenges she faces?

- ✔ **Go:** Because coaching is not a spectator sport, you next have to send the coachee to go and do the work. Coaching is not just theory; it's based on real-life situations, which also means that coaching can't happen only once in a blue moon.

- ✔ **Evaluate:** Finally, after you and the coachee have experienced some real-life examples that utilize everything you've created, you can evaluate the impact together. Because coaching is an open discussion and a cycle, take the time to see what worked and what did not.

Coaching in business and in sport has very similar paths: Although the coach may have a tremendous amount of knowledge about what works and what doesn't, the coach can't do the work. The coach's main goal is to make the coachee shine and perform better.

For more on coaching models, pick up a copy of *Coaching and Mentoring For Dummies,* by Marty Brounstein (Wiley).

Asking What Energizes Them

Throughout this chapter and book we provide a number of ideas on how to motivate and reward employees. However, the single most powerful reward and energizing tool you have is rewarding MVPs with what they want. So ask them a simple question: *What is most important to you?*

Although some top players may jump at the chance to gain more visibility and responsibility to showcase their talents, others would jump through hoops for you if you let them take the afternoon off to volunteer in their kid's classroom. Asking MVPs what motivates them should always be one of your first questions during a performance review or when you are asking them to take on more work during the business change.

When you are asking what energizes your MVPs, be sure to ask how they prefer to be rewarded and recognized, because you're likely to be doing it quite frequently for this group of employees. Some people prefer private recognition, whereas others want public recognition. Don't embarrass people who are more private.

Being Honest

So many leaders have to do more with less these days, and as a result, employees (even your best) may feel unmotivated and burned out. If you have done all you can to motivate and energize your star players and it still seems like something is missing, check to see how honest you're being with your team and superstars. Whether the news is that no raises are in the budget this year or that you can't guarantee everyone a job in the new organization, it is hard to give bad news to employees, let alone to your best employees. Whether you are delivering tough news or genuine thanks, be honest in your communication to your MVPs (and everyone, for that matter).

> *Being authentic is easiest when you speak from the heart. Your MVPs will know when you are trying to pretend things are better than they really are or just telling half the truth. Trust and credibility take time to develop, and being honest, even with negative messages, can build a more trusting environment. You, as a manager, need to invest in building an atmosphere of trust if the changes are significant and impact the MVP. Respect, openness, empowerment, and more help create this trust.*

Treating your MVPs like the mature adults they are and giving them as much information as legally allowed empowers them with the autonomy to continue to make sound decisions for themselves.

Asking for Feedback and Using It

Most people have heard the saying that feedback is a gift. But asking for a gift is always hard. Classes upon classes can tell you how to give feedback to employees, but what about asking them for feedback on how you're doing? Asking for feedback develops mutually rewarding relationships energizing both you and your employees to make change happen. Even your superstars may not feel comfortable giving the boss feedback, but that just means you need to find ways to get honest and open feedback to use in your job and during your change project.

Being genuinely curious about others' views, opinions, and experiences will help you make better decisions and will help make sure your MVPs have their opinions and ideas heard.

One option for getting feedback is to change your point of view on how you ask for it. Just asking for what you can do better leads to something of a dead end; most leaders ask what they can change or do better, and because few people like giving negative feedback, how much information you receive is often limited. Instead, try asking questions like: What would our "world-class" team look like to you? How can I support the team? How can I support you?

When asking for feedback from your MVPs, be clear on how you plan to use the feedback going forward. Then close the loop with your MVPs; not all suggestions are practical to implement, but make sure they know you considered their input.

Another way to ask for feedback is through a more comprehensive 360-degree feedback process. It works like this: Leaders choose a group of employees, peers, and managers to provide detailed feedback in many areas, which could include effectiveness, coaching skills, communications skills, and team-building capability. This feedback is gathered, often confidentially, by an external facilitator and then presented to the leaders to help improve their performance by learning what is working and what is not.

Building a Positive Work Environment

To help energize your top-performing employees, involve them in designing a positive environment. In addition to the resulting benefit from working in a positive environment, the involvement will create empowerment and job satisfaction.

Provide ownership for projects and delegate tasks based on the interests and motivation of MVPs. Connecting interests to the work that needs to get done creates positive energy where superstars work with efficiency and enthusiasm. You may even develop an interest matrix for your MVPs so you can quickly align projects to the person who would be happiest doing it.

Creating a positive environment for your MVPs involves also creating a positive work environment for all your employees. Continually rewarding your best and brightest may seem like a good idea, but it can create hostility in the workplace. Managing individual performance, not preferential treatment, is the fastest way to create a positive workplace for everyone. By making your own leadership style fair and equitable, all your employees will feel like they too can be seen as high performers if they work hard. In other words, set clear goals and objectives, reward accomplishing these objectives appropriately, and be open, honest, and authentic, all the time.

Index

fear as reaction to change, 151–152
feedback
  asking for and using, 344
  messages to leadership, 331
  offering, 141–142
finalizing change and recognizing results, 97
financial risks, 91
firefighting/nonvalue tasks, 83
fit of companies as factor in success of
      mergers and acquisitions, 241
flattening organization
  employee's point of view, 220–221
  management's point of view, 222
flavor-of-the-month syndrome, 305
flexibility, providing, 154, 341
flipping the switch, 30
focus groups, 122
focusing on most important issues, 81–86
followers, 332
Ford Motor Company, 238
formal company-wide awards, 146
formal financial and nonfinancial awards, 146
formal influencers, 184
formula for change, 12
front-line council, 43
Fuji, 259
future successes
  centers of excellence, creating, 169
  change story, creating your, 170–171
  coaching and mentoring programs,
      developing, 170
  communities of practice, creating, 169
  confidence in, building, 168–171
  employees training other employees,
      169–170
  organizational knowledge, maintaining,
      169–170

• G •

gain sharing, 254
Geely, 238
Geico, 272
generations, working across, 128
global businesses impacting complex
      change, 309

goals
  and expectations, setting clear, 337–338
  in GRPI model, 77, 78
  and objectives, clarifying, 87
  of project, defining, 73–74
Google, 272
governance structure, outlining, 75
GRPI model
  communication in, 80
  conflicting opinions in, 80
  decision making in, 79
  goals in, 77, 78
  interpersonal relationships in, 78, 80–81
  overview, 77–78
  problem solving in, 80
  processes and actions, 78–80
  roles and responsibilities in, 78–79

• H •

helpers, leveraging, 190
helping other employees cope with
      change, 333
high-level buy-in, lack of, 187
hindrances
  common hindrances, handling, 187–188
  consistency used to minimize, 186
  effort used to minimize, 186
  helpers, leveraging, 190
  high-level buy-in, lack of, 187
  inadequate training/resources, 187
  inconsistent communication, 187
  intentions, honesty regarding, 189
  listening to manage, 189
  long-term issues, identifying, 189
  minimizing impact of, 186–190
  overview, 186
  patience used to minimize, 186
  respect, escalating issues with, 189
  scope creep, 187
  short-term issues, identifying, 189
  stragglers and naysayers, coaching,
      188–190
hiring
  new employees
    into new culture, 289–290

• *N* •

• *O* •

Apple & Mac

iPad 2 For Dummies,
3rd Edition
978-1-118-17679-5

iPhone 4S For Dummies,
5th Edition
978-1-118-03671-6

iPod touch For Dummies,
3rd Edition
978-1-118-12960-9

Mac OS X Lion
For Dummies
978-1-118-02205-4

Blogging & Social Media

CityVille For Dummies
978-1-118-08337-6

Facebook For Dummies,
4th Edition
978-1-118-09562-1

Mom Blogging
For Dummies
978-1-118-03843-7

Twitter For Dummies,
2nd Edition
978-0-470-76879-2

WordPress For Dummies,
4th Edition
978-1-118-07342-1

Business

Cash Flow For Dummies
978-1-118-01850-7

Investing For Dummies,
6th Edition
978-0-470-90545-6

Job Searching with Social
Media For Dummies
978-0-470-93072-4

QuickBooks 2012
For Dummies
978-1-118-09120-3

Resumes For Dummies,
6th Edition
978-0-470-87361-8

Starting an Etsy Business
For Dummies
978-0-470-93067-0

Cooking & Entertaining

Cooking Basics
For Dummies, 4th Edition
978-0-470-91388-8

Wine For Dummies,
4th Edition
978-0-470-04579-4

Diet & Nutrition

Kettlebells For Dummies
978-0-470-59929-7

Nutrition For Dummies,
5th Edition
978-0-470-93231-5

Restaurant Calorie Counter
For Dummies,
2nd Edition
978-0-470-64405-8

Digital Photography

Digital SLR Cameras &
Photography For Dummies,
4th Edition
978-1-118-14489-3

Digital SLR Settings
& Shortcuts
For Dummies
978-0-470-91763-3

Photoshop Elements 10
For Dummies
978-1-118-10742-3

Gardening

Gardening Basics
For Dummies
978-0-470-03749-2

Vegetable Gardening
For Dummies,
2nd Edition
978-0-470-49870-5

Green/Sustainable

Raising Chickens
For Dummies
978-0-470-46544-8

Green Cleaning
For Dummies
978-0-470-39106-8

Health

Diabetes For Dummies,
3rd Edition
978-0-470-27086-8

Food Allergies
For Dummies
978-0-470-09584-3

Living Gluten-Free
For Dummies,
2nd Edition
978-0-470-58589-4

Hobbies

Beekeeping
For Dummies,
2nd Edition
978-0-470-43065-1

Chess For Dummies,
3rd Edition
978-1-118-01695-4

Drawing For Dummies,
2nd Edition
978-0-470-61842-4

eBay For Dummies,
7th Edition
978-1-118-09806-6

Knitting For Dummies,
2nd Edition
978-0-470-28747-7

Language & Foreign Language

English Grammar
For Dummies,
2nd Edition
978-0-470-54664-2

French For Dummies,
2nd Edition
978-1-118-00464-7

German For Dummies,
2nd Edition
978-0-470-90101-4

Spanish Essentials
For Dummies
978-0-470-63751-7

Spanish For Dummies,
2nd Edition
978-0-470-87855-2

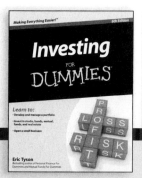

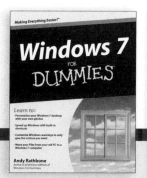

Math & Science

Algebra I For Dummies,
2nd Edition
978-0-470-55964-2

Biology For Dummies,
2nd Edition
978-0-470-59875-7

Chemistry For Dummies,
2nd Edition
978-1-1180-0730-3

Geometry For Dummies,
2nd Edition
978-0-470-08946-0

Pre-Algebra Essentials
For Dummies
978-0-470-61838-7

Microsoft Office

Excel 2010 For Dummies
978-0-470-48953-6

Office 2010 All-in-One
For Dummies
978-0-470-49748-7

Office 2011 for Mac
For Dummies
978-0-470-87869-9

Word 2010
For Dummies
978-0-470-48772-3

Music

Guitar For Dummies,
2nd Edition
978-0-7645-9904-0

Clarinet For Dummies
978-0-470-58477-4

iPod & iTunes
For Dummies,
9th Edition
978-1-118-13060-5

Pets

Cats For Dummies,
2nd Edition
978-0-7645-5275-5

Dogs All-in One
For Dummies
978-0470-52978-2

Saltwater Aquariums
For Dummies
978-0-470-06805-2

Religion & Inspiration

The Bible For Dummies
978-0-7645-5296-0

Catholicism For Dummies,
2nd Edition
978-1-118-07778-8

Spirituality For Dummies,
2nd Edition
978-0-470-19142-2

Self-Help & Relationships

Happiness For Dummies
978-0-470-28171-0

Overcoming Anxiety
For Dummies,
2nd Edition
978-0-470-57441-6

Seniors

Crosswords For Seniors
For Dummies
978-0-470-49157-7

iPad 2 For Seniors
For Dummies, 3rd Edition
978-1-118-17678-8

Laptops & Tablets
For Seniors For Dummies,
2nd Edition
978-1-118-09596-6

Smartphones & Tablets

BlackBerry For Dummies,
5th Edition
978-1-118-10035-6

Droid X2 For Dummies
978-1-118-14864-8

HTC ThunderBolt
For Dummies
978-1-118-07601-9

MOTOROLA XOOM
For Dummies
978-1-118-08835-7

Sports

Basketball For Dummies,
3rd Edition
978-1-118-07374-2

Football For Dummies,
2nd Edition
978-1-118-01261-1

Golf For Dummies,
4th Edition
978-0-470-88279-5

Test Prep

ACT For Dummies,
5th Edition
978-1-118-01259-8

ASVAB For Dummies,
3rd Edition
978-0-470-63760-9

The GRE Test For
Dummies, 7th Edition
978-0-470-00919-2

Police Officer Exam
For Dummies
978-0-470-88724-0

Series 7 Exam
For Dummies
978-0-470-09932-2

Web Development

HTML, CSS, & XHTML
For Dummies, 7th Edition
978-0-470-91659-9

Drupal For Dummies,
2nd Edition
978-1-118-08348-2

Windows 7

Windows 7
For Dummies
978-0-470-49743-2

Windows 7
For Dummies,
Book + DVD Bundle
978-0-470-52398-8

Windows 7 All-in-One
For Dummies
978-0-470-48763-1

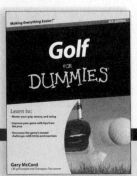

Available wherever books are sold. For more information or to order direct: U.S. customers visit www.dummies.com or call 1-877-762-297.
U.K. customers visit www.wileyeurope.com or call (0) 1243 843291. Canadian customers visit www.wiley.ca or call 1-800-567-4797.

Connect with us online at www.facebook.com/fordummies or @fordummies